ISBN: 9781314564006

Published by:
HardPress Publishing
8345 NW 66TH ST #2561
MIAMI FL 33166-2626

Email: info@hardpress.net
Web: http://www.hardpress.net

e Voyages of the English Nation to America
before the year 1600.

THE VOYAGES

OF

THE ENGLISH NATION TO AMERICA.

Collected by

RICHARD HAKLUYT, Preacher,

AND

Edited by

EDMUND GOLDSMID, F.R.H.S.

VOL. IV.

Edinburgh:

E. & G. GOLDSMID.

1890.

Nauigations, Voyages, Traffiques, and Discoueries

OF THE

ENGLISH NATION IN AMERICA.

The relation of the nauigation and discouery which Captaine Fernando Alarchon made by the order of the right honourable Lord Don Antonio de Mendoça Vizeroy of New Spaine, dated in Colima, an hauen of New Spaine.

Chap. 1.

Fernando Alarchon after he had suffered a storme, arriued with his Fleete at the hauen of Saint Iago, and from thence at the hauen of Aguaiaual : he was in great perill in seeking to discouer a Bay, and getting out of the same he discouered a riuer on the coast with a great current, entring into the same, and coasting along he descried a great many of Indians with their weapons : with signes hee hath traffique with them, and fearing some great danger returneth to his ships.

ON Sunday the ninth of May in the yeere 1540. I set saile with two ships, the one called Saint Peter being Admirall, and the other Saint Catherine, and wee set forward meaning to goe to the hauen of Saint Iago of good hope : but before wee arriued there wee had a terrible storme, wherewith they which were in the ship called Saint Catherine, being more afraid then was neede, cast ouer boord nine pieces of Ordinance, two ankers and one cable, and many other things as needfull for the enterprise wherein we went, as the ship it selfe. Assoone as we were arriued at the hauen of Saint Iago I repaired my losse which I had receiued, prouided my selfe of things necessary, and tooke aboord my people which looked for my comming, and directed my course toward the hauen of Aguaiauall. And being there arriued I vnderstood that the Generall Francis Vazquez de Coronado was departed with all his people : whereupon taking the ship called Saint Gabriel which carried victuals for the armie I led her with mee to put in execution your Lordships order. Afterward I followed my course along the coast without departing from the same, to see if I could find any token, or any Indian which could giue me knowledge of him : and in sailing so neere the shore I discouered other very good hauens, for the ships whereof Captaine Francis de Vllua was General for the Marquesse de Valle * neither sawe nor found them. And when we

---

* Hernando Cortes. After the conquest of Mexico, which had followed the battle of Otumba (7th July 1520) and the celebrated siege of seventy-five days, Cortes returned to Spain in 1528, where, though he had many enemies, he was received with much respect, and made marquis of the rich Valle de Oajaca,

He was very disappointed that the Court of Spain did not confer on him the post of Governor-General of Mexico, but it was never the custom of the Spanish Government to allow any of those who gained colonies for the Crown to retain power there.

In 1530 he had to return to Mexico, when he paid some attention to maritime discovery and visited the Gulf of California. He returned to Spain in 1540, when he was received by Charles V. with cold civility and by his ministers with insolent neglect. He, however, accompanied this prince in 1541 as a volunteer in the disastrous expedition to Algiers, and his advice, had it been listened to, would have saved the Spanish arms from disgrace and delivered Europe three centuries earlier from maritime barbarians.

Cortes was born in 1485 at Medellin, a village of Estremadura, in Spain. He was first sent to study law at Salamanca, but in 1504 he joined his relative, Ovando, governor of Hispaniola. In 1511 he distinguished himself under Velasquez in the conquest of Cuba, and in 1518 was selected by him to undertake the conquest of Mexico, which had just been discovered by Grijalva. He died near Seville, 2nd December, 1547, in the sixty-third year of his age. ("Life of Hernando Cortes," by Sir Arthur Helps ; and "Conquest of Mexico," by Prescott.)

were come to the flats and shoals from whence
the foresaid fleete returned, it seemed as well to me These shoalds are the bottome of mar Bermejo, or the Bay of California.
as to the rest, that we had the firme land before vs,
and that those shoalds were so perilous and fearefull,
that it was a thing to be considered whither with our
skiffes we could enter in among them : and the
Pilotes and the rest of the company would haue had vs done as
Captaine Vllua did, and haue returned backe againe. But
because your Lordship commanded mee, that I should bring you
the secret of that gulfe, I resolued, that although I had knowen I
should haue lost the shippes, I would not haue ceased for any
thing to haue seene the head thereof : and therefore I commanded Nicolas Zamorano Pilote maior, and Dominico del
Castello that eche of them should take a boate, and their lead
in their hands, and runne in among those shoalds, to see if
they could find out the chanell whereby the shippes might enter
in : to whom it seemed that the ships might saile vp higher
(although with great trauell and danger) and in this sort I and
he began to follow our way which they had taken, and within a
short while after wee found our selues fast on the sands with all
our three ships, in such sort that one could not helpe another,
neither could the boates succour vs, because the current was so
great that it was impossible for one of vs to come vnto another :
whereupon we were in such great ieopardie that the decke
of the Admirall was oftentimes vnder water, and if a great surge
of the sea had not come and driuen our ship right vp, and gaue
her leaue as it were to breath a while, we had there bin drowned :
and likewise the other two shippes found themselves in very
great hazard, yet because they were lesser and drewe lesse
water, their danger was not so great as ours. Nowe it pleased God
vpon the returne of the flood that the shippes came on flote, and
so wee went forward. And although the company would haue
returned backe, yet for all this I determined to goe forwarde,
and to pursue our attempted voyage : and we passed The bot-tome of the Bay of Cali-fornia.
forward with much adoe, turning our stemmes now
this way, now that way, to seeke to find the chanel.
And it pleased God that after this sort we came to
the very bottome of the Bay : where we found a very mightie
riuer, which ranne with so great fury of a streame, that we could
hardly saile against it.* In this sort I determined as wel as I

* Rio Colorado.

could to go vp this riuer, and with two boates, leauing the
third with the ships, and twenty men, my selfe being in one of
them with Roderigo Maldonado treasurer of this fleet, and
Gaspar de Castilleia comptroller, and with certaine small pieces
of artillerie I began to saile vp the river, and charged all my
company, that none of them should stirre nor vse any signe, but
he whom I appointed, although wee found Indians.
They goe vp The same day, which was Thursday the sixe and
the riuer of
Buena guia twentieth of August, following our voyage with draw-
the 26. of ing the boats with halsers we went about some 6
August. leagues: and the next day which was Friday by the
breake of day thus following our way vpward, I saw certaine
Indians which went toward certaine cottages neere vnto the
water, who assoone as they saw vs, ten or twelue of them rose vp
furiously, and crying with a loud voyce, other of their companions
came running together to the number of 50 which with all haste
carried out of their cottages such things as they had, and layd
them vnder certaine shrubs and many of them came running
toward that part whether wee approched, making great signes
vnto vs that we should goe backe againe, ·vsing great
threatnings against vs, one while running on this side and an
other while on that side.   I seeing them in such a rage, caused
our boates to lanch from the shore into the middes of the riuer,
that the Indians might be out of feare, and I rode at anker, and
set my people in as good order as I could, charging them that no
man should speake, nor make any signe nor motion, nor stirre
out of his place, nor should not be offended for any thing that
the Indians did, nor should shewe no token of warre : and by
this meanes the Indians came euery foote neere the riuers side
to see vs : and I gate by little and little toward them where the
riuer seemed to be deepest.   In this meane space there were
aboue two hundred and fiftie Indians assembled together with
bowes and arrowes, and with certaine banners in warrelike sort
in such maner as those of New Spayne doe vse : and perceiuing that I drewe toward the shore, they came with great
cryes toward vs with bowes and arrowes put into them, and with
their banners displayed.   And I went vnto the stemme of my
boate with the interpreter which I carried with me, whom I
commanded to speake vnto them, and when he spake, they
neither vnderstood him, nor he thém, although because they
sawe him to be after their fashion, they stayed themselues :

and seeing this I drewe neerer the shore, and they with great cryes came to keepe mee from the shore of the riuer, making signes that I should not come any further, putting stakes in my way betweene the water and the land : and the more I lingered, the more people still flocked together. Which when I had considered I beganne to make them signes of peace, and taking my sword and target, I cast them downe in the boate and set my feete vpon them, giuing them to vnderstand with this and other tokens that I desired not to haue warre with them, and that they should doe the like. Also I tooke a banner and cast it downe, and I caused my company A very good that were with mee to sit downe likewise, and taking to appease the wares of exchange which I carried with mee, I unknowen called them to giue them some of them': yet for all Sauages. this none of them stirred to take any of them, but rather flocked together, and beganne to make a great murmuring among themselues : and suddenly one came out from among them with a staffe wherein certayne shelles were set, and entred into the water to giue them vnto mee, and I tooke them, and made signes vnto him that hee should come neere me, which when he had done, I embraced him, and gaue him in recompence certaine beades and other things, and he returning with them vnto his fellowes, began to looke vpon them, and to parley together, and within a while after many of them came toward me, to whom I made signes to lay downe their banners, and to -leaue their weapons : which they did incontinently, then I made signes that they should lay them altogether, and should goe aside from them, which likewise they did : and they caused those Indians which newly came thither to leaue them, and to lay them together with the rest. After this I called them vnto me, and to all them which came I gaue some smal trifle, vsing them gently, and by this time they were so many that came thronging about mee, that I thought I could not stay any longer in safety among them, and I made signes vnto them that they should withdraw them-selues, and that they should stand al vpon the side of an hill which was there betweene a plaine and the riuer, and that they should not presse to me aboue ten at a time. And immediately the most ancient among them called vnto them with a loud voyce, willing them to do so : and some ten or twelue of them came where I was : whereupon seeing my selfe in some securitie, I determined to goe on land the more to put them out of feare :

and for my more securitie, I made signes vnto them, to sit downe on the ground which they did : but when they saw that ten or twelue of my companions came a shore after me, they began to be angry, and I made signes vnto them that we would be friends, and that they should not feare, and herewithal they were pacified, and sate down as they did before, and I went vnto them, and imbraced them, giuing them certain trifles, commanding mine interpreter to speake vnto them, for I greatly desired to vnderstand their maner of speech, and the cry which they made at mee.   And that I might knowe what maner of foode they had, I made a signe vnto them, that wee would gladly eate, and they brought mee certaine cakes of Maiz, and a loafe of Mizquiqui, and they made signes vnto mee that they desired to see an harquebuse shot off, which I caused to be discharged, and they were all wonderfully afraid, except two or three olde men among them which were not mooued at all, but rather cried out vpon the rest, because they were afrayd : and through the speach of one of these olde men, they began to rise vp from the ground, and to lay hold on their weapons : whom when I sought to appease, I would haue giuen him a silken girdle of diuers colours, and hee in a great rage bitte his nether lippe cruelly, and gaue mee a thumpe with his elbowe on the brest, and turned in a great furie to speake vnto his company.   After that I saw them aduance their banners, I determined to returne my selfe gently to my boates, and with a small gale of wind I set sayle, whereby wee might breake the current which was very great, although my company were not well pleased to goe any farther.   In the meane space the Indians came following vs along the shore of the riuer, making signes that I should come on land, and that they would giue mee food to eate, some of them sucking their fingers, and others entred into the water with certaine cakes of Maiz, to giue me them in my boate.

Chap. 2.

Of the habite, armour and stature of the Indians.. A relation of
    many others with whom he had by signes traffique, victuals
    and many courtesies.   .   ҆

IN this sort we went vp two leagues, and I arriued neere a

cliffe of an hill, whereupon was an arbour made newly, where they made signes vnto me, crying that I should go thither, shewing me the same with their handes, and telling mee that there was meate to eate. But I would not goe thither, seeing the place was apt for some ambush, but followed on my voyage, within a while after issued out from thence aboue a thousand armed men with their bowes and arrowes, and after that many women and children shewed themselues, toward whom I would not goe, but because the Sunne was almost set, I rode in the middest of the riuer. These Indians came decked after sundry fashions, some came with a painting that couered their face all ouer, some had their faces halfe couered, but all besmouched with cole, and euery one as it liked him best. Others carried visards before them of the same colour which had the shape of faces. They weare on their heads a piece of a Deeres skinne two spannes broad set after the maner of a helmet, and vpon it certaine small sticks with some sortes of fethers. Their weapons were bowes and arrowes of hard wood, and two or three sorts of maces of wood hardened in the fire. This is a mightie people, well feitured, and without any grossenesse. They haue holes bored in their nostrels whereat certaine pendents hang : and others weare shelles, and their eares are full of holes, whereon they hang bones and shelles. All of them both great and small weare a girdle about their waste made of diuerse colours, and in the middle is fastened a round bunch of feathers, which hangeth downe behind like a tayle. Likewise on the brawne of their armes they weare a streit string, which they wind so often about that it becommeth as broad as ones hand. They weare certaine pieces of Deeres bones fastened to their armes, wherewith they strike off the sweate, and at the other certaine small pipes of canes. They carry also certaine little long bagges about an hand broade tyed to their left arme, which serue them also instead of brasers for their bowes, full of the powder of a certaine herbe, whereof they make a certaine beuerage. They haue their bodies traced with coles, their haire cut before, and behind it hangs downe to their wast. The women goe naked, and weare a great wreath of fethers behind them, and before painted and glued together, and their haire like the men. There were among these Indians three or foure men in womens apparell. Nowe the next day being Saturday very

Good forecast.

Pipes and bagges of tobacco.

C

early I went forward on my way vp the riuer, setting on shore
two men for eache boate to drawe them with the rope, and
about breaking foorth of the Sunne, wee heard a mightie
crie of Indians on both sides of the riuer with their weapons,
but without any banner. I thought good to attend their
comming, aswell to see what they woulde haue, as also to try
whither our interpreter could vnderstand them. When they
came ouer against vs they leapt into the riuer on both sides
with their bowes and arrowes, and when they spake, our interpreter vnderstoode them not: whereupon I beganne to make
a signe vnto them that they should lay away their weapons,
as the other had done. Some did as I willed them, and some
did not, and those which did, I willed to come neere me and
gaue them some things which we had to trucke withall, which
when the others perceiued, that they might likewise haue their
part, they layd away their weapons likewise. I iudging my selfe
to be in securitie leaped on shore with them, and stoode in the
middest of them, who vnderstanding that I came not to fight with
them, began to giue some of those shels and beades, and some
brought me certaine skinnes well dressed, and others Maiz and a
roll of the same naughtily grinded, so that none of them came
vnto me that brought mee not something, and before they gaue
it me going a little way from mee they began to cry out amayne,
and made a signe with their bodies and armes, and afterward they
approached to giue me that which they brought. And now that
the Sunne beganne to set I put off from the shore, and rode in
the middest of the riuer. The next morning before break of day
on both sides of the riuer wee heard greater cries and of more
Indians, which leaped into the riuer to swimme, and they came
to bring mee certaine gourdes full of Maiz, and of those wrethes
which I spake of before. I shewed vnto them Wheate and
Beanes, and other seedes, to see whether they had any of those
kindes: but they shewed me that they had no knowledge of
them, and wondred at all of them, and by signes I came to
vnderstand that the thing which they most esteemed and
reuerenced was the Sunne: and I signified vnto them
that I came from the Sunne. Whereat they maruelled, and then they began to beholde me from the
toppe to the toe, and shewed me more favour then they did
before ; and when I asked them for food, they brought me such
aboundance that I was inforced twise to call for the boates to put

A notable policie.

it into them, and from that time forward of all the things which
they brought me they flang vp into the ayre one part vnto the
Sunne, and afterward turned towards me to giue mee the other
part : and so I was always better serued and esteemed of them
as well in drawing of the boats vp the riuer, as also in giuing me
food to eat : and they shewed me so great loue, that when I
stayed they would have carried vs in their armes vnto their
houses : and in no kind of thing they would breake my com-
mandment : and for my suretie, I willed them not to carry any
weapons in my sight : and they were so careful to doe so, that if
any man came newly thither with them, suddenly they
would goe and meete him to cause him to lay them downe
farre from mee : and I shewed them that I tooke great pleasure
in their so doing : and to some of the chiefe of them
I gaue certaine little napkins and other trifles ; for if *Swarmes of people.*
I should haue giuen somewhat to euery one of them
in particular, all the small wares in New Spayne would not haue
sufficed.   Sometimes it fell out (such was the great loue and
good wil which they shewed me) that if any Indians came thither
by chance with their weapons, and if any one being warned to
leaue them behind him, if by negligence, or because he vnderstood them not at the first warning, he had not layd them away,
they would runne vnto him, and take them from him by force,
and would breake them in pieces in my presence.   Afterward
they tooke the rope so louingly, and with striuing one with
another for it, that we had no need to pray them to doe it.
Wherefore if we had not had this helpe, the current of the riuer
being exceeding great, and our men that drew the rope being not
well acqainted with that occupation, it would haue beene impossible for vs to haue gotten vp the riuer so against the streame.
When I perceiued that they vnderstood mee in all things, and
that I likewise vnderstoode them, I thought good to try by some
way or other to make a good entrance to find some good issue
to obtaine my desire : And I caused certaine crosses to be made
of certaine small sticks and paper, and among others when I gaue
any thing I gaue them these as things of most price and kissed
them, making signes vnto them that they should honour them
and make great account of them, and that they should weare
them at their necks : giuing them to vnderstand that this signe
was from heauen, and they tooke them and kissed them, and
lifted them vp aloft, and seemed greatly to reioyce thereat when

they did so, and sometime I tooke them into my boate, shewing
them great good will, and sometime I gaue them of those trifles
which I caried with me.   And at length the matter grew to such
issue, that I had not paper and stickes ynough to make crosses.
In this matter that day I was very well accompanied, vntill that
when night approched I sought to lanch out into the riuer, and
went to ride in the middest of the streame, and they came to
aske leaue of me to depart, saying that they would returne the
next day with victuals to visite me, and so by litle and little they
departed, so that there stayed not aboue fiftie which made fires
ouer against vs, and stayed there al night calling vs, and before
the day was perfectly broken, they leapt into the water and
swamme vnto vs asking for the rope, and we gaue it them with a
good will, thanking God for the good prouision which he gaue vs
to go vp the riuer : for the Indians were so many, that if they
had gone about to let our passage, although we had bene many
more then wee were, they might haue done it.

Chap. 3.

One of the Indians vnderstanding the language of the interpreter,
     asketh many questions of the originall of the Spaniards,
     he telleth him that their Captaine is the child of the
     Sunne, and that he was sent of the Sunne vnto them, and
     they would haue receiued him for their king.   They take
     this Indian into their boat, and of him they haue many
     informations of that countrey.

IN this manner we sailed vntill Tuesday at night, going as we
were wont, causing mine interpreter to speak vnto the people to
see if peraduenture any of them could vnderstand him, I perceiued that one answered him, whereupon I caused the boates to
be stayed, and called him, which hee vnderstoode, charging mine
           interpreter that hee should not speake nor answere
A wise   him any thing else, but onely that which I said vnto
deuise.   him : and I saw as I stood still that that Indian
began to speake to the people with great furie : whereupon all of
them beganne to drawe together, and mine interpreter vnderstood, that he which came to the boate sayd vnto them, that he
desired to knowe what nation we were, and whence wee came,
and whither we came out of the water, or out of the earth, or

from heauen : And at this speech an infinite number of people came together, which maruelled to see mee speake : and this Indian turned on this side and on that side to speake vnto them in another language which mine interpreter vnderstood not. Whereas he asked me what we were, I answered that we were Christians, and that we came from farre to see them : and answering to the question, who had sent me, I said, I was sent by the Sunne, pointing vnto him by signes as at the first, because they should not take mee in a lye. He beganne againe to ask mee, how the Sunne had sent me, seeing he went aloft in the skie and never stoode still, and seeing these many yeeres neither he nor their olde men had euer seene such as we were, of whome they euer had any kind of knowledge, and that Sunne till that houre had neuer sent any other. I answered him that it was true that the Sunne made his course aloft in the skie, and did neuer stand still, yet neuertheless that they might well perceiue that at his going downe and rising in the morning hee came neere vnto the earth, where his dwelling was, and that they euer sawe him come out of one place, and that hee had made mee in that land and countrey from whence hee came, like as hee had made many others which hee had sent into other parties, and that nowe hee had sent me to visitie and view the same riuer, and the people that dwelt neere the same, that I should speake vnto them, and should ioyne with them in friend-shippe, and should giue them things which they had not, and that I should charge them that they should not make warre one against another. Whereunto he answered, that I should tell him the cause why the Sunne had not sent mee no sooner to pacifie the warres which had continued a long time among them, wherein many had beene slaine. I tolde him the cause hereof was, because at that time I was but a child. Then he asked the interpreter whether wee tooke him with vs perforce hauing taken him in the war, or whether he came with vs of his own accord. He answered him that he was with vs of his owne accord, and was very wel appaid of our company. He returned to enquire, why we brought none saue him onely that vnderstood vs, and wherefore we vuderstood not all other men, seeing we were the children of the Sunne : he answered, that the Sunne also had begotten him, and giuen him a language to vnderstand him, and me, and others : that the Sunne knew well that they dwelt there, but that because he had many other businesses, and

because I was but yong hee sent me 'no sooner. And
he turning vnto me sayd suddenly : Comest thou therefore
hither to bee our Lord, and that wee should serue thee ? I
supposing that I should not please him if I should haue said yea,
answered him, not to be their Lord, but rather to be their
brother, aud to giue them such things as I had. He asked me,
whether the Sunne had begotten me as he had begotten others,
and whether I was his kinsman or his sonne : I answered him
that I was. his sonne. / He proceeded to aske me whether the
rest that were with me were also the children of the Sunne, I
answered him no, but that they were borne all with me in one
countrey, where I was brought vp. Then he cryed out with a
loud voyce and sayd, seeing thou doest vs so much good, and
wilt not haue vs to make warre, and art the child of the Sunne,
wee will all receiue thee for our Lord, and alwayes serue thee,
therefore wee pray thee that thou wilt not depart hence nor leaue
vs : and suddenly hee turned to the people, and beganne to tell
them, that I was the childe of the Sunne, and that therefore they
should all chuse me for their Lord. Those Indians hearing this,
were astonied beyond measure, and came neerer still more and
more to behold me. That Indian also asked mee other questions,
which to auoyd tediousnesse I doe not recite : and in this wise
we passed the day, and seeing the night approch, I began by
all meanes I could deuise to get this fellow into our boat with vs :
and he refusing to goe with vs, the interpreter told him that wee
would put him on the other side of the riuer, and vpon this condition he entred into our boate, and there I made very much of
him, and gaue him the best entertaynement I could, putting him
alwayes in securitie, and when I iudged him to be out of all
suspition, I thought it good to aske him somewhat of that
countrey. And among the first things that I asked him this
was one, whether 'hee had euer seene any men like vs, or had
heard any report of them. Hee answered mee no, sauing that
Newes of   hee had sometime hearde of olde men, that very farre
bearded and from that Countrey there were other white men, and
white men,   with beardes like vs, and that hee knewe nothing else.
I asked him also whether hee knewe a place called Ceuola, and a
Riuer called Totonteac, and hee answered mee no. Whereupon
perceiuing that hee coulde not giue mee any knowledge of Francis
Vazquez nor of his company, I determined to aske him other
things of that countrey, and of their maner of life : and beganne

to enquire of him, whether they helde that there was one God, creator of heauen and earth, or that they worshipped any other Idol. And hee answered mee no: but that they esteemed and reuerenced the Sunne aboue all other things, because it warmed them and made their croppes to growe: and that of all things which they did eate, they cast a little vp into the ayre vnto him. I asked him next whether they had any Lorde, and hee sayde no: but that they knewe well that there was a great Lorde, but they knewe not well which way hee dwelt. And I tolde him that hee was in heauen, and that hee was called Iesus Christ, and I went no farther in diuinitie with him. I asked him whether they had any warre, and for what occasion. Hee answered that they had warre and that very great, and vpon exceeding small occasions: for when they had no cause to make warre, they assembled together, and some of them sayd, let vs goe to make warre in such a place, and then all of them set forward with their weapons. I asked them who commanded the armie: he answered the eldest and most valiant, and that when they sayd they should proceede no farther, that suddenly they retired from the warre. I prayed him to tell me what they did with those men which they killed in battell: he answered me that they tooke out the hearts of some of them, and eat them, and others they burned; and he added, that if it had not bene for my comming, they should haue bin now at warre: and because I commanded them that they should not war, and that they should cease from armes, therefore as long as I should not command them to take armes, they would not begin to wage warre against others, and they said among themselues, that seeing I was come vnto them, they had giuen ouer their intention of making warre, and that they had a good mind to liue in peace. He complained of certaine people which dwelt behind in a mountaine which made great war vpon them, and slew many of them: I answered him, that from henceforward they should not need to feare any more, because I had commanded them to be quiet, and if they would not obey my commandement, I would chasten them and kill them. He enquired of me how I could kill them seeing we were so few, and they so many in number. And because it was now late and that I saw by this time he was weary to stay any longer with me, I let him goe out of my boat, and therewith I dismissed him very well content.

The Sunne worshipped as God.

Certaine warlike people behind a mountaine.

Chap. 4.

Of Naguachato and other chiefe men of those Indians they
    receiue great store of victuals, they cause them to set vp a
    crosse in their countreys, and hee teacheth them to worship
    it.   They haue newes of many people, of their diuers
    languages, and customes in matrimony, how they punish
    adultery, of their opinions concerning the dead, and of
    the sicknesses which they are subiect vnto.

THe next day betimes in the morning came the chiefe man
among them called Naguachato, and wished me to come on land
because he had great store of victuals to giue me.   And because
I saw my selfe in securitie I did so without doubting; and
incontinently an olde man came with rols of that Maiz, and
certaine litle gourds, and calling me with a loud voyce and
vsing many gestures with his body and armes, came neere vnto
me, and causing me to turne me vnto that people, and hee himselfe also turning vnto them sayd vnto them, Sagueyca, and all
the people answered with a great voyce, Hu, and hee offred to
the Sunne a little of euery thing that he had there, and likewise
a little more vnto me (although afterward he gaue me all the
rest) and did the like to all that were with me : and calling out
mine interpreter, by meanes of him I gaue them thanks, telling
them that because my boats were litle I had not brought many
things to giue them in exchange, but that 1 would come againe
another time and bring them, and that if they would go with me
in my boates vnto my ships which I had beneath at the riuers
mouth, I would giue them many things.   They answered that
they would do so, being very glad in countenance.   Here by the
helpe of mine interpreter I sought to instruct them what the
sign of the crosse meant, and willed them to bring me a piece of
timber, wherof I caused a great crosse to be made, and commanded al those that were with mee that when it was made
they should worship it, and beseech the Lord to grant his
grace that so great a people might come to the knowledge of
his holy Catholike faith : and this done I told them by mine
interpreter that I left them that signe, in token that I tooke
them for my brethren, and that they should keepe it for me
carefully vntill I returned, and that euery morning at the
Sunne rising they should kneele before it.   And they tooke it

incontinently, and without suffering it to touch the ground, they carried it to set it vp in the middest of their houses, where all of them might beholde it; and I willed them alwayes to worshippe it because it would preserue them from euill. They asked me how deep they should set in the ground, and I shewed them. Great store of people followed the same, and they that stayed behinde *These people* inquired of mee, how they should ioyne their handes, *are greatly* and how they should kneele to worship the same; *inclined to* and they seemed to haue great desire to learne it. *learne the Christian faith.* This done, I tooke that chiefe man of the Countrey, and going to our boates with him, I followed my iourney vp the Riuer, and all the company on both sides of the shoare accompanied me with great good will, and serued me in *The Riuer in* drawing of our boates, and in halling vs off the sands *diuers places* whereupon we often fel: for in many places we *full of shelfes.* found the riuer so shoald, that we had no water for our boats. As wee thus went on our way, some of the Indians which I had left behind me, came after vs to pray mee that I would throughly instruct them, how they should ioyne their hands in the worshipping of the crosse: others shewed me whether they were well set in such and such sort, so that they would not let me be quiet. Neere vnto the other side of the riuer was greater store of people, which called vnto me very often, that I would receiue the victuals which they had brought me. And because I perceiued that one enuied the other, because I would not leaue them discontented, I did so. And here came before me another old man like vnto the former with the like ceremonyes and offrings: and I sought to learne something of him as I had done of the other. This man said likewise to the rest of the people, This is our lord. Now you see how long ago our ancesters told vs, that there were bearded and white people in the world, and we laughed them to scorne. I which am old and the rest which are here, haue neuer seene any such people as these. And if you wil not beleeue me, behold these people which be in this riuer: let vs giue them therefore meate, seeing they giue vs of their victuals: let vs willingly serue this lord, which wisheth vs so well, and forbiddeth vs to make warre, and imbraceth all of vs: and they haue mouth, handes and eyes as we haue, and speake as we doe. I gaue these likewise another crosse as I had done to the others beneath, and said vnto them the selfe same words: which they

D

listened vnto with a better will, and vsed greater diligence to learne that which I said.   Afterward as I passed farther vp the riuer, I found another people, whom mine interpreter vnderstood not a whit : wherefore I shewed them by signes the selfe same ceremonies of worshipping the crosse, which I had taught the rest.   And that principal old man which I tooke with me, told me that farthur vp the riuer I should find people which would vnderstand mine interpreter : and being now late, some of those men called me to giue me victuals, and did in all poynts as the others had done, dauncing and playing to shew me pleasure.   I desired to know what people liued on the banks of this riuer : and I vnderstood by this man that it was inhabited by 23 languages, and these were bordering vpon the riuer, besides others not farre off, and that there were besides these 23. languages, other people also which hee knewe not, aboue the riuer.   I asked him whether euery people were liuing in one towne together : and he answered me, No : but that they had many houses standing scattered in the fieldes, and that euery people had their Countrey seuerall and distinguished, and that in euery habitation there were great store of people.   He shewed me a towne which was in a mountaine, and told me that there was there great store of people of bad conditions, which made continual warre vpon them : which being without a gouernour, and dwelling in that desert place, where small store of Maiz groweth, came downe into the playne to buy it in trucke of Deeres skinnes, wherewith they were apparelled with long garments, which they did cutte with rasors, and sewed with needles made of Deeres bones : and that they had great houses of stone.   I asked them whether there were any there of that Countrey ; and I found one woman which ware a garment like a little Mantle, which clad her from the waste downe to the ground, of a Deeres skin well dressed. Then I asked him whether the people which dwelt on the riuers side, dwelt alwayes there, or els sometime went to dwell in some other place : he answered me, that in the summer season they aboade there, and sowed there ; and after they had gathered in their croppe they went their way, and dwelt in other houses which they had at the foote of the mountaine farre from the riuer. And hee shewed me by signes that the houses were of wood com-

[marginal note:] Another nation.

[marginal note:] People of 23. languages dwelling along this riuer.

[marginal note:] Acuco as Gomara writeth is on a strong mountaine.

passed with earth without, and I vnderstood that they made a round house, wherein the men and women liued all together. I asked him whether their women were common or no : he tolde me no, and that hee which was married, was to haue but one wife only. I desired to know what order they kept in marying : and he tolde me, that if any man had a daughter to marry, he went where the people kept, and said, I haue a daughter to marry, is there any man here that wil haue her ? And if there were any that would haue her, he answered that he would haue her : and so the mariage was made. And that the father of him which would have her, brought something to giue the yong woman ; and from that houre forward the mariage Dancing and was taken to be finished, and that they sang and singing at danced : and that when night came, the parents tooke mariages of them, and left them together in a place where no body the Sauages. might see them. And I learned that brethren, and sisters, and kinsfolk married not together : and that maydes before they were married conuersed not with men, nor talked not with them, but kept at home at their houses and in their possessions, and wrought : and that if by chance any one had company with men before she were married, her husband forsooke her, and went away into other Countreyes : and that those women which fell into this fault, were accompted naughty packs. And 'that if after they were maried, any man were taken in adultery with another woman, they put him to death : and that no They burne man might haue more that one wife, but very secretly. their dead. They tolde mee that they burned those which dyed : and such as remayned widowes, stayed halfe a yeere, or a whole yeere before they married. I desired to know what they thought of such as were dead. Hee told me that they went to another world, but that they had neither punishment nor glory. The greatest sicknesse that this people dye of is vomitiug of blood by the mouth : and they haue Physicions which cure them with charmes and blowing which they make. The Pipes to apparell of these people were like the former : they drinke Tab- carried their pipes with them to perfume themselues, acco with. like as the people of New Spaine vse Tabacco. I inquired whether they had any gouernour, and found that Maize, they had none, but that every family had their seuerall gourds, Mill. gouernour. These people haue besides their Maiz certaine gourds, and another corne like vnto Mill : they haue

Grindestones, grindstones and earthern pots, wherein they boyle those
earthern   gourds, and fish of the riuer, which are very good.   My
pots, good interpreter could goe no farther then this place: for he
fish.   said that those which we should find farther on our way,
were their enemies, and thefore I sent him backe very well con-
teuted.   Not long after I espied many Indians to come crying
with a loude voice, and running after me.   I stayed to know what
they would haue ; and they told me that they had set vp the
crosse which I had giuen them, in the midst of their dwellings
This riuer   as I had appointed, but that I was to wit, that when
ouerfloweth the riuer did ouerflow, it was wont to reach to that
his banks at place, therefore they prayed mee to giue them leaue
certaine   to remove it, and to set it in another place where the
seasons.   riuer could not come at it, nor carry it away : which
I granted them.

Chap. 5.

Of an Indian of that countrey they haue relation of the state of
    Ceuola, and of the conditions and customes of these
    people, and of their gouernour : and likewise of the
    countreys not farre distant from thence, whereof one was
    called Quicoma, and the other Coama : of the people of
    Quicoma, and of the other Indians not farre distant they
    receiue courtesie.

THus sayling I came where were many Indians, and another
interpreter, which I caused to come with me in my boat.   And
because it was cold, and my people were wet, I leapt on shore,
and commanded a fire to be made, and as we stood thus warming
our selues, an Indian came and strooke me on the arme, pointing
with his finger to a wood, out of which I saw two companies of
men come wt their weapons, and he told me that they came to
set vpon vs : and because I meant not to fall out with any of
them, I retired my company into our boats, and the Indians
which were with me swam into the water, and saued themselues
on the other side of the riuer.   In the meane season I inquired
of that Indian which I had with me, what people they were that
came out of ye wood : and he told me that they were their
enemies, and therefore these others at their approch without
saying any word leapt into the water : and did so, because they

meant to turne backe againe, being without weapons, because they brought none with them, because they vnderstood my wil and pleasure, that they should cary none. I inquired the same things of this interpreter which I had done of the other of the things of that countrey, because I vnderstood that among some people one man vsed to haue many wiues, and among others but one. Now I vnderstood by him, that he had bin at Ceuola, and that it was a moneths iourney from his country, and that from that place by a path that went along that riuer a man might easily trauel thither in xl. daies, and that the occasion that moued him to go thither, was only to see Ceuola, because it was a great thing, and had very hie houses of stone of 3. or 4. lofts, and windowes on ech side; that the houses were compassed about with a wall con-teining the height of a man and an halfe, and that aloft and beneath they were inhabited with people, and that they vsed the same weapons, that others vsed, which we had seene, that is to say, bowes and arrowes, maces, staues and bucklers: and that they had one gouernor, and that they were apparelled with mantles, and with oxe-hides, and that their mantles had a painting about them, and that their gouernour ware a long shirt very fine girded vnto him, and ouer the same diuers mantles: and that the women ware very long garments, and that they were white, and went all couered: and that euery day many Indians wayted at the gate of their gouernour to serue him, and that they did weare many Azure or blew stones, which were digged out of a rocke of stone, and that they had but one wife, with whom they were maried, and that when their gouernors died, all the goods that they had were buried with them. And likewise all the while they eate, many of their men waite at their table to court them, and see them eate, and that they eate with napkins, and that they haue bathes. On Thursday morning at breake of day the Indians came with the like cry to the banke of the riuer, and with greater desire to serue vs, bringing me meat to eat, and making me the like good cheere, which the others had done vnto me, hauing vnderstood what I was: and I gaue them crosses, with the self same order which I did vnto the former. And going farther vp the riuer I came to a country where I found better gouernment: for the inhabitants are wholly obedient vnto one only. But returning againe to conferre with mine interpreter

Ceuola 40 dayes iourney from thence by the riuer.

Turqueses in Ceuola.

touching the dwellings of those of Ceuola, he tolde me, that the lord of that countrey had a dog like that which I caried with me. Afterward when I called for dinner, this interpreter saw certaine dishes caried in the first and later seruice, whereupon he told me that the lord of Ceuola had also such as those were, but that they were greene, and that none other had of them sauing their gouernour, and that they were 4, which he had gotten together with that dogge, and other things, of *This was the Negro that* a blacke man which had a beard, but that he knew *went with* not from what quarter he came thither, and that the *Frier Marco de Niza.* king caused him afterward to be killed, as he heard say. I asked him whether he knew of any towne that was neere vnto that place: he tolde me that aboue the riuer he knew some, and that among the rest there was a lord of a towne called Quicoma, and another of a towne called Coama: and that they had great store of people vnder them. And after he had giuen me this information, he craued leaue of me to returne vnto his companions. From hence I began againe to set saile, and within a dayes sayling I found a towne dispeopled: where assoone as I was entred, by chance there arriued there 500. Indians with their bowes and arrowes, and with them was that principal Indian called Naguachato, which I had left behind, and brought with them certaine conies and yucas: and after I had friendly interteined them all, departing from them, I gaue them license to returne to their houses. As I passed further by the desert, I came to certain cotages, out of which much people came toward me with an old man before them, crying in a language which mine interpreter wel vnderstood, and he said vnto those men: Brethren, you see here that lord; let vs giue him such as we haue, seeing he dooth vs pleasure, and hath passed through so many discourteous people, to come to visit vs. And hauing thus said, he offred to the Sunne, and then to me in like sort as the rest had done. These had certaine great bags and well made of the skins of fishes called Sea-bremes. And I vnderstood that this was a towne belonging vnto the lord of Quicoma, which people came thither onely to gather the fruit of their haruest in summer; and among them I found one which vnderstood mine interpreter very well: whereupon very easily I gaue them the like instruction of the crosse which I, had giuen to others behind. These people had cotton, but they were not very carefull to vse the same: because there was none among them that knew the arte of weauing, and to make apparel thereof. They asked me how they should set vp their crosse when they were come to their dwelling which was in the mountaine, and whether it were best to make an house about it, that it might not be wet, and whether they should hang any thing vpon the armes therof. I said no; and that it sufficed to set it in a place where it might be seene of all men, vntill I returned: and lest peraduenture any men of warre should come that way, they offred mee more men to goe with me, saying that they were naughty men which I should finde aboue; but I would haue none: neuerthelesse 20. of them went with me, which when I drew neere vnto those which were their enemies, they warned mee thereof: and I found their centinels set vpon their guarde on their borders. On Saturday morning I found a great squadron of people sitting vnder an exceeding great arbour, and another part of them without: and when I saw that they rose not vp, I passed along on my voyage: when they beheld this an old man rose vp which said vnto me, Sir, why doe you not receiue victuals to eate of vs, seeing you haue taken food of others? I answered, that I tooke nothing but that which was giuen me, and that I went to none but to such as requested me. Here without any stay they brought me victuals, saying vnto me, that because I entred not into their houses, and stayed all day and all night in the riuer, and because I was the sonne of the Sunne, all men were to receiue me for their lord. I made them signes to sit down, and called that old man which mine interpreter vnderstood, and asked him whose that countrey was, and whether the lord thereof was there, he said yes: and I called him to me; and when he was come, I imbraced him, shewing him great loue: and when I saw that all of them tooke great pleasure at the friendly interteinment which I gaue him, I put a shirt vpon him, and gaue him other trifles, and willed mine interpreter to vse the like speaches to that lord which he had done to the rest; and that done, I gaue him a crosse, which he receiued with a very good wil, as the others did: and this lord went a great way with me, vntill I was called vnto from the other side of the riuer, where the former old man stood with much people: to whom I gaue another crosse, vsing the like speach to them which I had vnto the rest, to wit, how they should vse it. Then following my way, I mette with another great company of people, with whom came that very same olde man whom mine interpreter vnderstood; and when I saw their lord which he shewed vnto me, I prayed him to come with me into my boat, which he did very willingly, and so I went still vp the riuer, and the olde man came and shewed me who were the chiefe lords: and I spake vnto them alwayes with great courtesie, and all of them shewed that they reioyced much thereat, and spake very wel of my comming thither. At night I withdrew my selfe into the midst of the riuer, and asked him many things concerning that country: and I found him as willing and wel disposed to shew them me,

Ceuola a goodly thing. as I was desirous to know them. I asked him of Ceuola: and he told me he had bin there, and that it was a goodly thing, and that the lord thereof was very wel obeyed: and that there were other lords thereabout, with whom he was at continual warre. I asked him whether they had siluer and gold, and he beholding certain bels, said they had metal of their colour. I inquired whether they made it

Gold and siluer in a mountaine neere Ceuola. there, and he answered me no, but that they brought it from a certain mountaine, where an old woman dwelt. I demanded whether he had any knowledge of a riuer called Totonteac, he answered me no, but of another exceeding mighty riuer, wherein there were such huge Crocodiles, that of their hides they made bucklers, and that they worship the Sunne neither more nor lesse then those which I had passed: and when they offer vnto him the fruits of the

This riuer seemeth to bee Northward by the colde. earth, they say: Receiue hereof, for thou hast created them, and that they loued him much, because he warmed them; and that when he brake not foorth, they were acolde. Herein reasoning with him, he began somewhat to complaine, saying vnto me, I know not wherefore the Sunne vseth these termes with vs, because he giueth vs not clothes, nor people to spin nor to weaue them, nor other things which he giueth to many other, and he complayned that those of that country would not suffer them to come there, and would not giue them of their corne. I told him that I would remedie this, whereat he remayned very well satisfied.

Chap. 6.

They are aduertised by the Indians, wherefore the lorde of Ceuola killed the Negro, which went with Frier Marco, and of many other things : And of an old woman called Guatazaca, which liueth in a lake and eateth no food. The description of a beast, of the skinne whereof they make targets. The suspition that they conceiue of them, that they are of those Christians which were seene at Ceuola, and how they cunningly saue themselues.

THe next day which was Sunday before breake of day, began their cry as they were woont : and this was the cry of 2. or 3. sorts of people, which had lyen all night neere the riuers side, wayting for me : and they tooke Maiz and other corne in their mouth, and sprinkled me therewith, saying that that was the fashion which they vsed when they sacrificed vnto the Sunne : afterward they gaue me of their victuals to eat, and among other things, they gaue me many white peason. I gaue them a crosse as I had done to the rest : and in the meane season that old man tolde them great matters of my doing, and poynted me out with his finger, saying, this is the lord, the sonne of the Sunne : and they made me to combe my beard, and to set mine apparel handsomely which I ware vpon my backe. And so great was the confidence that they had in me, that all of them told me what things had passed, and did passe among them, and what good or bad mind they bare one toward another. I asked them wherefore they imparted vnto me all their secrets, and that old man answered mee : Thou art our lord, and we ought to hide nothing from our lord. After these things, following on our way, I began againe to inquire of him the state of Ceuola, and whether he knewe that those of this countrey had euer seene people like vnto vs : he answered me no, sauing one Negro which ware about his legs and armes certain things which did ring. Your lordship is to cal to mind how this Negro which went with frier Marco was wont to weare bels, and feathers on his armes and legs, and that he caried plates of diuers colours, and that it was not much aboue a yeere agoe since he came into those parts. I demanded vpon what occasion

The Negro that went with Frier Marco de Niza slaine.

E

he was killed; and he answered me, That the lord of Ceuola

The cause wherefore Stephan Do-rantez the Negro was slaine. inquired of him whether he had other brethren: he answered that he had an infinite number, and that they had great store of weapons with them, and that they were not very farre from thence. Which when he had heard, many of the chiefe men consulted together, and resolued to kil him, that he might not giue newes vnto these his brethren, where they dwelt, and that for this cause they slew him, and cut him into many pieces, which were diuided among all those chiefe lords, that they might know assuredly that he was dead: and also that he had a dogge like mine, which he likewise killed a great while after. I asked him whether they of Ceuola had any enemies, and he said they had. And he reckoned vnto me 14. or 15. lords which had warre with them: and that they had mantles, and bowes like those aboue mentioned: howbeit he told me that I should find going vp the riuer a people that had no warre neither with their neighbors, nor with any other. He told me that they had 3. or 4. sorts of trees bearing most excellent fruite to eate: and that in a certaine lake dwelt an olde woman, which was much honoured and worshipped of them: and that shee remayned in a litle house which was there, and that she neuer did eate any thing: and that there they made things which did sound, and that many mantles, feathers and Maiz were giuen vnto her. I asked what her name was, and he tolde me that she was called Guatuzaca, and that thereabout

Antonio d'Es-pejo speak-eth of such a great lake. were many lords which in their life and death, vsed the like orders which they of Ceuola did, which had their dwelling in the summer with painted mantles, and in the winter dwelt in houses of wood of 2. or 3. lofts hie: and that he had seene all these things, sauing the old woman. And when againe I began to aske him more questions, he would not answere me, saying that he was wearie of me: and many of those Indians comming about me, they said among themselues: Let vs marke him well, that we may knowe him when he commeth back againe. The Monday following, the riuer was beset with people like to them, and I began to request the old man to tell me what people were in that countrey, which told me he thought I would soone forget them: and here he reckoned vp vnto me a great number of lords, and people at the least 200. And discoursing with him of their armour, he said that some of them had certaine

very large targets of lether, aboue two fingers thicke. I
asked him of what beasts skinne they made them: and he
discribed vnto me a very great beast, like vnto an Oxe, *This might*
but longer by a great handfull, with broad feete, the *be the crooke*
legs as ˙bigge as the thigh of a man, and the head *backed oxe*
seuen handfuls long, the forehead of three spannes, *of Quiuira.*
and the eyes bigger then ones fist, and the hornes of the length
of a mans leg, out of which grew sharpe poynts, an handfull
long, the forfeete and hinderfeete aboue seuen handfuls bigge,
with a wrethed tayle, but very great; and holding vp his armes
aboue his head, he said the beast was higher then that. After
this hee gaue mee information of another olde woman which
dwelt toward the sea side. I spent this day in giuing crosses to
those people as I had done vnto the former. This old man that
was with me leapt on shore, and fell in conference with another
which that day had often called him; and here both of them
vsed many gestures in their speach, moouing their armes, and
poynting at me. Therefore I sent mine interpreter out, willing
him to drawe neere vnto them, and listen what they said; and
within a while I called him, and asked him whereof they talked,
and he sayd, that he which made those gestures said vnto the
other, that in Ceuola there were others like vnto vs with beards,
and that they said they were Christians, and that both of
them sayd that we were all of one company, and *The Sauages*
that it were a good deede to kill vs, that those others *treasons to*
might haue no knowledge of vs, lest they might *be taken*
come to doe them harme: and that the old *heede of.*
man had answered him, this is the sonne of the Sunne, and our
lord, he doth vs good, and wil not enter into our houses,
although we request him thereunto: he will take away nothing
of ours, he wil meddle with none of our women, and that to be
short, he had spoken many other things in my commendation
and fauour: and for all this the other stedfastly affirmed that we
were all one, and that the old man said, Let vs goe vnto him,
and aske him whether he be a Christian as the other be, or els
the sonne of the Sunne: and the old man came vnto me, and
sayd: In the countrey of Ceuola whereof you spake *Certaine*
vnto me doe other men like vnto you dwell. Then *newes of the*
I began to make as though I wondred, and answered *Spanyaads at*
him, that it was impossible; and they assured me *Ceuola.*
that it was true, and that two men had seene them which came

from thence, which reported that they had things which did shoote fire, and swords as we had.   I asked them whether they had seene them with their owne eyes?   and they answered no; but that certaine of their companions had seene them.   Then hee asked mee whether I were the sonne of the Sunne, I answered him yea.   They said that those Christians of Ceuola said so likewise.   And I answered them that it might well be. Then they asked mee if those Christians of Ceuola came to ioyne themselues with me, whether I would ioyne with them: and I answered them, that they needed not to feare any whit at all, for if they were the sonnes of the Sunne as they said, they must needes be my brethren, and would vse towards all men the like loue and courtesie which I vsed : whereupon hereat they seemed to be somewhat satisfied.

Chap. 7.

It is tolde him that they are ten dayes iourney distant from Ceuola, and that there be Christians there, which make warre against the lords of that countrey.   Of the Sodomie which those Indians vse with foure young men, appoynted for that seruice, which weare womens apparel.   Seeing they could not send newes of their being there to them of Ceuola, they went backe againe downe the riuer to their ships.

THen I prayed them to tel me how many dayes that kingdom of Ceuola, which they spake of, was distant from that riuer: and that man answered, that there was the space of tenne dayes iourney without habitation, and that he made none accompt of the rest of the way, because there were people to be found.   Vpon this aduertisement I was desirous to certifie Captaine Francis Vazquez of my being there, and imparted my mind with my souldiers, among whom I found none that was willing to goe thither, although I offered them many rewards in your lordships name, onely one Negro slaue though with an euil wil offred himselfe vnto me to go thither : but I looked for the comming of those two Indians which they tolde me of, and herewithall we went on our way vp the riuer against the streame in such sort as

Ceuola tenne dayes distant from this place.
A desert of ten dayes iourney.

we had done before.   Here that olde man shewed me as a
strange thing a sonne of his clad in womans apparel, exercising
their office : I asked him how many there were of these among
them, and he told me there were foure ; and that when any of
them died, there was a search made of all the women with child
which were in the country, and that the first sonne which was
borne of them, was appoynted to doe that duetie belonging vnto
women, and that the women clad him in their apparell, saying,
that seeing he was to doe that which belonged to them, he should
weare their apparel : these yong men may not haue carnall copu-
lation with any woman : but all the yong men of the countrey
which are to marrie, may company with them.   These men
receiue no kind of reward for this incestuous act of the people of
that countrey, because they haue libertie to take whatsoeuer they
find in any house for their food.   I saw likewise certaine women
which liued dishonestly among men : and I asked the old man
whether they were married, who answered me noe, but they were
common women, which liued apart from the married women.   I
came at length after these discourses to pray them to send for
those Indians, which they said had bin at Ceuola, and they
told me that they were eight dayes iourney distant from
that place, but that notwithstanding there was one among them
which was their companion and which had spoken with them, as he
met them on the way, whem they went to see the kingdome of
Ceuola, and that they told him that he were not best to goe any
farther, for he should find there a fierce nation like vs : and of the
same qualities and making, which had fought much with the
people of Ceuola, because they had killed a Negro of their company
saying, Wherefore haue yee killed him ? what did he to you ? did
he take any bread from you, or do you any other wrong ? and
such like speech.   And they said moreouer, that these people
were called Christians, which dwelt in a great house, and that
many of them had oxen like those of Ceuola, and other litle
blacke beastes with wooll and hornes, and that some of them had
beasts which they rode vpon, which ran very swiftly ; and that
one day before their departure, from sunne rising vntill sunne
setting these Christians were all day in comming thither, and all
of them lodged in that place where others had lodged, and that
these two met with two Christians, which asked them whence
they were, and whether they had fields sowen with corne : and
they told them that they dwelt in a farre country, and that they

had corne, and that then they gaue each of them a litle cap, and
they gaue them another to cary to their other companions, which
they promised to do, and departed quickly.   When I vnderstood
this, I spoke againe with my company, to see if any one of them
would go thither, but I found them vnwilling as at the first, and
they layd against me greater inconueniences.   Then I called the
old man to see if he would giue me any people to goe with me,
 A desert.   and victuals to trauel through that wildernes, but he
laid before me many inconueniences and dangers,
which I might incurre in that voyage, shewing me the danger
that there was in passing by a lord of Cumana, which threatned
to make warre vpon them, because his people had entred into
the others countrey to take a stagge, and that I should not there,
fore depart thence without seeing him punished.   And when I
replied that in any wise I must needes goe to Ceuola, he willed
me to surcease from that purpose, for they looked that that lord
without al doubt would come to annoy them, and that therefore
they could not leaue their countrey naked to goe with me, and
that it would be better, that I would make an end of that warre
betweene them; and that then I might haue their company
to Ceuola.   And vpon this point we grew to such variance,
that we began to grow into choler, and in a rage he
would haue gone out of the boat, but I stayed him,
and with gentle speeches began to pacifie him, seeing that it
imported mee much to haue him my friend : but for all my
courtesies which I shewed him, I could not alter him from his
mind, wherein he stil remained obstinate.   In the meane while
I sent a man away vnto my ships to giue them knowledge of the
iourney that I had determined to make.   After this I prayed the
old man that he would fetch him backe again, because I had
determined, that seeing I saw no meanes to be able to go to
Ceuola, and because I would stay no longer among those people,
because they should not discouer me, and likewise because I
meant in person to visit my ships, with determination to returne
againe vp the riuer, carying with me other companions, and
leaue there some which I had sicke, and telling the olde man
and the rest that I would returne, and leauing them satisfied the
best I could (although they alwayes said that I went away for
feare) I returned downe the riuer : and that way which I had
gone against the streame vp the riuer in 15 dayes and an halfe, I
made in my returne in 2. dayes and an halfe, because the streame

was great and very swift. In this wise going downe
the riuer, much people came to the banks, saying, Sir, IIe returneth in 2 dayes and
wherefore doe you leaue vs ? what discourtesie hath an halfe to
bin done vnto you ? did you not say that you would his ships.
remayne continually with vs, and be our Lord ;
And turne backe again ? if any man aboue the riuer hath done
you any wrong we will goe with our weapons with you and kill
him ; and such like words ful of loue and kindnes.

Chap. 8.

When they came to their shippes the Captaine named the coast
La Campanna de la Cruz, and builded a Chapel vnto our
Lady, and called the riuer El Rio de Buena Guia, and
returned vp the same againe ? when he came to Quicona
and Coama the Lords of those places vsed him very
courteously.

VPon mine arriuall at my ships I found all my people in
health, although very heauie for my long stay, and because the
current had fretted fower of their cables, and that they had lost
two ankers which were recouered. After we had brought our
ships together, I caused them to bring them into a good harbour,
and to giue the carena to the shippe called Sanct Peter, and to
mend all that were needfull. And here assembling all my company together, I opened vnto them what knowledge I had
receiued of Francis Vasquez ; and how it might be that in those
sixteeeene dayes space which I was in sayling vp the riuer he
might peraduenture haue some knowledge of me, and that I was
minded to returne vp the riuer once againe to try if I could
finde any means to ioyne myself with him : and although some
spake against my determination, I caused al my boates to bee
made ready, because the ships had no need of them.
I caused one of them to be filled with wares of ex- Mark what things the
change, with corne and other seedes, with hennes Spaniardes
and cockes of Castile, and departed vp the riuer, cary with them in newe
leauing order that in that prouince called Campanna discoueries.
de la Cruz they should build an Oratorie or Chapell,
and called it the Chappell of our Lady de la Buena Guia, and
that they should call this riuer Rio de Buena because that is your
Lordships Deuise : I carried with me Nicolas Zamorano Pilote

mayor, to take the height of the pole. And I departed on
Tuesday the fourteenth of September, and on Wednesday I came
vnto the first dwellings of the first Indians, which came running
to hinder my passage, supposing that we had bene other people,
for we caried with vs a fifer, and a drummer, and 1 was clad in
other apparell, then I went in before, when they saw me first of
all : and when they knew me they stayed, though I could not
grow vnto perfect friendship with them, whereupon I gaue some
of those seedes which I brought with mee ; teaching them how
they should sow them : and after I had sayled 3 leagues, my
first interpretour came euen to my boat to seeke me with great
ioy, of whom I demanded wherefore he had left me, he tolde me
that certaine companions of his had led him away. I made him
good countenance and better intertainment, because he should
beare me companie againe, considering howe much it did im-
porte me to haue him with me. He excused himselfe because

Parrats in these parts. he stayed there to bring mee certaine feathers of
Parrats, which he gaue me. I asked him what
people these were, and whether they had any Lord :
hee answered me yea ; and named three or foure vnto me, of
24 or 25 names of people which he knew and that they had

Two moones to Ceuola. houses painted within, and that they had trafficke
with those of Ceuola, and that in two moones he
came into the countrey. He told me moreouer
many other names of Lords, and other people,

Another booke writ- ten of the particulars of that countrey. which I haue written downe in a booke of mine,
which I will bring my selfe vnto your Lordship. But
I thought good to deliuer this brief relation to
Augustine Guerriero in this hauen of Colima, that he
might send it ouerland to your Lordshippe, to whom
I haue many other things to imparte.

But to returne to my iourney, I arriued at Quicama, where the
Indians came forth with great ioy and gladnes to receive me,
aduertizing me that their Lord waited for my comming ; to whom
when I was come I found that he had with him fiue or sixe
thousand men without weapons, from whom he went aparte with some
two hundred onely, all which brought victuals with them, and so
he came towards me, going before the rest with great authoritie,
and before him and on each side of him were certaine which
made the people stand aside, making him way to passe. Hee
ware a garment close before and behind and open on both sides,

fastened with buttons, wrought with white and blacke checker worke, it was very soft and well made, being of the skinnes of certaine delicate fishes called Sea breams. Assoone as he was come to the waters side his seruants tooke him vp in their armes, and brought him into my boate, where I embraced him and receiued him with great ioy, shewing vnto him much kindnesse: vpon which intertainment his people standing by and beholding the same seemed not a litle to reioyce. This Lord turning himselfe to his people willed them to consider my courtesie, and that he being of his owne accord come vnto me with a strange people, they might see how good a man I was, and with how great loue I had entertained him, and that therefore they should take me for their Lord, and that all of them should become my seruants, and doe whatsoeuer I would command them. There I caused him to sit downe, and to eat certaine conserues of sugar which I had brought with mee, and willed the interpreter to thanke him in my name for the fauour which he had done me in vouchsafing to come to see mee, recommending vnto him the worshipping of the crosse, and all such other things as I had recommended to the rest of the Indians; namely that they should liue in peace, and should leaue off warres, and should continue alwayes good friendes together: he answered that of long time they had continued in warres with their neighbours, but that from thence forward he would command his people that they should giue food to all strangers that passed through his kingdome, and that they should doe them no kinde of wrong, and that if any nation should come to inuade him, he said he would tell them howe I had commanded that they should liue in peace, and if they refused the same, he would defend himselfe, and promised me, that he would neuer goe to seeke warre, if others came not to invade him. Then I gaue him certaine trifles, as well of the seedes which I brought, as of the hens of Castile, wherewith he was not a litle pleased. And at my departure I caryed certaine of his people with me, to make friendship betweene them and those other people which dwelt aboue the Riuer: and here the interpreter came vnto me, to craue leaue to returne home: and I gaue him certaine gifts wherewith he departed greatly satisfied.

The next day I came to Coama, and many of them knew me not, seeing me clad in other apparel, but the old man which was there as soone as he knew me leapt into the water, saying vnto

F

me, Sir, lo here is the man which you left with me, which came
forth very ioyfull and pleasant declaring vnto me the great
courtesies which that people had shewed him, saying that they
had strouen together who should haue him to his house, and
that it was incredible to thinke what care they had at the rising
of the Sunne to hold vp their hands and kneele before the
Crosse.   I gaue them of my seedes and thanked them hartily for
the good entertainement which they had shewed my man, and
they besought me that I would leaue him with them, which I
granted them vntill my return, and he stayed among them very
willingly.   Thus I went forward vp the Riuer, taking that olde
man in my companie, which tolde mee, that two Indians came
from Cumana to enquire for the Christians, and that he had
answered them that he knew none such, but that he
Treason of the sauages. knew one which was the sonne of the Sunne, and
that they had perswaded him to ioyne with them to
kill mee and my companions.   I wished him to lend me two
Indians, and I would send word by them, that I would come
vnto them, and was desirous of their friendship, but that if they
on the contrary would haue warre, I would make such a warre
with them, that should displease them.   And so I passed
through all that people, and some came and asked me, why I
had not giuen them Crosses as well as the rest, and so I gaue
them some.

Chap. 9.

They goe on land, and see the people worship the Crosse
which they had giuen them.   The Captain causeth an
Indian to make a draught of the countrey : hee sendeth a
Crosse to the Lord of Cumana, and going down the
Riuer with the streame, he arriueth at his ships.   Of the
error of the Pilots of Cortez as touching the situation of
this Coast.

THe next day I went on land to see certaine cottages, and I
found many women and children holding vp their hands and
kneeling before a Crosse which I had giuen them.   When I
came thither I did the like my self; and conferring with the old

man, he began to informe me of as many people and Prouinces
as he knew.   And when euening was come I called the old man
to come and lodge with mee in my boate; hee answered that
hee would not goe with mee because I would wearie him with
asking him questions of so many matters : I told him that I
would request him nothing else but that he would set me downe
in a chart as much as he knew concerning that Riuer, and what
maner of people those were which dwelt vpon the banckes
thereof on both sides : which he did willingly.   And then he
requested me that I would describe my countrey vnto him, as
he had done his vnto me.   And for to content him, I caused a
draught of certaine things to be made for him.   The next day I
entred betweene certaine very high mountaines, through which
this Riuer passeth with a streight chanel, and the boats went vp
against the streame very hardly for want of men to draw the
same.   Here certaine Indians came and told me, that in the
same place there were certaine people of Cumana, and among
the rest an enchanter, who enquired which way we would passe;
and they telling him that we meant to passe by the Riuer, he set
certaine canes on both sides thereof, through which wee passed,
without receiuing any kinde of domage which they intended
against vs.   Thus going forward I came vnto the house of the
olde man which was in my company, and here I caused a very
high crosse to be set vp, whereupon I engraued certaine letters
to signifie that I was come thither: and this I did, that if by
chance any of the people of the generall Vasquez de Coronado
should come thither, they might haue knowledge of my being
there.   At length seeing I could not attaine to the knowledge of
that which I sought for, I determined to returne backe vnto my
ships.   And being ready to depart there arriued two Indians,
which by meanes of the interpreters of the old man, told me that
they were sent to me, and that they were of Cumana, and that
their Lord could not come himselfe, because he was farre from
that place, but desired me to signifie vnto him what my pleasure
was.   I told them, that I wished that he would alwayes imbrace
peace, and that I was comming to see that countrey, but being
inforced to returne backe downe the Riuer I could not now doe
it, but that hereafter I would returne, and that in the meane
season they should giue that Crosse vnto their Lorde, which
they promised me to do, and they went directly to cary him that
Crosse with certaine feathers which were on the same.   Of these

This Riuer ran much farther vp then he had trauelled. I sought to vnderstand what people dwelt vpward vpon the bankes of the Riuer, which gaue me knowledge of many people, and told me that the Riuer went farre more vp into the land then I had yet seene, but that they knew not the head thereof, because it was very far into the countrey, and that many other Riuers fell into the same.

Hauing learned thus much the next day morning I returned downe the Riuer, and the day following I came where I had left my Spaniard, with whom I spake, and told him that all things had gone well with me, and that at this* time and the former I had gone aboue 30 leagues into the countrey. The Indians of that place inquired of me what the cause was of my departure, and when I would returne; to whom 1 answered, that I would returne shortly. Thus sayling downe the streame, a woman leapt into the water crying vnto vs to stay for her, and shee came into our boate, and crept vnder a bench, from whence we could not make her to come out: I vnderstood that shee did this, because her husband had taken vnto him another wife, by whom hee had children, saying that she ment not to dwell any longer with him, seeing he had taken another wife. Thus shee and another Indian came with me of their owne accord, and so I came into my ships, and making them ready we proceeded home on our voyage, coasting and oftentimes going on land, and entering a great way into the countrey, to see if I could learne any newes of Captaine Francis Vasquez and his companie; of whom I could haue no other knowledge, but such as I learned in the aforesaide Riuer. I bring with me many actes of taking possession of all that Coast. And by the situation of the Riuer, and the height which I tooke, I finde that that which the Masters and Pilots of the Marquesse tooke is false, and that they were deceiued by 2 degrees, and I haue sayled beyond them aboue 4 degrees. I sayled vp the Riuer 85 leagues, where I saw and learned all the particulars before mentioned, and many other things; whereof when it shall please God to giue me leaue to kisse your Lordships hands, I will deliuer you the full and perfect relation. I thinke my selfe to haue had very good fortune, in that I found Don Luis de Castilia, and Augustine Ghenero in the port of Colima: for the Galiot of the Adelantado came vpon mee, which was there with the rest of his fleet, and commanded me to strike sayle, which seeming a strange thing vnto me, and

not vnderstanding in what state things were in Nueua Espanna, I
went about to defend my selfe, and not to doe it. In the meane
while came Don Luis de Castilia in a boate and conferred with
mee, and I lay at anchor on the other side of the hauen where
the saide fleete road, and I gaue vnto him this relation (and to
auoyd striffe I determined to sayle away by night) which relation
I caryed about me briefly written ; for I alwayes had a purpose
to send the same, as soone as I should touch vpon Nueua
Espanna, to aduertise your Lordship of my proceedings.

An extract of a Spanish letter written from Pueblo de los Angeles
in Nueua Espanna in October 1597, touching the discouerie of the rich Isles of California, being distant eight
dayes sayling from the maine.

WE haue seene a letter written the eight of October 1597, out
of a towne called Pueblo de los Angeles situate eighteene leagues
from Mexico, making mention of the Ilands of California situate
two or three hundreth leagues from the maine land of Nueua
Espanna, in Mar del Sur : as that thither haue bene sent before
that time some people to conquer them : which with losse of some
twentie men were forced backe. After that they had wel visited
and found those Islands or countreys to be very rich of gold and
siluer mynes, and of very fayre Orientall pearles, which were
caught in good quantitie vpon one fathome and an halfe passing
in beautie the pearles of the Island Margarita : the report thereof
caused the Vice-roy of Mexico to send a citizen of Mexico with
two hundreth men to conquer the same. Therein also was
affirmed that within eight dayes they could sayle thither from the
mayne.

The course which Sir Francis Drake held from the hauen of
Guatulco in the South sea on the backe side of Nueua
Espanna, to the North-west of California as far as fourtie
three degrees : and his returne back along the said Coast
to thirtie eight degrees : where finding a faire and goodly
hauen, he landed, and staying there many weekes, and
discouering many excellent things in the countrey and
great shewe of rich minerall matter, and being offered the
dominion of the countrey by the Lord of the same, hee
tooke possession thereof in the behalfe of her Maiestie,
and named it Noua Albion.

WEe kept our course from the Isle of Cano (which lyeth in

eight degrees of Northerly latitude, and within two leagues of the maine of Nicaragua, where wee calked and trimmed our ship) along the Coast of Nueua Espanna, vntill we came to the Hauen and Towne of Guatulco, which (as we were informed) had but seuenteene Spaniards dwelling in it, and we found it to stand in fifteene degrees and fiftie minutes.

Assoone as we were entred this Hauen we landed, and went presently to the towne, and to the Towne house, were we found a Iudge sitting in iudgement, he being associate with three other officers, vpon three Negroes that had conspired the burning of the Towne : both which Iudges, and prisoners we tooke, and brought them a shippeboord, and caused the chiefe Iudge to write his letter to the Towne, to command all the Townesmen to auoid, that we might safely water there. Which being done, and they departed, wee ransaked the Towne, and in one house we found a pot of the quantitie of a bushell full of royals of plate, which we brought to our ship.

And here one Thomas Moone one of our companie, took a Spanish gentleman as he was flying out of the Towne, and searching him he found a chaine of Gold about him, and other iewels, which we tooke and so let him goe.

At this place our Generall among other Spaniards, set ashore his Portugall Pilote, which he tooke at the Island of Cape Verde, out of a ship of Saint Marie port of Portugall, and hauing set them ashoore, we departed thence.

The Portugal Pilote set on land.

Our General at this place and time thinking himselfe both in respect of his priuate iniuries receiued from the Spaniards, as also of their contempts and indignities offered to our Countrey and Prince in generall, sufficiently satisfied, and reuenged : and supposing that her Maiestie at his returne would rest contented with this seruice, purposed to continue no longer vpon the Spanish coastes, but began to consider and to consult of the best way for his Countrey.

He thought it not good to returne by the Streights, for two speciall causes : the one, least the Spaniards should there waite, and attend for him in great number and strength, whose handes he being left but one ship, could not possibly escape. The other cause was the dangerous situation of the mouth of the Streits of the South side, with continuall stormes raining and blustring, as he found by experience, besides the shoals and sands vpon the coast, wherefore he thought it not a good course to aduenture that way : he resolued therefore to auoide these hazards, to goe forward to the Islands of the Malucos, and therehence to saile the course of the Portugales by the Cape of Bona Sperança.

Vpon this resolution, he began to thinke of his best way for the Malucos, and finding himselfe, where hee now was, becalmed, hee sawe that of necessitie hee must bee enforced to take a Spanish course, namely to saile somewhat Northerly to get a good winde, and thus much we sayled from the 16 of Aprill after our olde stile till the third of Iune.

The fift day of Iune being in fortie three degrees towardes the pole Arcticke, being speedily come out of the extreame heate, wee found the ayre so colde, that our men being pinched with the same, com-playned of the extremitie thereof, and the further we went, the more the colde increased vpon vs, where-upon we thought it best for that time to seeke land, and did so, finding it not mountainous, but low plaine land, and we drew backe againe without landing, til we came within thirtie eight degrees towardes the line. In which height it pleased God to send vs into a faire and good Bay, with a good winde to enter the same.

Sir Francis Drake sayled on the backe side of America, to 43 degrees of Northerly latitude.

38 degrees.

In this Bay wee ankered the seuententh of Iune, and the people of the Countrey, hauing their houses close by the waters side, shewed themselues vnto vs, and sent a present to our Generall.

When they came vnto vs, they greatly wondred at the things which we brought, but our Generall (according to his naturall and accustomed humanitie) curteously intreated them, and liberally bestowed on them necessarie things to couer their nakednesse, whereupon they supposed vs to be gods, and would not be perswaded to the contrary : the presentes which they sent vnto our Generall were feathers, and cals of net worke. .

Their houses are digged round about with earth, and haue from the vttermost brimmes of the circle clifts of wood set vpon them, ioyning close together at the toppe like a spire steeple, which by reason of that closenesse are very warme.

A description of the people and Countrey of Noua Albion.

Their bed is the ground with rushes strawed on it, and lying about the house, they haue the fire in the middest. The men goe naked, the women take bulrushes and kembe them after the maner of hempe, and thereof make their loose garments, which being knit about their middles, hang downe about their hippes, hauing also about their shoulders a skinne of Deere, with the haire vpon it.   These women are very obedient and seruiceable to their husbands.

After they were departed from vs, they came and visited vs the second time, and brought with them feathers and bags of Tabacco for presents : And when they came to the toppe of the hil (at the bottome whereof wee had pitched our tents) they stayed themselues, where one appointed for speaker, wearied himselfe with making a long oration, which done, they left their bowes vpon the hill and came downe with their presents.

In the meane time the women remaining on the hill, tormented themselues lamentably, tearing their flesh from their cheekes, whereby we perceiued that they were about a sacrifice.   In the meane time our Generall, with his companie, went to prayer, and to reading of the Scriptures, at which exercise they were attentiue and seemed greatly to be affected with it : but when they were come vnto vs they restored againe vnto vs those things which before we had bestowed vpon them.

The newes of our being there being spread through the countrey, the people that inhabited round about came downe, and amongst them the king himself, a man of a goodly stature, and comely personage, with many other tall and warlike men : before whose comming were sent two Ambassadours to our Generall, to signifie that their king was comming, in doing of which message, their speech was continued about halfe an howre. This ended, they by signes requested our Generall to send some-thing by their hand to their king, as a token that his comming might bee in peace : wherein our Generall hauing satisfied them, they returned with glad tidings to their king, who marched to vs with a princely Maiestie, the people crying continually after their maner, and as they drewe neere vnto vs, so did they striue to behaue themselues in their actions with comelinesse.

In the fore front was a man of a goodly personage, who bare the scepter, or mace before the king, whereupon hanged two crownes, a lesse and a bigger, with three chaines of a marueilous length : the crownes were made of knit work wrought artificially with feathers of diuers colours : the chaines were made of a bony substance and few be the persons among them that are admitted

These are like chaines of Esurnoy in Canada and Hochelage.

to weare them : and of that number also the persons are stinted, as some ten, some twelue, &c. Next vnto him which bare the scepter, was the king himselfe, with his Guarde about his person, clad with Conie skinnes, and other skinnes : after them followed the naked common sort of people, euery one hauing his face painted, some with white, some with blacke, and other colours, and hauing in their hands one thing or other for a present, not so much as their children, but they also brought their presents.

In the meane time, our Generall gathered his men together, and marched within his fenced place, making against their approching, a very warlike shewe. They being trooped togéther in their order, and a general salutation being made, there was presently a generall silence. When he that bare the scepter before the king, being informed by another, whome they assigned to that office, with a ·manly and loftie voice, proclaimed that which the other spake to him in secret, continuing halfe an houre : which ended, and a generall Amen as it were giuen, the king with the whole number of men, and women (the children excepted) came downe without any weapon, who descending to the foote of the hill, set themselues in order.

In comming towards our bulwarks and tents, the scepter bearer began a song, obseruing his measures in a dance, and that with a stately countenance, whom the king with his Garde, and euery degree of persons following, did in like maner sing and dance, sauing onely the women which daunced and kept silence. The General permitted them to enter within our bulwark, where they continued their song and daunce a reasonable time. When they had satisfied themselues, they made signes to our Generall to sit downe, to whom the king, and diuers others made seuerall orations, or rather supplication, that he would take their prouince and kingdom into his hand, and become their king, making signes that they would resigne vnto him their right and title of the whole land, and become his subiects. In which to perswade vs the better, the king and the rest, with one consent and with great reuerence, ioyfully singing a song, did set the crowne vpon his head, inriched his necke with all their chaines, and offered vnto him many other things, honouring him by the name of Hioh, adding thereunto as it seemed a signe *The king resignes his crowne and kingdome to Sir Francis Drake. Great riches in Noua Albion.*
of triumph : which thing our Generall thought not meete to reiect, because hee knewe not what honour and profite it might

G

bee to our countrey.   Wherefore in the name, and to the vse of
her Maiestie, he tooke the scepter, crowne and dignitie of the
said Countrey in his hands, wishing that the riches and treasure
thereof might so conueniently be transported to the inriching of
her kingdome at home, as it aboundeth in the same.

The common sort of the people leauing the king and his
Guarde with our Generall, scattered themselues together with
their sacrifices among our people, taking a diligent viewe of
euery person ; and such as pleased their fancie, (which were the
yongest) they inclosing them about offred their sacrifices vnto
them with lamentable weeping, scratching, and tearing the flesh
from their faces with their nayles, whereof issued abundance of
blood.   But wee vsed signes to them of disliking this, and stayed
their hands from force, and directed them vpwardes to the
liuing God, whome onely they ought to worshippe.   They
shewed vnto vs their wounds, and craued helpe of them at our
handes, whereupon wee gaue them lotions, plaisters, and
ointments agreeing to the state of their griefes, beseeching God
to cure their deseases.   Euery thirde day they brought their
sacrifices vnto vs, vntill they vnderstoode our meaning, that we
had no pleasure in them : yet they could not be long absent from
vs, but daily frequented our company to the houre of our departure, which departure seemed so grieuous vnto them, that
their ioy was turned into sorrow.   They intreated vs, that being
absent wee would remember them, and by stelth prouided a
sacrifice, which we misliked.

Our necessarie businesse being ended, our Generall with his
companie traueiled vp into the Countrey to their villages, where
we found heardes of Deere by a thousand in a companie, being
most large and fat of body.

We found the whole countrey to bee a warren of a strange
kinde of Conies, their bodyes in bignes as be the Barbary
Abundance of Conies, their heads as the heades of ours, the feet of
strange   a Want, and the taile of a Rat being of great length :
conies.   vnder her chinne on either side a bagge, into the
which shee gathereth her meate when she hath filled her belly
abroad.   The people eate their bodies, and make great account
of their skinnes, for their Kings coate was made of them.

Our Generall called this countrey, Noua Albion, and that for
two causes : the one in respect of the white bankes and cliffes,
which ly towardes the sea : and the other, because it might haue

some affinitie with our Countrey in name, which sometimes was so called.

There is no part of earth heere to be taken vp, wherein there is not some special likelihood of gold or siluer. Golde and siluer in the earth of Noua Albion.

At our departure hence our Generall set 'vp a monument of our being there; as also of her Maiesties right and title to the same, namely a plate nailed vpon a faire great poste, whereupon was ingrauen her Maiesties name, the day and yeere of our arriuall there, with the free giuing vp of the Prouince and people into her Maiesties hands, together with her highnes picture and armes, in a piece of sixe pence of current English money vnder the plate, where vnder was also written the name of our Generall.

It seemeth that the Spaniards hitherto had neuer bene in this part of the countrey, neither did euer discouer the land by many degrees to the Southwards of this place.

THE DISCOVERIE

OF THE LARGE, RICH, AND BEAUTIFULL EMPIRE OF GUIANA, WITH
A RELATION OF THE GREAT AND GOLDEN CITIE OF MANOA
(WHICH THE SPANIARDS CALL EL DORADO) AND THE PRO-
UINCES OF EMERIA, AROMAIA, AMAPAIA, AND OTHER
COUNTRIES, WITH THEIR RIUERS ADIOYNING. PERFORMED
IN THE YEERE 1595 BY SIR WALTER RALEGH KNIGHT,
CAPTAINE OF HER MAIESTIES GUARD, LORDE WARDEN OF
THE STANNERIES, AND HER HIGHNESSE LIEUTENANT
GENERALL OF THE COUNTIE OF CORNE-WALL.

To the right Honourable my singular good Lord and kinsman
Charles Howard, Knight of the Garter, Baron and
Counceller, and of the Admirals of England the most
renowmed: and to the right Honourable Sir Robert
Cecyll knight, Counceller in her Highnesse Priuie
Councils.

FOr your Honours many Honourable and friendly partes, I
haue hitherto onely returned promises, and now for answere of
both your adventures, I haue sent you a bundle of papers, which
I haue deuided betwene your Lordship, and Sir Robert Cecyll in
these two respects chiefly : First for that it is reason, that wastful
factors, when they haue consumed such stockes as they had in
trust, doe yeeld some colour for the same in their account;
secondly for that I am assured, that whatsoeuer shall bee done,
or written by me, shall neede a double protection and defence.
The triall that I had of both your loues, when I was left of all,
but of malice and reuenge, makes me still presume, that you wil
be pleased (knowing what litle power I had to performe ought,
and the great aduantage of forewarned enemies) to answer that
out of knowledge, which others shal but obiect out of malice.
In my more happy times as I did especially Hon. you both, so I
found that your loues sought mee out in the darkest shadow of
aduersitie, and the same affection which accompanied my better

fortune, sored not away from me in my many miseries : al which though I can not requite yet I shal euer acknowledge : and the great debt which I haue no power to pay, I can do no more for a time but confesse to be due. It is true that as my errors were great, so they haue yeelded very grieuous effects, and if ought might haue bene deserued in former times to haue conterpoysed any part of offences, the fruit thereof (as it seemeth) was long before fallen from the tree, and the dead stocke onely remained. I did therefore euen in the winter of my life, vndertake these trauels, fitter for bodies lesse blasted with mis-fortunes, for men of greater abilitie, and for minds of better incouragement, that thereby, if it were possible, I might recouer but the moderation of excesse, and the least tast of the greatest plenty formerly possessed. If I had knowen other way to win, if I had imagined how greater aduentures might haue regained, if I could conceiue what farther meanes I might yet vse, but euen to appease so powerful displeasure, I would not doubt but for one yeere more to hold fast my soule in my teeth, till it were performed. Of that litle remaine I had, I haue wasted in effect all herein.   I haue vndergone many constructions.   I haue been accompanyed with many sorrows, with labour, hunger, heat, sicknes, and perill : It appeareth notwithstanding that I made no other brauado of going to the sea, then was ment, and that I was neuer hidden in Cornewall, or els where, as was supposed. They haue grosly belied me, that foreiudged, that I would rather become a seruant to the Spanish King, then returne, and the rest were much mistaken, who would haue perswaded, that I was too easefull and sensuall to vndertake a iourney of so great trauell.   But, if what I haue done, receiue the gracious construction of a painefull pilgrimage, and purchase the least remission, I shall thinke all too litle, and that there were wanting to the rest many miseries. But if both the times past, the present, and what may be in the future, doe all by one grain of gall continue in eternall distast ; I doe not then know whether I should bewaile my selfe, either for my too much trauell and expence, or condemne my selfe for doing lesse then that, which can deserue nothing. From my selfe I haue deserued no thankes, for I am returned a begger, and withered, but that I might haue bettred my poore estate, it shall appeare by the following discourse, if I had not onely respected her Maiesties future Honour, and riches. It became not the former fortune in which I once liued, to goe iourneys of picory,

it had sorted ill with the offices of Honour, which by her
Maiesties grace I hold this day in England, to run from Cape to
Cape, and from place to place, for the pillage of ordinaries prizes.
Many yeeres since, I had knowledge by relation, of that mighty,
rich and beautifull Empier of Guiana, and of that great and
golden Citie, which the Spaniards call El Dorado, and the
naturals Manoa, which Citie was conquered, reedified, and in-
larged by a yonger sonne of Guainacapa Emperour of Peru, at
such time as Francisco Piçarro and others conquered the said
Empire, from his two elder brethren, Guascar, and Atabalipa,
both then contending for the same, the one being fauoured by
the Orejones of Cuzco, the other by the people of Caxamalca.
I sent my seruant Iacob Whiddon the yere before, to get knowledge of the passages, and I had some light from Captaine
Parker, sometime my seruant, and nowe attending on your Lordship, that such a place there was to the Southward of the great
Bay of Charuas, or Guanipa: but I found that it was 600 miles
farther off then they supposed, and many other impediments to
them vnknowen and vnheard.   After I had displanted Don
Antonio de Berreo, who was vpon the same enterprize, leauing
my ships at Trinidad at the Port called Curiapan, I wandred 400
miles into the said countrey by lande and riuer: the particulars I
will leaue to the following discourse.   The countrey hath more
quantity of gold by manifolde, then the best partes of the Indies,
or Peru: All the most of the kings of the borders are already
become her Maiesties vassals: and seeme to desire nothing more
then her Maiesties protection and the returne of the English
nation.   It hath another ground and assurance of riches and
glory, then the voyages of the West Indies, an easier way to inuade the best parts thereof, then by the common course.   The
king of Spaine is not so impouerished, by taking three or foure
Port townes in America, as wee suppose, neither are the riches of
Peru, or Nueua Espanna so left by the sea side, as it can bee
easily washt away with a great flood, or springtide, or left dry
vpon the sandes on a lowe ebbe.   The Port townes are fewe and
poore in respect of the rest within the lande, and are of litle
defence, and are onely rich, when the Fleets are to receiue the
treasure for Spaine: and we might thinke the Spaniards very
simple, hauing so many horses and slaues, if they could not vpon
two dayes warning cary all the golde they haue into the land, and
farre enough from the reach of our foote-men, especially the

Indies being (as they are for the most part) so mountanous, so full of woodes, riuers, and marishes. In the Port townes of the Prouince of Veneçuela, as Cumana, Coro and S. Iago (whereof Coro and S. Iago were taken by Captaine Preston, and Cumana and S. Iosepho by vs) we found not the value of one riall of plate in either: but the Cities of Barquasimeta, Valencia, S. Sebastian, Cororo, S. Lucia, Laguna, Maracaiba, and Truxillo, are not so easely inuaded : neither doeth the burning of those on the coast impouerish the king of Spaine any one ducat : and if we sacke the riuer of Hacha, S. Marta, and Cartagena, which are the Portes of Nueuo reyno, and Popayan ; there are besides within the land, which are indeed riche and populous the townes and Cities of Merida, Lagrita, S. Christophoro, the great Cities of Pamplon, S. Fe de Bogota, Tunxa and Mozo where the Esmeralds are found, the townes and Cities of Marequita, Velez, la Villa de Leua, Palma, Vnda, Angustura, the great citie of Timana, Tocaima, S. Aguila, Pasto, Iuago, the great Citie of Popaian it selfe, Los Remedios, and the rest. If we take the Ports and villages within the Bay of Vraba in the kingdom or riuers of Dariene, and Caribana, the Cities and townes of S. Iuan de Roydas, of Cassaris, of Antiocha, Caramanta, Cali, and Anserma haue gold enough to pay the kings part, and are not easily inuaded by the way of the Ocean : or if Nombre de Dios and Panama be taken in the Prouince of Castilla del oro, and the villages vpon the riuers of Cenu and Chagre ; Peru hath besides those and besides the magnificent cities of Quito and Lima so many ylands, ports, cities, and mines, as if I should name 'them with the rest, it would seem incredible to the reader : of all which, because I haue written a particular treatise of the West Indies, I wil omit the repetition at this time, seeing that in the said treatise I haue anatomised the rest of the sea-townes, aswel of Nicaragua, Iucatan, Nueua Espanna, and the ylands, as those of the Inland, and by what meanes they may be best inuaded, as far as any meane iudgment can comprehend. But I hope it shal appeare that there is a way found to answer euery mans longing, a better Indies for her Maiestie then the King of Spaine hath any : which if it shal please her highnes to vndertake, I shall most willingly end the rest of my daies in folowing the same : if it be left to the spoile and sackage of common persons, if the loue and seruice of so many nations be dispised, so great riches, and so mighty an empire refused, I hope her maiesty wil yet take my humble desire and my labor therin in gracious part, which, if it had not bin in respect of her highnes future honor and riches, could haue laid hands on and ransomed many of the kings and Casiqui of the country, and haue had a reasonable proportion of gold for their redemption : but I haue chosen rather to beare the burden of pouerty, then reproch, and rather to endure a second traue and the chances therof, then to haue defaced an enterprise of so great assurance, vntil I knew whether it pleased God to put a disposition in her princely and royal heart either to folow or foreslow the same : I wil therefore leaue it to his ordinance that hath only power in all things, and do humbly pray that your honors wil excuse such errors, as without the defence of art, ouerrun in euery part of the folowing discourse, in which I haue neither studied phrase, forme or fashion, that you will be pleased to esteeme mee as your owne (though ouer dearly bought) and I shall euer remaine ready to do you all honour and seruice.

W. R.

¶ To the Reader.

BEcause there haue bin diuers opinions conceiued of the gold oare broght from Guiana, and for y^t an Alderman of London and an officer of her Maiesties Mint, hath giuen out that the same is of no price, I haue thought good by the addition of these lines to giue answer aswel to the said malicious slander, as to other obiections. It is true that while we abode at the yland of Trinidad, I was informed, by an Indian, that not far from the Port, where we ancored, there were found certaine mineral stones which they esteemed to be gold, and were thereunto perswaded the rather for that they had seene both English and Frenchmen gather, and imbark some quantities therof : vpon this likelyhood I sent 40. men and gaue order that each one should bring a stone of that mine to make trial of ye goodnes : which being performed, I assured them at their returne that the same was Marcasite, and of no riches or value : notwithstanding diuers, trusting more to their owne sence, then to my opinion, kept of the said Marcasite, and haue tried therof since my returne in diuers places. In Guiana it selfe I neuer saw Marcasite, but al the rocks, mountains, al stones in ye plaines, woods, and by the riuers side are in effect throughshining, and seem maruelous rich, which being tried to be no Marcasite, are the true signes of rich minerals, but are no other then El madre del oro (as the Spaniards terme them) which is the mother of gold, or as it is said by others the scum of gold : of diuers sorts of these many of my company brought also into England, euery one taking yᵉ fairest for the best, which is not general.   For mine own part I did not countermand any mans desire, or opinion, and I could haue aforded them litle if I should haue denied them the pleasing of their owne fancies therein : but I was resolued that gold must be found either in graines separate from the stone (as it is in most of the riuers in Guiana) or els in a kind of hard stone, which we call The white spar, of which I saw diuers hils, and in sundry places, but had neither time nor men, nor instruments fit for labour.   Neere vnto one of the riuers I found of the said White sparre or flint a very great ledge or banke, which I endeuoured to breake by al the meanes I could, because there appeared on the outside some smal graines of golde, but finding no meane to worke the same vpon the vpper part, seeking the sides and circuit of the said rocke, I found a clift in the same from whence with daggers, and with the head of an axe, we got out some smal quantitie therof, of which kind of white stone (wherin gold engendred) we saw diuers hils and rocks in euery part of Guiana, wherein we traueiled.   Of this there haue bin made many trials, and in London it was first assaid by M. Westwood a refiner dwelling in Woodstreet, and it held after the rate of 12000. or 13000. pounds a tunne. Another sort was afterward tried by M. Bulmar and M. Dimock Assay-master, and it held after the rate of 23000 li. a tunne. There was some of it againe tried by M. Palmer comptroller of the Mint, and M. Dimock in goldsmiths hal, and it held after 26900. li. a tun.   There was also at the same time, and by the same persons a trial made of the dust of the said mine which held 8. li. 6. ounces weight of gold in the 100 : there was likewise at the same. time a triall of an image of copper made in Guiana, which held a third part of gold, besides diuers trials made in the countrey, and by others in London.   But because there came ill with the good, and belike the said Alderman was not presented with the best, it hath pleased him therefore to scandall all the rest, and to deface the enterprize as much as in him lieth.   It hath also bene concluded by diuers, that if there had bin any such oare in Guiana, and the same discouered, that I would haue

H

brought home a greater quantitie thereof: first I was not bound to satisfie any man of the quantitie, but such only as aduentured, if any store had bin returned thereof: but it is very true that had al their mountaines bene of massie gold, it was impossible for vs to haue made any longer stay to haue wrought the same: and whosoeuer hath seene with what strength of stone the best gold oare is inuironed, hee will not thinke it easy to be had out in heapes, and especially by vs, who had neither men, instruments, nor time (as it is said before) to performe the same. There were on this discouery no lesse then 100. persons, who can all witnesse, that when we past any branch of the riuer to view the land within, and staied from our boats but 6. houres, wee were driuen to wade to the eyes, at our returne: and if we attempted the same, the day following it was impossible either to ford it, or to swim it, both by reason of the swiftnesse, and also for that the borders were so pestred with fast woods, as neither boat nor man could find place, either to land or to imbarke: for in Iune, Iuly, August and September, it is impossible to nauigate any of those riuers: for such is the fury of the current, and there are so many trees and woods ouerflowne, as if any boat but touch vpon any tree or stake, it is impossible to saue any one person therein: and yer* we departed the land it ranne with such swiftnes, as wee draue downe most commonly against the wind, little lesse then 100. miles a day: Besides our were no other then whirries, one little barge, a small cockboat, and a bad Galiota, which we framed in hast for that purpose at Trinidad, and those little boats had 9. or 10. men a piece, with all their victuals, and armes. It is further true, that we were about 400. miles from our ships, and had bene a moneth from them, which also we left weakly manned in an open road, and had promised our returne in 15. dayes. Others haue deuised that the same oare was had from Barbary, and that we caried it with vs into Guiana: surely the singularitie of that deuice I doe not well comprehend: for mine owne part, I am not so much in loue with these long voyages, as to deuise, therby to cozen my selfe, to lie hard, to fare worse, to be subiected to perils, to diseases, to ill sauors, to be parched and withered, and withall to sustaine the care and labour of such an enterprize, except the same had more comfort, then the fetching of Marcasite in Guiana,

---

* Be fore.

or buying of gold oare in Barbary. But I hope the better sort wil iudge me by themselues, and that the way of deceit is not the way of honour or good opinion: I haue herein consumed much time, and many crownes, and I had no other respect or desire then to serue her Maiestie and my country thereby. If the Spanish nation had bene of like beliefe to these detracters, we should litle haue feared or doubted their attempts, wherewith we now are daily threatned. But if we now consider of the actions both of Charles the 5. who had the maidenhead of Peru, and the abundant treasures of Atabalipa, together with the affaires of the Spanish king now liuing, what territories he hath ·purchased, what he hath added to the acts of his predecessors, how many kingdoms he hath indangered, how many armies, garisons, and nauies he hath and doth mainteine, the great losses which he hath repaired, as in 88. aboue 100. saile of great ships with their artillery, and that no yere is lesse vnfortunate but that many vessels, treasures, and people are deuoured, and yet notwithstanding he beginneth againe like a storme to threaten shipwrack to vs all : we shall find that these abilities rise not from the trades of sacks, and Siuil oringes, nor from ought els that either Spaine, Portugal, or any of his other prouinces produce : it is his Indian gold that indangereth and disturbeth all the nations of Europe, it purchaseth intelligence, creepeth into counsels, and setteth bound loyaltie at libertie, in the greatest Monarchies of Europe. If the Spanish king can keepe vs from forren enterprizes, and from the impeachment of. his trades, either by offer of inuasion, or by besieging vs in Britaine, Ireland, or elsewhere, hee hath then brought the worke of our peril in great forwardnes. Those princes which abound in treasure haue great aduantages ouer the rest, if they once constraine them to a defensiue war, where they are driuen once a yere or oftener to cast lots for their own garments, and ·from such shal all trades, and entercourse be taken away, to the general losse and impouerishment of the kingdom and common weale so reduced : besides when our men are constrained to fight, it hath not the like hope, as when they are prest and incouraged by the desire of spoile and riches. Farther, it is to be douted how those that in time of victory seeme to affect their neighbor nations, wil remaine after the first view of misfortunes, or il successe ; to trust also to the doubtfulnes of a battel, is but a fearefull and vncertaine aduenture, seeing therein fortune is as likely to preuaile, as vertue. It shall not be necessary to alleage all that might bee said, and therefore I will thus conclude, that whatsoeuer kingdome shall be inforced to defend it selfe, may be compared to a body dangerously diseased, which for a season may be preserued with vulgar medicines, but in a short time, and by litle and litle, the same must needs fall to the ground, and be dissolued.   I haue therefore laboured all my life, both according to my smal power, and perswasion, to aduance al those attempts, that might either promise return of profit to our selues, or at least be a let and impeachment to the quiet course and plentifull trades of the Spanish nation, who in my weake iudgement by such a warre were as easily indangered and brought from his powerfulnes, as any prince of Europe, if it be considered from how many kingdoms and nations his reuenues are gathered, and those so weake in their owne beings, and so far seuered from mutual succour.   But because such a preparation and resolution is not to be hoped for in hast, and that the time which our enemies imbrace, cannot be had againe to aduantage, I wil hope that these prouinces, and that Empire now by me discouered shal suffice to inable her Maiestie and the whole kingdome, with no lesse quantities of treasure, then the king of Spaine hath in all the Indies East and West, which he possesseth, which if. the same be considered and followed, ere the Spaniards enforce the same, and if her Maiestie wil vndertake it, 1 wil be contented to lose her highnesse fauour and good opinion for euer, and my life withall, if the same be not found rather to exceed, then to equal whatsoeuer is in this discourse promised or declared.   I will now referre the Reader to the following discourse, with the hope that the perillous and chargeable labours and indeuors of such as thereby seeke the profit and honour of her Maiestie, and the English nation, shall by men of qualitie and vertue receiue such construction, and good acceptance, as themselues would looke to be rewarded withall in the like.

W. R.

¶ The discouerie of Guiana.

ON Thursday the 6. of February in the yeere 1595. we departed England, and the Sunday following had sight of the North cape of Spaine, the winter for the most part continuing prosperous : we passed in sight of the Burlings, and the Rocke,

and so onwards for the Canaries, and ·fel with Fuerte ventura
the 17 of the same moneth, where we spent two or three dayes,
and relieued our companies with some fresh meat. From thence
we coasted by the Grand Canaria, and so to Tenerif, and stayed
there for the Lions whelpe your Lordships ship, and for Captaine
Amyas Preston and the rest. But when after 7. or 8. dayes
wee found them not, we departed and directed our
course for Trinidad with mine owne ship, and a small   The yle of
barke of Captaine Crosses onely (for we had before   Trinidad.
lost sight of a small Galego on the coast of Spaine, which came
with vs from Plimmouth) we arriued at Trinidad the 22. of
March, casting ancker at point Curiapan, which the Spaniards
call punta de Gallo, which is situate in 8. degrees or there
abouts : we abode there 4. or 5. dayes, and in all that time we
came not to the speach of any Indian or Spaniard : on the
coast we saw a fire, as we sailed from the point Caroa towards
Curiapan, but for feare of the Spaniards none durst come to
speake with vs. I my selfe coasted it in my barge close abord
the shore and landed in euery Coue, the better to know the
yland, while the ships kept the chanell. From Curiapan after a
fewe dayes we turned vp Northeast to recouer that place which
the Spaniards call Puerto de los Espannoles, and the inhabitants
Conquerabia, and as before (reuictualling my barge) I left the
ships and kept by the shore, the better to come to speach with
some of the inhabitants, and also to vnderstand the riuers, watering places, and ports of the yland, which (as it is rudely done)
my purpose is to send your Lordship after a few dayes. From
Curiapan I came to a port and seat of Indians called Parico,
where we found a fresh water riuer, but saw no people. From
thence I rowed to another port, called by the naturals Piche,
and by the Spaniards Tierra de Brea: In the way betweene both
were diuers little brookes of fresh water and one salt riuer that
had store of oisters vpon the branches of the trees, and were
very salt and well tasted. All their oisters grow vpon those
boughs and spraies, and not on the ground : the like is commonly seene in other places of the West Indies, and else where.
This tree is described by Andrew Theuet in his French Antarc-
tique, and the forme figured in the booke as a plant very strange,
and by Plinie in his 12. booke of his naturall historie. But in
this yland, as also in Guiana there are very many of them.
    At this point called Tierra de Brea or Piche there is that

abundance of stone pitch, that all the ships of the world may be therewith loden from thence, and we made trial of it in trimming our shippes to be most excellent good, and melteth not with the Sunne as the pitch of Norway, and therefore for shippes trading the South parts very profitable.   From thence wee went to the mountaine foote called Anniperima, and so passing the riuer Carone on which the Spanish Citie was seated, we met with our ships at Puerto de los Espannoles or Conquerabia.

This yland of Trinidad hath the forme of a sheephooke, and is but narrow, the North part is very mountainous, the soile is very excellent and will beare suger, ginger, or any other commoditie that the Indies yeeld.   It hath store of deere, wilde porks, fruits, fish and foule : It hath also for bread sufficient maiz, cassaui, and of those rootes and fruites which are common euery where in the West Indies.   It hath diuers beastes which the Indies haue not : the Spaniards confessed that they found graines of golde in some of the riuers, but they hauing a purpose to enter Guiana (the Magazin of all rich mettals) cared not to spend time in the search thereof any further.   This yland is called by the people thereof Cairi, and in it are diuers nations : those about Parico are called Iaio, those at Punta de Carao are of the Arwacas, and betweene Carao and Curiapan they are called Saluajos, betwene Carao and Punta de Galera are the Nepoios, and those about the Spanish citie terme themselues Carinepagotes : Of the rest of the nations, and of other ports and riuers I leaue to speake here, being impertinent to my purpose, and meane to describe them as they are situate in the particular plot and description of the yland, three parts whereof I coasted with my barge, that I might the better describe it.

Meeting with the ships at Puerto de los Espannoles, we found at the landing place a company of Spaniards who kept a guard at the descent, and they offering a signe of peace, I sent Captaine Whiddon to speake with them, whom afterward to my great griefe

The death of Captaine Whiddon. I left buried in the said yland after my returne from Guiana, being a man most honest and valiant.   The Spaniards seemed to be desirous to trade with vs, and to enter into termes of peace, more for doubt of their owne strength then for ought else, and in the ende vpon pledge, some of them came abord : the same euening there stale also abord vs in a small Canoa two Indians, the one of them being a Casique or Lord of the people called Cantyman, who had the yeere before bene with Captaine Whiddon, and was of his acquaintance. By this Cantyman, wee vnderstood what strength the Spaniards had, howe farre it was to their Citie, and of Don Antonio de Berreo the gouernor, who was said to be slaine in his second attempt of Guiana, but was not.

While we remained at Puerto de los Espannoles some Spaniards came abord vs to buy linnen of the company, and such other things as they wanted, and also to view our ships and company, all which I entertained kindly and feasted after our maner : by meanes whereof I learned of one and another as much of the estate of Guiana as I could, or as they knew for those poore souldiers hauing bene many yeeres without wine, a few draughts made them merrie, in which mood they vaunted of Guiana and of the riches thereof, and all what they knewe of the wayes and passages, my selfe seeming to purpose nothing lesse then the enterance or discouerie thereof, but bred in them an opinion that I was bound onely for the reliefe of those English which I had planted in Virginia, whereof the bruite was come among them ; which I had performed in my returne, if extremitie of weather had not forst me from the said coast.

I found occasions of staying in this place for two causes : the one was to be reuenged of Berreo, who the yere before 1594. had betraied eight of Captaine Whiddons men, and tooke them while he departed from them to seeke the Edward Bonauenture, which arriued at Trinidad the day before from the East Indies : in whose absence Berreo sent a Canoa abord the pinnesse onely with Indians and dogs inuiting the company to goe with them into the woods to kill a deare, who like wise men in the absence of their Captaine followed the Indians, but were no sooner one harquebuze shot 8 Englishmen betrayed by Antony Berreo. from the shore, but Berreos souldiers lying in ambush had them al, notwithstanding that he had giuen his word to Captaine Whiddon that they should take water and wood safely : the other cause of my stay was, for that by discourse with the Spaniards I dayly learned more and more of Guiana, of the riuers and passages, and of the enterprise of Berreo, by what meanes or fault he failed, and how he meant to prosecute the same.

While wee thus spent the time I was assured by another Casique of the North side of the yland, that Berreo had sent to Margarita and Cumana for souldiers, meaning to haue giuen mee a cassado at parting, if it had bene possible. For although he

had giuen order through all the yland that no Indian should
come abord to trade with me vpon paine of hanging and
quartering, (hauing executed two or them for the same, which I
afterwards founde) yet euery night there came some with most
lamentable complaints of his crueltie, how he had diuided the
yland and giuen to euery souldier a part, that hee made the
ancient Casiques which were Lords of the countrey to be their
slaues, that he kept them in chaines, and dropped their naked
bodies with burning bacon, and such other torments, which I
found afterwards to be true : for in the citie after I entred the
same there were 5. of ye lords or litle kings (which they cal
Casiques in the West Indies) in one chaine almost dead of
famine, and wasted with torments : these are called in their owne
language Acarewana, and now of the late since English, French
and Spanish are come among them, they call themselues
Capitaines, because they perceiue that the chiefest of euery ship
is called by that name.   Those fiue Capitaines in the chaine
were called Wannawanare, Carroaori, Maquarima, Tarroopanama,
and Aterima.   So as both to be reuenged of the former wrong,
as also considering that to enter Guiana by small boats, to depart
400. or 500. miles from my ships, and to leaue a garison in my
backe interrested in the same enterprize, who also dayly expected
supplies out of Spaine, I should haue sauoured very much of the
asse : and therefore taking a time of most aduantage I set vpon
the Corps du guard in the euening, and hauing put them to the

sword, sent Captaine Calfield onwards with 60.
souldiers, and my selfe followed with 40. more and
so tooke their new City which they called S. Ioseph
by breake of day : they abode not any fight after a
fewe shot, and all being dismissed but onely Berreo

*The Citie of
S. Ioseph
taken.*

*Antony
Berreo taken
prisoner.*

and his companion, I brought them with me abord,
and at the instance of the Indians I set their new citie of S.
Ioseph on fire.

The same day arriued Captaine George Gifford with your
Lordships ship, and Captaine Keymis whom I lost on the coast
of Spaine with the Galego, and in them diuers gentlemen and
others, which to our little armie was a great comfort and supply.

We then hasted away towards our purposed discouery, and
first I called all the Captaines of the yland together that were
enemies t ﹑ the Spaniards : for there were some which Berreo had
brought out of other countreys, and planted there to eate out and

wast those that were naturall of the place, and by my Indian
interpreter, which I caried out of England, I made them vnderstand that I was the seruant of a Queene, who was the great
Casique of the North, and a virgine, and had more Casiqui vnder
her then there were trees in that yland : that shee was an
enemie to the Castellani in respect of their tyrannie and
oppression, and that she deliuered all such nations about her, as
were by them oppressed, and hauing freed all the coast of the
Northren world from their seruitude, had sent mee to free them
also, and withall to defend the countrey of Guiana from their
inuasion and conquest. I shewed them her Maiesties picture
which they so admired and honourèd, as it had bene easie to haue
brought them idolatrous thereof.

The like and a more large discourse I made to the rest of the
nations both in my passing to Guiana, and to those of the
borders, so as in that part of the world her Maiestie is very
famous and admirable, whom they now call Ezrabeta Cassipuna
Aquerewana, which is as much as Elizabeth, the great princesse
or greatest commander. This done we left Puerto de los
Espannoles, and returned to Curiapan, and hauing Berreo my
prisoner I gathered from him as much of Guiana as he knew.

This Berreo is a gentleman wel descended, and had long
serued the Spanish king in Millain, Naples, the Low countreis
and elsewhere, very valiant and liberall, and a gentleman of great
assurednes, and of a great heart : I vsed him according to his
estate and worth in all things I could, according to the small
meanes I had.

I sent Captaine Whiddon the yeere before to get what
knowledge he could of Guiana, and the end of my
iourney at this time was to discouer and enter the
same, but my intelligence was farre from trueth, for
the countrey is situate aboue 600. English miles
further from the Sea, then I was made beleeue it had bin, which
afterward vnderstanding to be true by Berreo, I kept it from the
knowledge of my company, who else would neuer haue bene
brought to attempt the same : of which 600. miles I passed 400.
leauing my ships so farrè from mee at ancker in the Sea, which
was more of desire to performe that discouery, then of reason,
especially hauing such poore and weake vessels to transport our
selues in ; for in the bottom of an old Galego which I
caused to be fashioned like a galley, and in one barge, two

Sir W. Ralegh passed 400. miles toward Guiana.

whirries, and a shipboat of the Lions whelpe, we caried 100. persons and their victuals for a moneth in the same, being al driuen to lie in the raine and weather, in the open aire, in the burning Sunne, and vpon the hard bords, and to dresse our meat, and to cary all maner of furniture in them, wherewith they were so pestered and unsauory, that what with victuals being most fish, with wette clothes of so many men thrust together, and the heat of the Sunne, I will vndertake there was neuer any prison in England, that could bee found more vnsauorie and lothsome, especially to my selfe, who had for many yeeres before bene dieted and cared for in a sort farre more differing.

If Captaine Preston had not bene perswaded that he should haue come too late to Trinidad to haue found vs there (for the moneth was expired which I promised to tary for him there ere hee coulde recouer the coast of Spaine) but that it had pleased God hee might haue ioyned with vs, and that we had entred the countrey but some ten dayes sooner ere the Riuers were ouer-flowen, wee had aduentured either to haue gone to the great Citie of Manoa, or at least taken so many of the other Cities and townes neerer at hand, as would haue made a royall returne: but it pleased not God so much to fauour mee at this time: if it shall be my lot to prosecute the same, I shall willingly spend my life therein, and if any else shalbe enabled thereunto, and con-quere the same, I assure him thus much, he shall perfourme more then euer was done in Mexico by Cortez, or in Peru by Piçarro, whereof the one conquered the Empire of Mutezuma, the other of Guascar, and Atabalipa, and whatsoeuer prince shall possesse it, that Prince shall be Lord of . more golde, and of a more beautifull Empire, and of more Cities . and people, then either the King of Spaine, or the great Turke.

But because there may arise many doubts, and how this Empire of Guiana is become so populous, and adorned with so many great Cities, townes, temples and treasures, I thought good to make it knowen, that the Emperour now reigning is descended from those magnificent princes of Peru, of whose large territories, of whose policies, conquests, edifices, and riches Pedro de Cieça, Francisco Lopez, and others haue written large discourses: for when Francisco ∙Piçarro, Diego Almagro and others con-quered the said Empire of Peru, and had put to death Atabalipa sonne to Guaynacapa, which Atabalipa had formerly caused his eldest brother Guascar to bee slaine, one of the yonger sonnes of

Guaynacapa fled out of Peru, and tooke with him many thousands of those souldiers of the Empire called Oreiones, and with those and many others which followed him, he vanquished all that tract and valley of America which is situate betweene the great riuer of Amazones, and Baraquan, otherwise called Orenoque and Marannon.

The Empire of Guiana is directly East from Peru towards the Sea, and lieth under the Equinoctial line, and it hath more abundance of golde then any part of Peru, and as many or moe great Cities then euer Peru had when it flourished most : it is gouerned by the same lawes, and the Emperour and people obserue the same religion, and the same forme and policies in gouernment as were vsed in Peru, not differing in any part : and I haue bene assured by such of the Spaniards as haue seene Manoa the Imperiall Citie of Guiana, which the *The state-*
Spaniards call El Dorado, that for the greatnesse, for *lines of*
the riches, and for the excellent seat, it farre exceedeth *Manoa.*
any of the world, at least of so much of the world as is knowen to the Spanish nation : it is founded vpon a lake of salt water of 2oo. leagues long like vnto Mare Caspium.   And if we compare it to that of Peru, and but read the report of Fran- *Fran. Lopez*
cisco Lopez and others, it will seeme more ·then *de Gomera*
credible : and because we may iudge of the one by *hist. gen.*
the other, I thought good to insert part of the 12o. *cap. 12o.*
Chapter of Lopez in his generall historie of the Indies, wherein he describeth the Court and magnificence of Guaynacapa, ancestour to the Emperor of Guiana, whose very wordes are these.   Todo el seruicio de su casa, mesa, y cozina, era de oro, y de plata, y quando menos de plata, y cobre por mas rezio. Tenia en su recamara estatuas huecas de oro, que parecian gigantes, y las figuaras al propio, y tamanno de quantos animales, aues, arboles, y yeruas produze la tierra, y de quantos peces cria la mar y aguas de sus reynos.   Tenia assi mesmo sogas, costales, cestas, y troxes de oro y plata, rimeros de palos de oro, que parecissen lenna raiada para quemar.   En fin no auia cosa en su tierra, que no la tuuiesse do oro contrahecha : y aun dizen, que tenian los Ingas vn vergel en vna Isla cerca de la Puna, donde se yuan a holgar, quando querian mar, que tenia la ortaliza, las flores, y arboles de oro y plata, inuencion y grandeza hasta entonces nunca vista.   Allende de todo esto tenia infini-tissima, cantitad de plata, y oro por labrar en el Cuzco, que se

perdio por la muerte de Guascar, car los Indios lo escondieron, viendo que los Espannoles se lo tomauan, y embiauan a Espanna. That is, All the vessels of his house, table and kitchin were of gold and siluer, and the meanest of siluer and copper for strength and hardnesse of metall. He had in his wardrobe hollow statues of gold which seemed giants, and the figures in proportion and bignesse of all the beasts, birds, trees and hearbes, that the earth bringeth foorth : and of all the fishes that the sea or waters of his kingdome breedeth. He had also ropes, budgets, chestes and troughs of golde and siluer, heapes of billets of gold, that seemed wood marked out to burne. Finally, there was nothing in his countrey, whereof he had not the counterfait in gold : Yea and they say, The Ingas had a garden of pleasure in an yland neere Puna, where they went to recreat themselues, when they would take the aire of the Sea, which had all kinde of garden-hearbs, flowers and trees of golde and siluer, an inuention, and magnificence till then neuer seene. Besides all this, he had an infinite quantitie of siluer and golde vnwrought in Cuzco which was lost by the death of Guascar, for the Indians hid it, seeing that the Spaniards tooke it, and sent it into Spaine.

And in the 117. chapter Francisco Piçarro caused the gold and siluer of Atabalipa to be weyed after he had taken it, which Lopez setteth downe in these words following. Hallaron cinquenta y dos mil marcos de buena plata, y vn millon y trezientos veinte y seys mil, y quinientos pesos de oro, Which is : They found fiftie and two thousand markes of good siluer, and one million, and three hundred twenty and sixe thousand and fiue hundred pezos of golde.*

Now although these reports may seeme strange, yet if we consider the many millions which are dayly brought out of Peru into Spaine, wee may easily beleeue the same : for we finde that by the abundant treasure of that countrey the Spanish king

---

* These quotations show the riches of *Peru*, not of *El Dorado*. This was the name given by the Spaniards in the sixteenth century to an imaginary region somewhere in the interior of South America, between the Orinoco and the Amazon, where gold and precious stones were supposed to be in such abundance as to be had for merely picking them up. This story was communicated by an Indian cacique to Gonzalo Pizarro, brother of the conqueror, who sent Francisco Orellana down the Amazon River to discover this wonderful land. Orellana followed the course of the Amazon down to the sea, but he did not find El Dorado. The story, however, continued to be credited for many years afterwards.

vexeth all the princes of Europe, and is become, in a few yeeres, from a poore king of Castile, the greatest monarch of this part of the world, and likely euery day to increase, if other princes forslow the good occasions offered, and suffer him to adde this empire to the rest, which by farré exceedeth all the rest : if his golde now endanger vs, hee will then be vnresistable. Such of the Spanyards as afterward endeuoured the conquest thereof (whereof there haue bene many, as shall be declared hereafter) thought that this Inga (of whom this emperour now liuing is descended) tooke his way by the riuer of Amazones, by that branch which is called Papamene : for by that way followed Orellana (by the commandement of Gonzalo Piçarro, in the yere 1542) whose name the riuer also beareth this day, which is also by others called Marannon, although Andrew Theuet doeth affirme that betweene Marannon and Amazones there are 120 leagues : but sure it is that those riuers haue one head and beginning, and the Marannon, which Thuet describeth, is but a branch of Amazones or Orellana, of which I will speake more in another place. It was attempted by Ordas ; but it is now little lesse then 70 yeres since that Diego Ordas, a knight of the order of Saint Iago attempted the same: and it was in the yeere 1542 that Orellana discouered the riuer of Amazones ; but the first that euer saw Manoa was Iuan Martinez master of the munition to Ordas. At a port called Morequito in Guiana there lieth at this day a great anker of Ordas his ship ; and this port is some 300 miles within the land, vpon the great riuer of Orenoque. *Iuan Martinez the first that euer saw Manoa.*

I rested at this port foure dayes : twenty dayes after I left the ships at Curiapan. The relation of this Martinez (who was the first that discouered Manoa) his successe and ende are to bee seene in the Chancery of Saint Iuan de Puerto rico, whereof Berreo had a copy, which appeared to be the greatest incouragement aswell to Berreo as to others that formerly attempted the discouery and conquest. Orellana after he failed of the discouery of Guiana by the sayd riuer of Amazones, passed into Spaine, and there obteined a patent of the king for the inuasion and conquest, but died by sea about the Islands, and his fleet seuered by tempest, the action for that time proceeded not. Diego Ordas followed the enterprise, and departed Spaine with 600 souldiers, and 30 horse, who arriuing on the coast of Guiana, was slaine *Diego de Ordas went foorth with 600 souldiers 1531.*

in a mutiny, with the most part of such as fauoured
him, as also of the rebellious part, insomuch as his ships
perished, and few or none returned, neither was it certeinly knowen what became of the sayd Ordas, vntill
Berreo found the anker of his ship in the riuer of Orenoque ;
but it was supposed, and so it is written by Lopez, that he

Fran. Lopez perished on the seas, and of other writers diuersely
hist. gen. de conceiued and reported.   And hereof it came that
las Ind. cap. Martines entred so farre within the land, and arriued
    87.   at that city of Inga the emperour ; for it chanced that
while Ordas with his army rested at the port of Morequito (who
was either the first or second that attempted Guiana) by some
negligence, the whole store of powder prouided for the seruice
was set on fire ; and Martinez hauing the chiefe charge, was condemned by the Generall Ordas to be executed foorthwith :
Martinez being much fauoured by the souldiers, had all the
meanes possible procured for his life ; but it could not be obtened
in other sort then this : That he should be set into a canao alone
without any victuall, onely with his armes, and so turned loose
into the great riuer : but it pleased God that the canoa was
caried downe the streame, and that certeine of the Guianians
mette it the same euening ; and hauing not at any time seene
any Christian, nor any man of that colour, they caried Martinez
into the land to be woondred at, and' so from towne to towne,

The great city vntill he came to the great city of Manoa, the seat
of Manao or and residence of Inga the emperour.   The emperour
El Dorado. after he had beheld him, knew him to be a Christian
(for it was not long before that his brethren Guascar and Atabalipa were vanquished by the Spanyards in Peru) and caused him
to be lodged in his palace, and well interteined.   Hee liued
seuen moneths in Manoa, but was not suffered to wander into
the countrey any where.   He was also brought thither all the
way blindfold, led by the Indians, vntill he came to the entrance
of Manoa it selfe, and was fourteene or fifteene dayes in the
passage.   He auowed at his death that he entred the city at
Noon, and then they vncouered his face, and that he trauelled
all that day till night thorow the city, and the next day from Sun
rising to Sun setting yer he came to the palace of Inga.   After
that Martinez had liued seuen moneths in Manoa, and began to
vnderstand the language of the countrey, Inga asked him whether
he desired to returne into his owne countrey, or would willingly

abide with him. But Martinez not desirous to stay, obteined the fauour of Inga to depart : with whom he sent diuers Guianians to conduct him to the riuer of Orenoque, all loden with as much golde as they could cary, which he gaue to Martinez at his departure : but when he was arriued neere the riuers side, the borderers which are called Orenoqueponi robbed him and his Guianians of all the treasure (the borderers being at that time at warres, which Inga had not conquered) saue only of two great bottels of gourds, which were filled with beads of golde curiously wrought, which those Orenoqueponi thought had bene no other thing then his drinke or meat, or graine for food, with which Martinez had liberty to passe : and so in canoas hee fell downe from the riuer of Orenoque to Trinidad, and from thence to Margarita, and also to Saint Iuan de puerto rico, where remaining a long time for passage into Spaine, he died. In the time of his extreme sicknesse, and 'when he was without hope of life, receiuing the Sacrament at the hands of his Confessor, he deliuered these things, with the relation of his trauels, and also called for his calabaças or gourds of the golde beads which he gaue to the church and friers to be *The author of* prayed for. This Martinez was he that Christened *the name of* the city of Manoa by the name of El Dorado, and as *El Dorado.* Berreo informed mee, vpon this occasion : Those Guianians, and also the borderers, and all other in that tract which I haue seene are maruellous great drunkards ; in which vice, I thinke no nation can compare with them : and at the times of their solemne feasts, when the emperour caroweth with his captaines, tributaries, and gouernours, the maner is thus : All those that pledge him are first stripped naked, and their bodies anointed all ouer with a kind of white balsamum (by them called curca) of which there is great plenty, and yet very deare amongst them, and it is of all other the most precious, whereof wee haue had good experience : when they are anointed all ouer, certeine seruants of the emperour, hauing prepared golde made into fine powder, blow it thorow hollow canes vpon their naked bodies, vntill they be all shining from the foot to the head : and in this sort they sit drinking by twenties and hundreds, and continue in drunkennesse sometimes sixe or seuen dayes together. The same is also confirmed by a letter written into Spaine, which was intercepted, which M. Robert Duddeley tolde me he had seene. *Sir Robert* Vpon this sight, and for the abundance of golde *Duddeley.*

which he saw in the city, the images of golde in their
temples, the plates, armours, and shields of gold which they vse
in the warres, he called it El Dorado. After the death of Ordas
and Martinez, and after Orellana, who was imployed by Gonzalo
Piçarro, one Pedro de Osua a knight of Nauarre attempted
Guiana, taking his way from Peru, and built his brigandines vpon
a riuer colled Oia, which riseth to the Southward of Quito, and
is very great. This riuer falleth into Amazones, by which Osua
with his companies descended, and came out of that prouince
which is called Mutylonez: and it seemeth to mee that this
empire is reserued for her Maiesty and the English nation, by
reason of the hard success which all these and other Spanyards

Reade Iosephus Acosta. found in attempting the same, whereof I will speake
briefly, though impertinent in some sort to my
purpose. This Pedro de Osua had among his troups
a Biscain, called Agiri, a man meanly borne, who bare no
other office then a sergeant or alferez: but after certaine moneths,
when the souldiers were grieued with trauels, and consumed
with famine, and that no entrance could be found by the
branches or body of Amazones, this Agiri raised a mutiny, of
which hee made himselfe the head, and so preuailed, as he put
Osua to the sword, and all his followers, taking on him the whole
charge and commandement, with a purpose not onely to make himselfe emperour of Guiana, but also of Peru, and of all that side
of the West Indies: he had of his party seuen hundred souldiers,
and of those many promised to draw in other captaines and
companies, to deliuer vp townes and forts in Peru: but neither
finding by ye sayd riuer any passage into Guiana, nor any possi-
bility to returne towards Peru by the same Amazones, by reason
that ye descent of the riuer made so great a current, he was
inforced to disemboque at the mouth of the sayd Amazones, which
can not be lesse then a thousand leagues from the place
where they imbarked: from thence he coasted the land
till he arriued at Margarita: to the North of Mompatar,
which is at this day called Puerto de Tyranno, for that he
there slew Don Iuan de villa Andreda, gouernour of Margarita

The voyage of sir Iohn Burgh to the West Indies. when sir Iohn Burgh landed there and attempted the
Island. Agiri put to the sword all other in the
Island that refused to be of his party, and tooke with
him certeine Simerones, and other desperate companions. From thence he went to Cumana, and there slew

the gouernour, and dealt in all as at Margarita : hee spoiled all the coast of Caracas, and the prouince of Venezuela, and of Rio de la hacha ; and as I remember, it was the same yere that sir Iohn Hawkins sailed to Saint Iuan de Vllua in the Iesus of Lubeck : for himselfe tolde me that he met with such a one vpon the coast that rebelled, and had sailed downe all the riuer of Amazones. Agiri from thence landed about Sancta Marta, and sacked it also, putting to death so many as refused to be his followers, purposing to inuade Nueuo reyno de Granada, and to sacke Pamplon, Merida, Lagrita, Tunxa, and the rest of the cities of Nueuo reyno, and from thence againe to enter Peru : but in a fight in the sayd Nueuo reyno he was ouerthrowen, and finding no way to escape, he first put to the sword his owne children, foretelling them that they should not liue to be defamed or vp-braided by the Spanyards after his death, who would haue termed them the children of a traitour or tyrant ; and that si-thence hee could not make them princes, hee would yet deliuer them from shame and reproche. These were the ends and tragedies of Ordas, Martinez, Orellana, Ozua, and Agiri.

Also soone after Ordas followed Ieronimo Ortal de Saragosa with 130 souldiers, who failing his entrance by sea, was cast with the current on the coast of Paria, and peopled about S. Miguel de Neueri. It was then attempted by Don Pedro de Silua, a Portugues of the family of Ruigomes de Silua, and by the fauour which Ruigomes had with the king, he was set out, but he also shot wide of the marke ; for being departed from Spaine with his fleete, he entered by Marannon and Amazones, where by the nations of the riuer, and by the Amazones hee was vtterly ouerthrowen, and himselfe and all his armie defeated, only seuen escaped, and of those but two returned.

1534.
Gomar. cap.
84 and 86.

After him came Pedro Hernandez de Serpa, and landed at Cumaná in the West Indies, taking his iourney by land towards Orenoque, which may be some 120 leagues : but yer he came to the borders of the sayd riuer, hee was set vpon by a nation of the Indians called Wikiri, and ouerthrowen in such sort, that of 300 souldiers, horsemen, many Indians, and Negros, there returned but 18. Others affirme, that he was de-feated in the very entrance of Guiana, at the first ciuil towne of the empire called Macureguarai. Captaine Preston in taking S. Iago de Leon (which was by him and his companies very

K

resolutely performed, being a great towne, and farre within the
land) held a gentleman prisoner, who died in his ship, that was
one of the company of Hernandez de Serpa, and saued among
those that escaped, who witnessed what opinion is held among
the Spanyards thereabouts of the great riches of Guiana, and El
Dorado the city of Inga.   Another Spanyard was brought aboord
me by captaine Preston, who told me in the hearing of himselfe
and diuers other gentlemen, that he met with Berreos campe-
master at Caracas, when he came from the borders of Guiana,
and that he saw with him forty of most pure plates of golde
curiously wrought, and swords of Guiana decked and inlaye'd
with gold, feathers garnished with golde, and diuers rarities which
he carried to the Spanish king.

After Hernandez de Serpa, it was vndertaken by the Adelantado, Don Gonzales Ximenes de Casada, who was one of the
chiefest in the conquest of Nueuo reino, whose daughter and
heire Don Antonio de Berreo maried.   Gonzales sought the
passage also by the riuer called Papamene, which riseth by Quito
in Peru, and runneth Southeast 100 leagues, and then falleth into
Amazones, but he also failing the entrance, returned with the
losse of much labour and cost.   I tooke one captaine George
a Spanyard that followed Gonzales in this enterprise.   Gonzales
gaue his daughter to Berreo, taking his oth and honour to follow
the enterprise to the last of his substance and life, who since, as
he hath sworne to me, hath spent 300000 ducats in the same,
and yet neuer could enter so far into the land as my selfe with
that poore troupe or rather a handfull of men, being in all about
100 gentlemen, souldiers, rowers, boat-keepers, boyes, and of all
sorts : neither could any of the forepassed vndertakers, nor
Berreo himselfe, discouer the countrey, till now lately by conference with an ancient king called Carapana, he got the true
light thereof : for Berreo came about 1500 miles yer he vnderstood ought, or could finde any passage or entrance into any
part thereof, yet he had experience of al these forenamed, and
diuers others, and was perswaded of their errors and mistakings.
Berreo sought it by the riuer Cassamar,* which falleth into a great
riuer called Pato : Pato falleth into Meta, and Meta into Baraquan,
which is also called Orenoque.

He tooke his iourney from Nueuo reyno de Granada where he

---

* Casanare.

dwelt, hauing the inheritance of Gonzales Ximenes in those parts: he was followed with 700 horse, he draue with him 1000 head of cattell, he had also many women, Indians, and slaues. How all these riuers crosse and encounter, how the countrey lieth and is bordered, the passage of Ximenes and Berreo, mine owne discouery, and the way that I entred, with all the rest of the nations and riuers, your lordship shall receiue in a large Chart or Map, which I haue not yet finished, and which I shall most humbly pray your lordship to secret, and not to suffer it to passe your owne hands; for by a draught thereof all may be preuented by other nations: for I know it is this very yeere sought by the French, although by the way that they now take, I feare it not much. It was also tolde me yer I departed from England, that Villiers the Admirall was in preparation for the planting of Amazones, to which riuer the French **A new and rich trade of** haue made diuers voyages, and returned much golde, **the French** and other rarities. I spake with the captaine of a **to the riuer of Amazones.** French ship that came from thence, his ship riding in Falmouth the same yere that my ships came first from Virginia.

There was another this yeere in Helford that also came from thence, and had bene foureteene moneths at an anker in Amazones, which were both very rich. Although, as I am perswaded, Guiana cannot be entred that way, yet no doubt the trade of gold from thence passeth by branches of riuers into the riuer of Amazones, and so it doth on euery hand far from the countrey it selfe; for those Indians of Trinidad haue plates of golde from Guiana, and those canibals of Dominica which dwell in the Islands by which our ships passe yerely to the West Indies, also the Indians of Paria, those Indians called Tucaris, Chochi, Apotomios, Cumanagotos, and all those other nations inhabiting neere about the mountaines that run from Paria thorow the prouince of Venezuela, and in Maracapana, and the canibals of Guanipa, the Indians called Assawai, Coaca, Aiai, and the rest (all which shall be described in my description as they are situate) haue plates of golde of Guiana. And vpon the riuer of Amazones, Theuet writeth that the people weare croissants of golde, for of that forme the Guianians most commonly make them: so as from Dominica to Amazones, which is aboue 250 leagues, all the chiefe Indians in all parts weare of those plates of Guiana. Vndoubtedly those that trade Amazones

returne much golde, which (as is aforesayd) commeth by trade
from Guiana, by some branch of a riuer that falleth from the
countrey into Amazones, and either it is by the riuer which
passeth by the nations called Tisnados, or by Carepuna.   I made
inquiry amongst the most ancient and best trauelled of the
Orenoqueponi, and I had knowledge of all the riuers betweene
Orenoque and Amazones, and was very desirous to vnderstand
the truth of those warlike women, because of some it is beleeued,
of others not.   And though I digresse from my purpose, yet I
will set downe that which hath bene deliuered me for trueth of
those women, and I spake with a casique or lord of people, that

The seat   told me he had bene in the riuer, and beyond it also.
of the   The nations of these women are on the South side
Amazones.   of the riuer in the prouinces of Topago, and their
chiefest strengths and retracts are in the Islands situate on the
South side of the entrance some 60 leagues within the mouth of
the sayd riuer.   The memories of the like women are very
ancient aswell in Africa and in Asia : In Africa those that had
Medusa for queene : others in Scithia nere the riuers of Tanais
and Thermodon : we finde also that Lampedo and Marthesia
were queenes of the Amazones : in many histories they are
verified to haue bene, and in diuers ages and prouinces : but
they which are not far from Guiana doe accompany with men
but once in a yere, and for the time of one moneth, which I
gather by their relation, to be in April : and that time all kings
of the borders assemble, and queenes of the Amazones ; and
after the queenes haue chosen, the rest cast lots for their Valen-
tines.   This one moneth, they feast, dance, and drinke of their
wines in abundance ; and the Moone being done, they all depart
to their owne prouinces.   If they conceiue, and be deliuered of
a sonne, they returne him to the father ; if of a daughter they
nourish it, and reteine it : and as many as haue daughters send
vnto the begetters a present ; all being desirous to increase their
owne sex and kind : but that they cut off the right dug of the
brest, I doe not finde to be true.   It was farther tolde me, that
if in these warres they tooke any prisoners that they vsed to
accompany with those also at what time soeuer, but in the end
for certeine they put them to death : for they are sayd to be
very cruell and bloodthirsty, especially to such as offer to inuade
their territories.   These Amazones haue likewise great store of
these plates of golde, which they recouer by exchange chiefly for

a kinde of greene stones, which the Spanyards call Piedras hijadas, and we vse for spleene stones : and for the disease of the stone we also esteeme them. Of these I saw diuers in Guiana : and commonly euery king or casique hath one, which their wiues for the most part weare ; and they esteeme them as great iewels.

But to returne to the enterprise of Bereo, who (as I haue sayd) departed from Nueuo reyno with 700 horse, besides the pro- uisions aboue rehearsed, he descended by the riuer called Cassanar, which riseth in Nueuo reyno out of the mountaines by the city of Tuuia, from which mountaine also springeth Pato ; both which fall into the great riuer of Meta : and Meta riseth from a mountaine ioyning to Pamplon in the same Nueuo reyno de Grenada. These, as also Guaiare, which issueth out of the mountaines by Timana, fall all into Baraquan, and are but of his heads ; for at their comming together they lose their names ; and Baraquan farther downe is also rebaptized by the name of Orenoque. On the other side of the city and hilles of Timana riseth Rio grande, which falleth in the sea by Sancta Marta. By Cassanar first, and so into Meta, Berreo passed, keeping his horsemen on the banks, where the countrey serued them for to march, and where otherwise, he was driuen to imbarke them in boats which he builded for the purpose, and so came with the current downe the riuer of Meta, and so into Baraquan. After he entred that great and mighty riuer, he began dayly to lose of his companies both men and horse ; for it is in many places violently swift, and hath forcible eddies, many sands, and diuers Islands sharp pointed with rocks : but after one whole yeere, iourneying for the most part by riuer and the rest by land, he grew dayly to fewer numbers ; for both by sicknesse, and by encountring with the people of those regions, thorow which he trauelled, his companies were much wasted, especially by diuers encounters with the Amapians : and in all this time hee neuer could learne of any passage into Guiana, nor any newes or fame thereof, vntill he came to a further border of the sayd Amapaia, eight dayes iourney from the riuer Caroli, which was the furthest riuer that he entred. Among those of Amapaia, Guiana was famous, but few of these people accosted Berreo, or would trade with him the first three moneths of the six, which he soiourned there. This Amapaia is also maruellous rich in golde (as both Berreo confessed and those of Guiana with whom I had most

conference) and is situate vpon Orenoque also.   In this countrey
Berreo lost 60 of his best souldiers, and most of all his horse that
remained in his former yeeres trauell : but in the end, after
diuers encounters with those nations, they grew to peace ; and
they presented Berreo with tenne images of fine golde among
diuers other plates and croissants, which, as he sware to me and
diuers other gentlemen, were so curiously wrought, as he had
not seene the like either in Italy, Spaine, or the Low-countreys :
and he was resolued, that when he came to the hands of the
Spanish king, to whom he had sent them by his campmaster,
they would appeare very admirable, especially being wrought by
such a nation as had no yron instruments at all, nor any of those
helps which our goldsmiths haue to worke withall.   The particular name of the people in Amapaia which gaue him these
pieces, are called Anebas, and the riuer of Orenoque at that place
is aboue 12 English miles broad, which may be from his out fall
into the sea 700 or 800 miles.

This prouince ot Amapaia is a very low and a marish ground
nere the riuer ; and by reason of the red water which issueth out
in small branches thorow the fenny and boggy ground, there
breed diuers poisonfull wormes and serpents : and the Spanyards
not suspecting, nor in any sort foreknowing the danger, were in-
fected with a grieuous kinde of fluxe by drinking thereof; and
euen the very horses poisoned therewith : insomuch as at the end
of the 6 moneths, that they abode their, of all there troups, there
were not left aboue 120 souldiers, and neither horse nor cattell :
for Berreo hoped to haue found Guiana by 1000 miles nerer then
it fel out to be in the end : by meanes whereof they susteined
much want and much hunger, oppressed with grieuous diseases,
and all the miseries that could be imagined.   I demanded of
those in Guiana that had trauelled Amapaia, how they liued with
that tawny or red water when they trauelled thither : and they
tolde me that after the Sun was neere the middle of the skie,
they vsed to fill their pots and pitchers with that water, but either
before that time, or towardes the setting of the Sun it was dangerous to drinke of, and in the night strong poison.   I learned also of
diuers other riuers of that nature among them, which were also (while
the Sun was in the Meridian) very safe to drinke, and in the
morning, euening, and night woonderfull dangerous and in-
fectiue.   From this prouince Berreo hasted away assoone as the
Spring and beginning of Summer appeared, and sought his

entrance on the borders of Orenoque˜ on the South side ; but there ran a ledge of so high and impassable mountaines, as he was not able by any meanes to march ouer them, continuing from the East sea into which Orenoque falleth, euen to Quito in Peru : neither had he meanes to cary victuall or munition ouer those craggie, high, and fast hilles, being all woody, and those so thicke and spiny, and so full of prickles, thornes, and briers, as it is impossible to creepe thorow them : hee had also neither friendship among the people, nor any interpreter to perswade or treat with them : and more, to his disaduantage, the casiques and kings of Amapaia had giuen knowledge of his purpose to the Guianians, and that he sought to sacke and conquer the empire, for the hope of their so great abundance and quantities of golde : he passed by the mouthes of many great riuers, which fell into Orenoque both from the North and South, which I forbeare to name for tediousnesse, and because they are more pleasing in describing then reading.

Berreo affirmed that there fell an hundred riuers into Orenoque from the North and South, whereof the least was as big as Rio grande, that passed betweene Popayan and Nueuo reyno de Granada (Rio *Many great riuers falling into Orenoque.* grande being esteemed one of the renowmed riuers in all the West Indies, and numbred among the great riuers of the world:) but he knew not the names of any of these, but Caroli onely ; neither from what nations they descended, neither to what prouinces they led ; for he had no meanes to discourse with the inhabitants at any time : neither was he curious in these things, being vtterly vnlearned, and not knowing the East from the West. But of all these I got some knowledge, and of many more, partly by mine owne trauell, and the rest by conference : of some one I learned one, of others the rest, hauing with me an Indian that spake many languages, and that of Guiana naturally. I sought out all the aged men, and such as were greatest trauellers, and by the one and the other I came to vnderstand the situations, the riuers, the kingdomes from the East sea to the borders of Peru, and from Orenoque Southward as farre as Amazones or Marannon, and the religions of Maria Tamball, and of all the kings of prouinces, and captaines of townes and villages, how they stood in tearmes of peace or warre, and which were friends or enemies the one with the other, without which there can be neither entrance nor conquest in those parts, nor elsewhere : for by the dissention betweene Guascar and Atabalipa, Piçarro conquered Peru, and by the hatred that the Tlaxcallians bare to Mutezuma, Cortez was victorious ouer Mexico; without which both the one and the other had failed of their enterprise, and of the great honour and riches which they atteined vnto.

Now Berreo began to grow into dispaire, and looked for no

The prouince other successe then his predecessor in this enterprise, **of Emeria** vntill such time as hee arriued at the prouince of **inhabited by** Emeria towards the East sea and mouth of the riuer, **gentle** where he found a nation of people very fauourable, **Indians.** and the countrey full of all maner of victuall. The king of this land is called Carapana, a man very wise, subtill, and of great experience, being little lesse then an hundred yeeres olde : in his youth he was sent by his father into the Island of Trinidad, by reason of ciuill warre among themselues, and was bred at a village in that island, called Parico : at that place in his youth hee had seene many Christians, both French and Spanish, and went diuers times with the Indians of Trinidad to Margarita and Cumana in the West Indies (for both those places haue euer beene relieued with victuall from Trinidad) by reason whereof he grew of more vnderstanding, and noted the difference of the nations, comparing the strength and armes of his countrey with those of the Christians, and euer after temporized so, as whosoeuer els did amisse, or was wasted by contention, Carapana kept himselfe and his countrey in quiet and plenty : he also held peace with the Caribes or Canibals his neighbours, and had free trade with all nations, whosoeuer els had warre.

Berreo soiourned and rested his weake troupe in the towne of Carapana sixe weeks, and from him learned the way and passage to Guiana, and the riches and magnificence thereof; but being then vtterly disable to proceed, he determined to try his fortune another yere, when he had renewed his prouisions, and re-gathered more force, which hee hoped for as well out of Spaine as from Nueuo reyno, where hee had left his sonne Don Antonio Ximenes to second him vpon the first notice giuen of his en-trance, and so for the present imbarked himselfe in canoas, and by the branches of Orenoque arriued at Trinidad, hauing from Carapana sufficient pilots to conduct him. From Trinidad he coasted Paria, and so recouered Margarita : and hauing made relation to Don Iuan Sermiento the gouernour, of his proceeding, and perswaded him of the riches of Guiana, he obteined from thence fifty souldiers, promising presently to returne to Carapana, and so into Guiana. But Berreo meant nothing lesse at that time; for he wanted many prouisions necessary for such an enterprise, and therefore departed from Margarita, seated him-selfe in Trinidad, and from thence sent his camp-master, and his sergeant-maior backe to the borders to discouer the neerest passage into the empire, as also to treat with the borderers, and to draw them to his party and loue; without which, he knew he could neither passe safely, nor in any sort be relieued with victuall or ought els. Carapana directed his company to a king called Morequito, assuring them that no man could deliuer so much of Guiana as Morequito could, and that his dwelling was but fiue dayes iourney from Macureguarai, the first ciuill towne of Guiana.

Now your lordship shall vnderstand, that this Morequito, one of the greatest lords or kings of the borders of Guiana, had two or three yeeres before bene at Cumana and at Margarita, in the West Indies, with great store of plates of golde, which he caried to exchange for such other things as he wanted in his owne countrey, and was dayly feasted, and presented by the gouernours of those places, and held amongst them some two moneths, in which time one Vides gouernour of Cumana wanne him to be his conductour into Guiana, being allured by those croissants and images of golde which hee brought with him to trade, as also by the ancient fame and magnificence of El Dorado: whereupon Vides sent into Spaine for a patent to dis-couer and conquer Guiana, not knowing of the pre-cedence of Berreos patent, which, as Berreo affirmeth, was signed before that of Vides: so as when Vides vnderstood of Berreo, and that he had made entrance into that territory, and forgone his desire and hope, it was verily thought that Vides practised with Morequito to hinder and disturbe Berreo in all he could, and not to suffer him to enter thorow his signorie, nor any of his companies; neither to victuall, nor guide them in any sort; for Vides gouernour of Cumana, and Berreo, were become mortall enemies, aswell for that Berreo had gotten Trinidad into his patent with Guiana, as also in that he was by Berreo preuented in the iourney of Guiana it selfe: howsoeuer it was, I know not, but Morequito for a time dissembled his disposition, suffered Spanyards, and a frier (which Berreo had sent to discouer

Vides the gouernour of Cumana competitor with Berreo in the con-quest of Guiana.

L

Manoa) to trauell thorow his countrey, gaue them a guide for
Macureguaray, the first towne of ciuill and apparelled people,
from whence they had other guides to bring them to Manoa the
great city of Inga : and being furnished with those things which
they had learned of Carapana were of most price in Guiana,
Ten Span-   went onward, and in eleuen dayes arriued at Manoa,
yards arriue as Berreo affirmeth for certaine : although I could
at Manoa.   not be assured thereof by the lord which now
gouerneth the prouince of Morequito, for he tolde me that they
got all the golde they had, in other townes on this side Manoa,
there being many very great and rich, and (as he sayd) built like
the townes of Christians, with many roomes.

When these ten Spaniards were returned, and ready to put out
of the border of Aromaia, the people of Morequito set vpon
them, and slew them all but one that swam the riuer, and tooke
from them to the value of forty thousand pezos of golde : and
one of them onely liued to bring the newes to Berreo, that both
his nine souldiers and holy father were benighted in the said
prouince.   I my selfe spake with the captaines of Morequito that
slew them, and was at the place where it was executed.   Berreo,
inraged heerewithall, sent all the strength he could make into
Aromaia, to be reuenged of him, his people, and countrey.   But
Morequito suspecting the same, fled ouer Orenoque, and thorow
the territories of the Saima, and Wikiri, recouered Cumana,
where he thought himself very safe, with Vides the gouernour.
But Berreo sending for him in the Kings name, and his
messengers finding him in the house of one Fashardo on the
sudden yer he was suspected, so as he could not then be conueyed away, Vides durst not deny him, aswell to avoid the
suspition of this practise, as also for that an holy father was slaine
by him and his people.   Morequito offered Fashardo the weight
            of three quintals in golde, to let him escape : but
Morequito   the poore Guianian, betrayed on all sides was de-
executed.   liuered to the camp-master of Berreo, and was presently executed.

After the death of this Morequito, the souldiers of Berreo
spoiled his territorie, and tooke diuers prisoners, among others
they tooke the vncle of Morequito, called Topiawari, who is now
king of Aromaia (whose sonne I brought with me into England)
and is a man of great vnderstanding and policy : he is aboue an
hundred yeeres olde, and yet of a very able body.   The Spaniards

ledde him in a chaine seuenteene dayes, and made him their guide from place to place betweene his countrey and Emeria, the prouince of Carapana, aforesayd, and he was at last redeemed for an hundred plates of golde, and diuers stones called Piedras Hijadas, or Spleene-stones. Now Berreo for executing of Morequito, and other cruelties, spoiles, and slaughters done in Armonaia, hath lost the loue of the Orenoqueponi, and all the borderers, and dare not send any of his souldiers any further into the land then to Carapana, which he called the port of Guiana : but from thence by the helpe of Carapana he had trade further into the countrey, and alwayes ap-pointed ten Spaniards to reside in Carapanas towne, by whose fauour, and by being conducted by his *The towne of Carapana is the port of Guiana.* people, those ten searched the countrey thereabouts, aswell for mines, as for other trades and commodities.

They also haue gotten a nephew of Morequito, whom they haue Christened, and named Don Iuan, of whom they haue great hope, endeuouring by all meanes to establish him in the sayd prouince. Among many other trades, those Spaniards vsed canoas to passe to the riuers of Barema, Pawroma, and Dissequebe, which are on the south side of the mouth of Orenoque, and there buy women and children from the Canibals, which are of that bar-barous nature, as they will for three or foure hatchets *Some fewe Spaniards are now seated in Dissequebe.* sell the sonnes and daughters of their owne brethren and sisters, and for somewhat more, euen their owne daughters. Hereof the Spaniards make great profit : for buying a maid of twelue or thirteene yeres for three or foure hatchets, they sell them againe at Margarita in the West Indies for fifty and an hundred pezos, which is so many crownes.

The master of my shippe, Iohn Dowglas, tooke one of the canoas which came laden from thence with people to be solde, and the most of them escaped ; yet of those he brought, there was one as well fauoured, and as well shaped as euer I saw any in England, afterward I saw many of them, which but for their tawnie colour may be compared to any of Europe. They also trade in those riuers for bread of Cassaui, of which they buy an hundred pound weight for a knife, and sell it at Margarita for ten pezos. They also recouer great store of Cotton, Brasill wood, and those beds which they call Hamcas or Brasill beds, wherein in hot countreyes all the Spaniards vse to lie commonly, and in no other, neither did we our selues while we were there. By meanes of which trades, for ransome of diuers of the Guianians, and for exchange of hatchets and kniues, Berreo recouered some store of golde plates, eagles of golde, and images of men and diuers birdes, and dispatched his campe-master for Spaine, with all that hee had gathered, therewith to leuie souldiers, and by the shew thereof to draw others to the loue of the enterprise. And hauing sent diuers images aswell of men as beasts, birds and fishes, so ˙curiously wrought in gold, he doubted not but to perswade the king to yeeld to him some further helpe, especially for that this land hath neuer beene sacked, the mines neuer wrought, and in the Indies their works were well spent, and the golde drawen out with great labour and charge. He also dispatched messengers to his sonne in Nueuo reyno to leuie all the forces he could, and to come downe the riuer Orenoque to Emeria, the prouince of Carapana, to meet him : he had also sent to Saint Iago de Leon on the coast of the Caracas, to buy horses and mules.

After I had thus learned of his proceedings past and purposed, I told him that I had resolued to see Guiana, and that it was the end of my iourney, and the cause of my comming to Trinidad, as it was indeed, (and for that purpose I sent Iacob Whiddon the yeere before to get intelligence with whom Berreo himselfe had speech at that time, and remembred how inquisitiue Iacob Whiddon was of his proceedings, and of the countrey of Guiana) Berreo was stricken into a great melancholy and sadnesse, and vsed all the arguments he could to disswade me, and also assured the gentlemen of my company that it would be labour lost, and that they should suffer many miseries if they proceeded. And first he deliuered that I could not enter any of the riuers with any barke or pinnesse, or hardly with any ships boat, it was so low, sandy, and full of flats, and that his companies were dayly grounded in their canoas, which drew but twelue inches water. He further sayde, that none of the countrey would come to speake with vs, but would all flie ; and if we followed them to their dwellings, they would burne their owne townes : and besides that, the way was long, the Winter at hand, and that the riuers beginning once to swell, it was impossible to stem the current, and that we could not in those small boats by any‘means cary victuall for halfe the time, and that (which indeed most discouraged my company) the kings and lords of all the borders of

Guiana had decreed that none of them should trade with any Christians for golde, because the same would be their owne ouerthrow, and that for the loue of gold the Christians meant to conquer and dispossesse them of all together.

Many and the most of these I found to be true, but yet I resoluing to make triall of all whatsoeuer happened, directed Captaine George Gifford my vice-admirall to take the Lions whelpe, and captaine Calfield his barke to turne to the Eastward, against the mouth of a riuer called Capuri, whose entrace I had before sent captaine Whiddon, and Iohn Dowglas the master, to discouer, who found some nine foot water or better vpon the flood, and fiue at low water, to whom I had giuen instructions that they should anker at the edge of the shoald, and vpon the best of the flood to thrust ouer, which shoald Iohn Dowglas bwoyed and beckoned for them before : but they laboured in vaine ; for neither could they turne it vp altogether so farre to the East, neither did the flood continue so long, but the water fell yer they could haue passed the sands ; as wee after found by a second experience : so as now wee must either give ouer our enterprise, or leauing our ships at aduenture foure hundred mile behinde vs, must run vp in our ships boats, one barge, and two wheries. But being doubtfull how to cary victuals for so long a time in such bables, or any strength of men, especially for that Berreo assured vs that his sonne must be by that time come downe with many souldiers, I sent away one King, master of the Lions whelpe, with his ship-boat to trie another branch of a riuer in the bottome of the bay of Guanipa, which was called Amana, to prooue if there were water to be found for either of the small ships to enter. But when he came to the mouth of Amana, he found it as the rest, but stayed not to discouer it thorowly, because he was assured by an Indian, his guide, that the Canibals of Guanipa would assaile them with many canoas, and that they shot poisoned arrowes ; so as if he hasted not backe, they should all be lost.

In the mean time, fearing the woorst, I caused all the carpenters we had, to cut downe a Galego boat, which we meant to cast off, and to fit her with banks to row on, and in all things to prepare her the best they could, so as she might be brought to draw but fiue foot, for so much we had on the barre of Capuri at low water. And doubting of Kings returne, I sent Iohn Dowglas againe in my long barge, aswell to relieue him, as also to make a perfect search in the bottome of that bay : for it hath bene held for infallible, that whatsoeuer ship or boat shall fall therein, can neuer disembogue againe, by reason of the violent current which setteth into the sayde bay, as also for that the brize and Easterly winde bloweth directly into the same.   Of which opinion I haue heard Iohn Hampton of Plymmouth, one of the greatest experience of England, and diuers other besides that haue traded to Trinidad.

I sent with Iohn Dowglas an old.casique of Trinidad for a pilot, who tolde vs that we could not returne againe by the bay or gulfe, but that he knew a by-branch which ran within the land to the Eastward, and that he thought by it we might fall into Capuri, and so returne in foure dayes.   Iohn Dowglas searched those riuers, and found foure goodly entrances, whereof the least was as bigge as the Thames at Wolwich ; but in the bay thitherward it was shoald, and but sixe foote water : so as we were now without hope of any ship or barke to passe ouer, and therefore resolued to go on with the boats,.and the bottome of the Galego, in which we thrust 60 men.   In the Lions whelps boat and whery we caried 20.   Captaine Calfield in his whery caried ten more, and in my barge other tenne, which made vp a hundred : we had no other meanes but to cary victuall for a moneth in the same, and also to lodge therein as we could, and to boile and dresse our meat.   Captaine Gifford had with him master Edward Porter, captaine Eynos, and eight more in his whery, with all their victuall, weapons, and prouisions.   Captaine Calfield had with him my cousin Butshead Gorges, and eight more.   In the galley, of gentlemen and officers my selfe had captaine Thin, my cousin Iohn Greenuile, my nephew Iohn Gilbert, captaine Whiddon, captaine Keymis, Edward Handcocke, captaine Clarke, lieutenant Hewes, Thomas Vpton, captaine Facy, Ierome Ferrar, Anthony Welles, William Connocke, and aboue fifty more.   We could not learne of Berreo any other way to enter but in branches, so farre to wind-ward, as it was impossibe for vs to recouer : for wee had as much sea to crosse ouer in our wheries, as betweene Douer and Calais, and in a great billow, the winde and current being both very strong, so as we were driuen to goe in those small boats directly before the winde into the bottome of the bay of Guanipa, and from thence to enter the mouth of some one of those riuers which Iohn Dowglas had last discouered, and had with vs for pilot an Indian of Barema, a riuer to the South of Orenoque, betweene that and Amazones, whose canoas we had formerly taken as hee was going from the sayd Barema, laden with Cassaui-bread, to sell at Margarita. This Arwacan promised to bring me into the great riuer of Orenoque, but indeed of that which he entred he was vtterly ignorant, for he had not seene it in twelue yeeres before; at which time he was very yoong, and of no iudgement: and if God had not sent vs another helpe, we might haue wandred a whole yere in that labyrinth of riuers, yer wee had found any way, either out or in, especially after wee were past ebbing and flowing, which was in foure dayes, for I know all the earth doeth not yeelde the like confluence of streames and branches, the one crossing the other so many times, and all so faire and large, and so like one to another, as no man can tell which to take : and if wee went by the Sunne or Compasse, *A wonderfull confluence of streames.* hoping thereby to goe directly one way or other, yet that way wee were also caried in a circle amongst multitudes of Islands, and euery Island so bordered with high trees, as no man coulde see any further then the bredth of the riuer, or length of the breach. But this it chanced, that entering into a riuer, (which because it had no name, wee called the riuer of the Red crosse, our selues being the first Christians that euer came therein) the two and twentieth of May, as wee were rowing vp the same, wee espied a small canoa with three Indians, which (by the swiftnesse of my barge, rowing with eight oares) I ouertooke yer they could crosse the riuer, the rest of the people on the banks shadowed vnder the thicke wood, gazed on with a doubtfull conceit what might befall those three which we had taken. But when they perceiued that we offered them no violence, neither entred their canoa with any of ours, nor tooke out of the canoa any of theirs, they then beganne to shew themselues on the banks side, and offered to traffique with vs for such things as they had. And as wee drew neere, they all stayed, and we came with our barge to the mouth of a little creeke which came from their towne into the great riuer.

As we abode there a while, our Indian pilot, called Ferdinando, would needs goe ashore their village to fetch some fruits, and to drinke of their artificiall wines, and also to see the place, and know the lord of it against another time, and tooke with him a brother of his, which hee had with him in the iourney: when they came to the village of these people the lord of the Island offered to lay hands on them, purposing to haue slaine them both, yeelding for reason that this Indian of ours had brought a strange nation into their territory, to spoile and destroy them. But the pilot being quicke, and of a disposed body, slipt their fingers, and ran into the woods, and his brother being the better footman of the two, recouered the creekes mouth, where we stayed in our barge, crying out that his brother was slaine : with that we set hands on one of them that was next vs, a very olde man, and brought him into the barge, assuring him that if we had not our pilot againe, we would presently cut off his head.   This olde man being resolued that he should pay the losse of the other, cried out to those in the woods to saue Ferdinando our pilot ; but they followed him notwithstanding, and hunted after him vpon the foot with the Deere-dogges, and with so maine a crie, that all the woods eckoed with the shout they made : but at the last this poore chased Indian recouered the riuer side, and got vpon a tree, and as we were coasting, leaped downe and swamme to the barge halfe dead with feare.   But our good happe was, that we kept the other olde Indian which we hand-fasted to redeeme our pilot withall ; for being naturall of those riuers, we assured our selues hee knew the way better then any stranger could.   And indeed, but for this chance, I thinke we had neuer found the way either to Guiana, or backe to our ships : for Ferdinando after a few dayes knew nothing at all, nor which way to turne, yea and many times the old man himselfe was in great doubt which riuer to take.   Those people which dwell in these broken islands and drowned lands, are generally called Tiuitiuas ; there are of them two sorts, the one called Ciawani, and the other Waraweete.

The great riuer of Orenoque or Baraquan hath nine branches which fall out on the North side of his owne maine mouth : on the South side it hath seuen other fallings into the sea, so it disemboqueth by sixteene armes in all, betweene Ilands and broken ground, but the Ilands are very great, many of them as bigge as the Isle of Wight, and bigger, and many lesse.   From the first branch on the North to the last of the South, it is at least 100 leagues, so as the riuers mouth is 300 miles wide at his entrance into the sea, which I take to be farre bigger then that of Amazones.   All those that inhabit in the mouth of this riuer vpon the seuerall North branches, are these Tiuitiuas, of which

A description of the mighty riuer of Oren-oque or Ba-raquan.

there are two chiefe lords which haue continuall warres one with the other. The Ilands which lie on the right hand, are called Pallamos, and the land on the left, Horotomaka, and the riuer by which Iohn Douglas returned within the land from Amana to Capuri, they call Macuri.

These Tiuitiaus are a very goodly people and very *What maner* valiant, and haue the most manly speech and most *of people the* deliberate that euer I heard, of what nation soeuer. *Tiuitiuas are.* In the Summer they haue houses on the ground, as in other places : in the Winter they dwell vpon the trees, where they build very artificiall townes and villages, as it is written in the Spanish story of the West Indies, that those people do in the low lands nere the gulfe of Vraba : for betweene May and September the riuer of Orenoque riseth thirty foot vpright, and then are those ilands ouerflowen twenty foot high aboue the leuell of the ground, sauing some few raised grounds in the middle of them : and for this cause they are inforced to liue in this maner. They neuer eat of any thing that is set or sowen : and as at home they vse neither planting nor other manurance, so when they come abroad, they refuse to feed of ought, but of that which nature without labour bringeth forth. They vse the tops of Palmitos for bread, and kill deere, fish, and porks, for the rest of their sustenance. They haue also many sorts of fruits that grow in the woods, and great variety of birds and fowle.

And if to speake of them were not tedious, and vulgar, surely we saw in those passages of very rare colours and formes, not elsewhere to be found, for as much as I haue either seene or read. Of these people those that dwell vpon the branches of Orenoque, called Capuri and Macureo, are for the most part carpenters of canoas, for they make the most and fairest canoas, and sel them into Guiana for golde, and into Trinidad for tobacco in the excessiue taking whereof, they exceed all nations ; and not withstanding the moistnesse of the aire in which they liue, the hardnesse of their diet, and the great labours they suffer to hunt, fish and fowle for their liuing in all my life, either in the Indies or in Europe, did I neuer behold a more goodly or better fauoured people or a more manly. They were woont to make warre vpon all nations, especially on the Canibals, so as none durst without a good strength trade by those riuers : but of late they are at peace with their neighbours, all holding the Spaniards

M

for a common enemy. When their commanders die, they vse great lamentation, and when they thinke the flesh of their bodies is putrified, and fallen from the bones, then they take vp the carcase againe, and hang it in the caciques house that died, and decke his scull with feathers of all colours, and hang all his golde plates about the bones of his armes, thighs, and legs. Those nations which are called Arwacas, which dwell on the South of Orenoque, (of which place and nation our Jndian pilot was) are dispersed in many other places, and doe vse to beat the bones of their lords into powder, and their wiues and friends drinke it all in their seuerall sorts of drinks.

After we departed from the port of these Ciawani, wee passed vp the riuer with the flood, and ankered the ebbe, and in this sort we went onward. The third day that we entred the riuer, our galley came on ground, and stucke so fast, as we thought that euen there our discouery had ended, and that we must haue left fourescore and ten of our men to haue inhabited like rooks vpon trees with those nations : but the next morning, after we had cast out all her ballast, with tugging and halling to and fro, we got her aflote, and went on. At foure dayes end wee fell into as goodly a riuer as euer I beheld, which was called The great Amana, which ranne more directly without windings and turnings then the other : but soone after the flood of the sea left vs ; and being inforced either by maine strength to row against a violent current, or to returne as wise as we went out, we had then no shift but to perswade the companies that it was but two or three dayes worke, and therefore desired them to take paines, euery gentleman and others taking their turnes to row, and to spell one the other at the houres end. Euery day we passed by goodly branches of riuers, some falling from the West, others from the East into Amana, but those I leaue to the description in the Cart of discouery, where euery one shalbe named with his rising and descent. When three dayes more were ouergone, our companies began to despaire, the weather being extreame hote, the riuer bordered with very high trees, that kept away the aire, and the current against vs euery day stronger then other : but we euermore commanded our pilots to promise an ende the next day, and vsed it so long, as we were driuen to assure them from foure reaches of the riuer to three, and so to two, and so to the next reach : but so long we laboured, that many dayes were spent, and wee driuen to drawe our selues to harder allowance, our bread euen at the last, and no drinke at all; and our men and our selues so wearied and scorched, and doubtfull withall, whether wee should euer performe it or no, the heat increasing as we drew towards the line; for wee were now in fiue degrees.

The further we went on (our victuall decreasing and the aire breeding great faintnesse) wee grew weaker and weaker, when wee had most need of strength and abilitie; for hourely the riuer ranne more violently then other against vs, and the barge, wheries, and shippes boat of captaine Gifford and captaine Calfield, had spent all their prouisions; so as we were brought into despaire and discomfort, had wee not perswaded all the company that it was but onely one dayes worke more to atteine the land where wee should be relieued of all wee wanted, and if we returned, that wee were sure to starue by the way, and that the world would also laugh vs to scorne. On the banks of these riuers were diuers sorts of fruits good to eat, flowers and trees of such variety, as were sufficient to make tenne volumes of herbals: we relieued our selues many times with the fruits of the countrey, and sometimes with fowle and fish. Wee saw birds of all colours, some carnation, some crimson, orenge-tawny, purple, watchet, and of all other sorts both simple and mixt, and it was vnto vs a great good passing of the time to beholde them, besides the reliefe we found by killing some store of them with our fowling pieces; without which, hauing little or no bread, and lesse drinke, but onely the thicke and troubled water of the riuer, we had beene in a very hard case.

Our olde pilot of the Ciawani (whom, as I sayd before, wee tooke to redeeme Ferdinando) tolde vs, that if we would enter a branch of a riuer on the right hand with our barge and wheries, and leaue the galley at anker the while in the great riuer, he would bring vs to a towne of the Arwacas, where we should finde store of bread, hennes, fish, and of the countrey wine; and perswaded vs, that departing from the galley at noone, we might returne yer night. I was very glad to heare this speech, and presently tooke my barke, with eight musketiers, captaine Giffords whery, with myselfe and foure musketiers and Captaine Calfield with his whery, and as many; and so we entred the mouth of this riuer: and because we were perswaded that it was so nere, we tooke no victuall with vs at all. When we had rowed three houres, we maruelled we saw no signe of any dwelling, and

asked the pilot where the towne was : he tolde vs a little further·
After three houres more, the Sun being almost set, we began to
suspect that he led vs that way to betray vs ; for hee confessed
that those Spaniards which fled from Trinidad, and also those
that remained with Carapana in Emeria, were ioyned together in
some village vpon that riuer.   But when it grew towards night ;
and wee demanded where the place was : hee tolde vs but foure
reaches more.   When we had rowed foure and foure, we saw no
signe ; and our poore water-men, euen heart-broken, and tired,
were ready to giue up the ghost : for we had now come from the
galley neere forty miles.

At the last we determined to hang the pilot ; and if wee had
well knowen the way backe againe by night, we had surely gone ;
but our owne necessities pleaded sufficiently for his safety : for it
was as darke as pitch, and the riuer began so to narrow it
selfe, and the trees to hang ouer from side to side, as wee were
driuen with arming swords to cut a passage thorow those
branches that couered the water.   Wee were very desirous to
finde this towne, hoping of a feast, because wee made but a short
breakefast aboord the galley in the morning and it was now
eight a clocke at night, and our stomacks began to gnawe apace :
but whether it was best to returne or goe on, we beganne to
doubt, suspecting treason in the pilot more and more : but the poore
olde Indian euer assured vs that it was but a little further, but
this one turning and that turning : and at the last about one a clocke
after midnight wee saw a light ; and rowing towards it, wee
heard the dogges of the village.   When we landed wee found
few people ; for the lord of that place was gone with diuers
canoas aboue foure hundred miles off, vpon a iourney towardes
the head of Orenoque to trade for golde, and to buy women of
the Canibals, who afterward vnfortunately passed by vs as wee
rode at an anker in the port of Morequito in the darke of the
night, and yet came so neere vs, as his canoas grated against our
barges : he left one of his company at the port of Morequito, by
whom wee vnderstood that hee had brought thirty yoong women,
diuers plates of golde, and had great store of fine pieces of
cotton cloth, and cotton beds.   In his house we had good store
of bread, fish, hennes, and Indian drinke, and so rested that
night, and in the morning after we had traded with such of his
people as came downe, we returned towards our gally, and
brought with vs some quantity of bread, fish, and hennes.

On both sides of this riuer we passed the most beautifull countrey that euer mine eyes beheld : and whereas all that we had seene before was nothing but woods, prickles, bushes, and thornes, here we beheld plaines A most beautifull countrey. of twenty miles in length, the grasse short and greene, and in diuers parts groues of trees by themselues, as if they had beene by all the arte and labour in the world so made of purpose : and still as we rowed, the deere came downe feeding by the waters side, as if they had beene vsed to a keepers call. Vpon this riuer there were great store of fowle, and of many sorts : we saw in it diuers sorts of strange fishes, and of maruellous bignes : but for lagartos it exceeded, for there were thousands of those vgly serpents ; and the people call it for the abundance The riuer of Lagartos, or Crocodiles. of them, The riuer of Lagartos, in their language. I had a Negro a very proper yoong fellow, who leaping out of the galley to swim in the mouth of this riuer, was in all our sights taken and deuoured with one of those lagartos. In the meane while our companies in the gally thought we had bene all lost, (for wee promised to returne before night) and sent the Lions whelps shippes boat with captaine Whiddon to follow vs vp the riuer ; but the next day, after we had rowed vp and downe some fourescore miles, we returned, and went on our way, vp the great riuer ; and when we were euen at the last cast for want of victuals, captaine Gifford being before the galley and the rest of the boats, seeking out some place to land vpon the banks to make fire, espied foure canoas comming downe the riuer ; and with no small ioy caused his men to trie the vttermost of their strengths, and after a while two of the foure gaue ouer, and ranne themselues ashore, euery man betaking himselfe to the fastnesse of the woods, the two other lesser got away, while he landed to lay hold on these : and so turned into some by-creeke, we knew not whither. Those canoas that Two canoas taken. were taken, were loaden with bread, and were bound for Margarita* in the West Indies, which those Indians (called Arwacas) purposed to cary thither for exchange : but in the lesser there were three Spanyards, who hauing heard Three Spanyards escaped. of the defeat of their gouernour in Trinidad, and that we purposed to enter Guiana, came away in those

* Margarita is an island situated in the Caribbean Sea. It was so called from its being supposed to produce many pearls *(Latin,* Margarita). It belongs to Venezuela, and its population in 1888 was 32,000.

canaos: one of them was a cauallero, as the captaine of the
Arwacas after tolde vs, another a souldier, and the third a
refiner.

THE DISCOVERIE

OF THE LARGE, RICH, AND BEAUTIFULL EMPIRE OF GUIANA, WITH A RELATION OF THE GREAT AND GOLDEN CITIE OF MANOA (WHICH THE SPANIARDS CALL EL DORADO) AND THE PRO-UINCES OF EMERIA, AROMAIA, AMAPAIA, AND OTHER COUNTRIES, WITH THEIR RIUERS ADIOYNING. PERFORMED IN THE YEERE 1595 BY SIR WALTER RALEGH KNIGHT, CAPTAINE OF HER MAIESTIES GUARD, LORDE WARDEN OF THE STANNERIES, AND HER HIGHNESSE LIEUTENANT GENERALL OF THE COUNTIE OF CORNE-WALL.

PART II.

In the meane time, nothing on the earth could haue bene more welcome to vs, next vnto gold, then the great store of very excellent bread which we found in these canoas; for now our men cried, Let vs goe on, we care not how farre. After that captaine Gifford had brought the two canoas to the galley, I tooke my barge, and went to the banks side with a dozen shot, where the canoas first ranne themselues ashore, and landed there, sending out captaine Gifford, and captaine Thyn on one hand, and captaine Calfield on the other, to follow those that were fled into the woods: and as I was creeping thorow the bushes, I sawe an Indian basket hidden, which was the refiners basket; for I found in it his quick-siluer, saltpeter, and diuers things for the triall of metals, and also the dust of such ore as he had refined, but in those canoas which escaped there was a good quantity of ore and gold. I then landed more men, and offered fiue hundred pound to what souldier soeuer could take one of those three Spanyards that we thought were landed. But our labours were in vaine in that behalfe; for they put themselues

The Spanish golde-finers basket and other things taken.

N

into one of the small canoas: and so while the greater canoas were in taking they escaped. But seeking after the Spanyards, we found the Arwacas hidden in the woods, which were pilots for the Spanyards, and rowed their canoas; of which I kept the chiefest for a pilot, and caried him with me to Guiana, by whom I vnderstood where and in what countreyes the Spaniards had laboured for golde, though I made not the same knowen to all: for when the springs began to breake, and the riuers to raise themselues so suddenly, as by no meanes wee could abide the digging of any mine, especially for that the richest are defended with rocks of hard stones, which wee call the White spar, and that it required both time, men, and instruments fit for such a worke, I thought it best not to houer thereabouts, least if the same had beene perceiued by the company, there would haue beene by this time many barks and shippes set out, and perchance other nations would also haue gotten of ours for pilots; so as both our selues might haue beene preuented, and all our care taken for good vsage of the people bene vtterly lost, by those that onely respect present profit, and such violence or insolence offered, as the nations which are borderers would haue changed their desire of our loue and defence into hatred and violence. And for any longer stay to haue brought a more quantity (which I heare hath beene often obiected) whosoeuer had seene or prooued the fury of that riuer after it beganne to arise, and had bene a moneth and odde dayes, as we were, from hearing ought from our shippes, leauing them meanly manned 400 miles off, would perchance haue turned somewhat sooner then we did, if all the mountaines had bene golde or rich stones. And to say the trueth, all the branches and small riuers which fell into Orenoque were raised with such speed, as if we waded them ouer the shooes in the morning outward, we were couered to the shoulders homeward the very same day: and to stay to digge out gold with our nailes, had bene Opus laboris but not Ingenij: such a quantitie as would haue serued our turnes we could not haue had, but a discouery of the Mines to our infinite disaduantage wee had made, and that could haue bene the best profite of farther search or stay: for those Mines are not easily broken, nor opened in hast, and I could haue returned a good quantity of gold ready cast, if I had not shot at another marke, then present profit.

This Arwacan Pilot with the rest, feared that wee would haue

Marginal note: The richest mines defended with the white spar.

eaten them, or otherwise haue put them to some cruel
death (for the Spaniards, to the end that none of the
people in the passage towards Guiana or in Guiana
it selfe might come to speach with vs, perswaded all the nations,
that we were men-eaters, and Canibals) but when the poore men
and women had seen vs, and that wee gaue them meate, and to
euery one something or other, which was rare and strange to
them, they beganne to conceiue the deceit and purpose of the
Spaniards, who indeed (as they confessed) tooke from them both
their wiues and daughters dayly, and vsed them for the satisfying
of their owne lusts, especially such as they tooke in this maner
by strength. But I protest before the Maiestie of the liuing
God, that I neither know nor beleeue, that any of our company
one or other, by violence or otherwise, euer knew any of their
women, and yet we saw many hundreds, and had many in our
power, and of those very yong, and excellently fauoured, which
came among vs without deceit, starke naked.

Nothing got vs more loue amongst them then this vsage: for
I suffered not any man to take from any of the nations so much
as a Pina, or a Potato roote, without giuing them contentment,
nor any man so much as to offer to touch any of their wiues or
daughters: which course so contrary to the Spaniards (who
tyrannize ouer them in all things) drewe them to admire her
Maiestie, whose commaundement I told them it was, and also
wonderfully to honour our nation.

But I confesse it was a very impatient worke to keepe the
meaner sort from spoyle and stealing, when wee came
to their houses: which because in all I coulde not
preuent, I caused my Indian interpreter at euery
place when wee departed, to knowe of the losse or wrong done,
and if ought were stolen or taken by violence, either the same
was restored, and the partie punished in their sight, or else was
payed for to their vttermost demand.

They also much wondered at vs, after they heard that we had
slaine the Spaniards at Trinidad, for they were before resolued,
that no nation of Christians durst abide their presence, and they
wondered more when I had made them know of the great ouerthrow that her Maiesties armie and Fleete had giuen them of
late yeeres in their owne Countreys.

After we had taken in this supply of bread, with diuers baskets
of rootes which were excellent meate, I gaue one of the Canoas

to the Arwacas, which belonged to the Spaniards that were escaped, and when I had dismissed all but the Captaine (who by the Spaniards was christened Martin) I sent backe in the same Canoa the olde Ciawan, and Ferdinando my first Pilot, and gaue them both such things as they desired, with sufficient victuall to cary them backe, and by them wrote a letter to the ships, which they promised to deliuer, and performed it, and then I went on with my newe hired Pilot Martin the Arwacan : but the next or second day after, wee came aground againe with our Galley, and were like to cast her away, with all our victuall and provision, and so lay on the sand one whole night and were farre more in despaire at this time to free her then before, because wee had no tide of flood to helpe vs, and therefore feared that all our hopes would haue ended in mishaps : but we fastened an anker vpon the lande, and with maine strength drewe her off : and so the fifteenth day wee discouered afarre off the mountaines of Guiana to our great ioy, and towards the euening had a slent of a Northerly winde that blewe very strong, which brought vs in sight of the great Riuer Orenoque ; out of which this riuer discended wherein wee were : wee descried afarre off three other Canoas as farre as wee could descerne them, after whom wee hastened with our barge and wherries, but two of them passed out of sight, and the thirde entered vp the great Riuer, on the right hande to the West-ward, and there stayed out of sight, thinking that wee meant to take the way Eastward towards the prouince of Carapana, for that way the Spaniards keepe, not daring to goe vpwards to Guiana, the people in those parts being all their enemies, and those in the Canoas thought vs to haue bene those Spaniards that were fled from Trinidad, and had escaped killing : and when wee came so farre downe as the opening of that branch into which they slipped, being neere them with our barge and wherries wee made after them, and ere they coulde land, came within call, and by our interpreter tolde them what wee were, wherewith they came backe willingly abord vs : and of such fish and Tortugas egges as they had gathered, they gaue vs, and promised in the morning to bring the Lord of that part with them, and to do vs all other seruices they could.

That night we came to an ancker at the parting of the three goodly Riuers (the one was the Riuer of Amana by which we came from the North, and ranne athwart towards the South, the other two were of Orenoque which crossed from the West and ranne to the Sea towardes the East) and landed vpon a faire sand, where wee found thousands of Tortugas egges which are very wholesome meate, and greatly restoring, so as our men were nowe well filled and highly contented both with the fare, and neerenesse of the land of Guiana which appeared in sight.

In the morning there came downe according to promise the Lord of that border called Toparimaca, with some thirtie or fourtie followers, and brought vs diuers sorts of fruites, and of his wine, bread, fish, and flesh, whom wee also feasted as wee could, at least wee dranke good Spanish wine (whereof wee had a'small quantitie in bottles) which aboue all things they loue. I conferred with this Toparimaca of the next way to Guiana, who conducted our galley and boates to his owne port, and caried vs from thence some mile and a halfe to his Towne, where some of our Captaines karoused of his wine till they were reasonable pleasant, for it is very strong with pepper, and the iuice of diuers hearbes, and fruites digested and purged, they keepe it in great earthern pots of tenne or twelue galons very cleane and sweete, and are themselues at their meetings and feastes the greatest karousers and drunkards of the world : when wee came to his towne wee found two Casiques, whereof one was a stranger that had bene vp the Riuer in trade, and his boates, people, and wife incamped at the port where wee anckered, and the other was of that countrey a follower of Toparimaca : they lay each of them in a cotten Hamaca, which wee call brasill beds, and two women attending them with sixe cuppes and a little ladle to fill them, out of an earthern pitcher of wine, and so they dranke each of them three of those cups at a time one to the other, and in this sort they drinke drunke at their feastes and meetings.

That Casique that was a stranger had his wife staying at the port where wee anckered, and in all my life I haue seldome seene a better fauoured woman : Shee was of good stature, with black eyes, fat of body, of an excellent countenance, her haire almost as long as her selfe, tied vp againe in pretie knots, and it seemed shee stood not in that awe of her husband, as the rest, for shee spake and discoursed, and dranke among the gentlemen and Captaines, and was very pleasant, knowing her owne comelinesse, and taking great pride therein. I haue seene a Lady in England so like to her, as but for the difference of colour, I would haue sworne might haue bene the same.

O

The seat of this Towne of Toparimaca was very pleasant, standing on a little hill, in an excellent prospect, with goodly gardens a mile compasse round aboute it, and two very faire and large ponds of excellent fish adioyning. This towne

The towne of Arowocay. is called Arowocai : the people are of the nation called Nepoios, and are followers of Carapana. In that place I sawe very aged people, that wee might perceiue all their sinewes and veines without any flesh, and but euen as a

The great breadth of the riuer Orenoque. case couered onely with skinne. The Lord of this place gaue me an old man for Pilot, who was of great experience and traueile, and knew the Riuer most perfectly both by day and night : and it shall bee requisite for any man that passeth it, to haue such a Pilot, for it is 'foure, fiue, and sixe miles ouer in many places, and twentie miles in other places, with wonderfull eddies, and strong currents, many great ylands, and diuers sholds, and many dangerous rockes, and besides vpon any increase of winde so great a bilowe, as wee were sometimes in great perill of drowning in the galley, for the small boates durst not come from the shoare, but when it was very faire.

They enter the riuer Orenoque, which run- neth East and West. The next day we hasted thence, and hauing an Easterly ·winde to helpe vs, we spared our armes from rowing : for after wee entred Orenoque, the Riuer lieth for the most part East and West, euen from the Sea vnto Quito in Peru. This Riuer is nauigable with barkes, litle lesse then a thousand miles, and from the place where we entred, it may be sailed vp in small pinnesses to many of the best parts of Nueuo reyno de Granada, and of Popayan : and from no place may the cities of these parts of the Indies be so easily taken and inuaded as from hence. All that day wee sailed vp a branch of that Riuer, hauing on the left hand a great yland which they call Assapana which may conteine some fiue and twentie miles in length, and sixe miles in breadth, the great body of the Riuer running on the other side of this yland. Beyond that middle branch there is also another yland in the Riuer called Iwana, which is twise as bigge as the yle of Wight, and beyond it, and betweene it and the maine of Guiana, runneth a thirde branch of Orenoque called Arraroopana : all three are goodly branches, and all nauigable for great ships. I iudge the riuer in this place to be at least thirty miles brode, reckoning the ylands which deuide the branches in it, for afterwards I sought also both the other branches.

After wee reached to the head of the yland, called Assapana, a little to the Westward on the right hand there opened a riuer which came from the North, called Europa, and fel into the great Riuer, and beyond it on the same side, wee anckered for that night, by another yland six miles long, and two miles broade, which they call Ocaywita: From hence in the morning wee landed two Guianians, which wee found in the Towne of Toparimaca, that came with vs, who went to giue notice of our comming to the Lord of that countrey called Putyma, a follower of Topiawari, chiefe Lord of Aromaia, who succeeded More-quito, whom (as you haue heard before) Berreo put to death: but his towne being farre within the land, he came not vnto vs that day, so as we ankered againe that night neere the bankes of another yland, of bignesse much like the other, which they call Putapayma, ouer against which yland, on the maine lande, was a very high mountaine called Oecope: we coueted to ancker rather by these ylands in the Riuer, then by the maine, because of the Tortugas egges, which our people found on them in great abundance, and also because the ground serued better for vs to cast our nets for fish, the maine bankes being for the most part stonie and high, and the rocks of a blue metalline colour, like vnto the best steele-ore, which I assuredly take it to be: of the same blew stone are also diuers great mountaines, which border this riuer in many places.

The next morning towards nine of the clocke, wee weighed ancker, and the brize increasing, we sailed alwayes West vp the riuer, and after a while opening the land on the right side, the countrey appeared to bee champaine, and the bankes shewed very perfect red. I therefore sent two of the little barges with Captaine Gifford, and with him Captaine Thyn, Captaine Calfield, my cosen Greenuile, my nephew Iohn Gilbert, Captaine Eynus, Master Edward Porter, and my cosen Butshead Gorges, with some fewe souldiers, to march ouer the bankes of that red land, and to discouer what maner of countrey it was on the other side, who at their return founde it all a plaine leuell, as farre as they went or could discerne, from the highest tree they could get vpon: And my old Pilot, a man of great trauell, brother to the Casique Toparimica tolde mee, that those were called the plaines of the Sayma, and that the same leuell reached to Cumana, and Caracas in the West Indies, which are a hundreth and twentie leagues to the North, and that there inhabited foure principall nations. The first were the Sayma, the next Assawai, the thirde and greatest the Wikiri, by whom Pedro Hernandez de Serpa before mentioned was ouerthrowen, as hee passed with three hundred horse from Cumana towards Orenoque, in his enterprize of Guiana : the fourth are called Aroras, and are as blacke as Negros, but haue smooth haire, and these are very valiant, or rather desperate people, and haue the most strong poyson on their arrowes, and most dangerous of all nations, of which poyson I will speake somewhat being a digression not vnnecessary.

Aroras a black people vsing venemous arrowes.

There was nothing whereof I was more curious, then to finde out the true remedies of these poysoned arrowes : for besides the mortalitie of the wound they make, the partie shotte indureth `the most insufferable torment in the world, and abideth a most vgly and lamentable death, sometimes dying starke mad, somtimes their bowels breaking out of their bellies : which are presently discoloured as blacke as pitch, and so vnsauory, as no man can endure to cure, or to attend them. And it is more strange ·to know, that in all this time there was neuer Spaniard either by gift or torment that could atteine to the true knowledge of the cure, although they haue martyred and put to inuented torture I know not how many of them. But euery one of these Indians knew it not, no not one among thousands, but their soothsayers and priestes, who doe conceale it, and onely teach it but from the father to the sonne.

Those medicines which are vulgar, and serue for the ordinarie poyson, are made of the iuice of a roote called Tupara : the same also quencheth marueilously the heate of burning feauers, and healeth inward wounds, and broken veines, that bleed within the body. But I was more beholding to the Guianians then any other : for Anthonio de Berreo tolde mee that hee could neuer attaine to the knowledge thereof, and yet they taught mee the best way of healing as well thereof, as of all other poysons. Some of the Spaniards haue bene cured in ordinary wounds, of the common poysoned arrowes with the iuice of the garlike : but this is a generall rule for all men that shall hereafter trauel the Indies where poisoned arrowes are vsed, that they must abstaine from drinke, for if they take any licour into their body,

The iuice of garlike good against ordinary poyson.

as they shall bee marueilously prouoked thereunto by drought
I say, if they drinke before the wound bee dressed, or soone
vpon it, there is no way with them but present death.

And so I will returne againe to our iourney which for this
thirde day we finished, and cast ancker againe neere the continent or the left hand betweene two mountaines, the one called
Aroami, and the other Aio: I made no stay here but till midnight, for I feared hourely least any raine should fall, and then it
had bene impossible to haue gone any further vp, notwithstanding that there is euery day a very strong brize, and Easterly
winde. I deferred the search of the countrey on Guiana-side,
till my returne downe the riuer.

The next day we sailed by a great yland in the middle of the
riuer called Manoripano, and as wee walked a while on the
yland, while the Galley got a head of vs, there came for vs from
the maine a small Canoa with seuen or eight Guianians, to
inuite vs to ancker at their port, but I deferred till my returne;
It was that Casique to whom those Nepoios went, which came
with vs from the towne of Toparimaca: and so the fift day we
reached as high vp as the prouince of Aromaia the countrey of
Morequito whom Berreo executed, and ankered to the West of
an yland called Murrecotima, tenne miles long and fiue broad:
and that night the Casique Aramiary, (to whose towne we made
our long and hungry voyage out of the riuer of Amana) passed
by vs.

The next day wee arriued at the port of Morequito, and
anckered there, sending away one of our Pilots to seeke the
king of Aromaia, vncle to Morequito slaine by Berreo as aforesaid. The next day following before noone hee came to vs on
foote from his house, which was fourteene English miles (himselfe being a hundreth and tenne yeeres olde) and returned on
foote the same day, and with him many of the borderers, with
many women and children, that came to wonder at our nation,
and to bring vs downe victuall, which they did in great plentie,
as venison, porke, hennes, chickens, foule, fish, with diuers sorts
of excellent fruites and rootes, and great abundance of Pinas, the
princes of fruites, that grow vnder the Sunne, especially those of
Guiana. They brought vs also store of bread, and of their wine,
and a sort of Paraquitos, no bigger then wrennes, and of all other
sorts both small and great; one of them gaue mee a beast called
by the Spaniards Armadilla, which they call Cassacam, which

seemeth to be all barred ouer with smal plates somewhat like to
a Rinoceros, with a white horne growing in his hinder parts, as
bigge as a great hunting horne, which they vse to winde in stead
of a trumpet.   Monardus writeth that a little of the powder of
that horne put into the eare, cureth deafenesse.

After this olde King had rested a while in a little tent, that I
caused to bee set vp, I beganne by my interpreter to discourse
with him of the death of Morequito his predecessour, and afterward of the Spaniards, and ere I went any farther I made him
knowe the cause of my comming thither, whose seruant I was,
and that the Queenes pleasure was, I should vndertake the
voyage for their defence, and to deliuer them from the tyrannie
of the Spaniards, dilating at large, (as I had done before to those
of Trinidad) her Maiesties greatnesse, her iustice, her charitie to
all oppressed nations, with as many of the rest of her beauties
and vertues, as either I could expresse, or they conceiue : all
which being with great admiration attentiuely heard, and marueilously admired, I beganne to sound the olde man as touching
Guiana, and the state thereof, what sort of common wealth it
was, how gouerned, of what strength and policie, howe farre it
extended, and what nations were friendes or enemies adioyning,
and finally of the distance and way to enter the same : hee tolde
mee that himselfe and his people with all those downe the Riuer
towards the Sea, as farre as Emeria, the prouince of Carapana,
were of Guiana, but that they called themselues Orenoqueponi,
and that all the nations betweene the riuer and those mountaines
in sight called Wacarima, were of the same cast and appellation :
and that on the other side of those mountaines of Wacarima
there was a large plaine (which after I discouered in my returne)
called the valley of Amariocapana, in all that valley the people
were also of the ancient Guianians.

I asked what nations those were which inhabited on the
farther side of those mountaines, beyond the valley of Amariocapana : hee answered with a great sigh (as a man which had
inward feeling of the losse of his Countrey and libertie, especially
for that his eldest sonne was slaine in a battell on that side of
the mountaines, whom hee most entirely loued) that he remembred in his fathers life time when hee was very olde, and
himselfe a yong man, that there came downe into that large
valley of Guiana, a nation from so farre off as the Sunne slept,
(for such were his owne wordes) with so great a multitude as

they coulde not bee numbred nor resisted, and that they wore
large coates, and hattes of crimson colour, which colour hee
expressed, by shewing a piece of red wood, wherewith my tent was supported, and that they were
called Orejones, and Epuremei, those that had slaine
and rooted out so many of the ancient people, as
there were leaues in the wood vpon all the trees,
and had nowe made themselues Lords of all, euen

Orejones are the gentle-men of Peru. Lop. de Gomar. Hist. gen. cap. 119.

to that mountaine foote called Curaa, sauing onely of two
nations, the one called Awarawaqueri, and the other Cassipagotos, and that in the last battell fought betweene the Epuremei,
and the Iwarawaqueri, his eldest sonne was chosen to carry to
the aide of the Iwarawaqueri, a great troupe of the Orenoqueponi,
and was there slaine with all his people and friendes, and that
hee had now remayning but one sonne : and farther tolde mee
that those Epuremei had built a great Towne called Macureguarai at the said mountaine foote, at the beginning of the
great plaines of Guiana, which haue no ende : and that their
houses haue many roomes, one ouer the other, and that therein
the great King of the Orejones and Epuremei kept three
thousande men to defend the borders against them, and withall
dayly to inuade and slay them : but that of late yeeres since the
Christians offered to inuade his territories, and those frontiers,
they were all at peace, and traded one with another, sauing onely
the Iwarawaqueri, and those other nations vpon the head of the
riuer of Caroli, called Cassipagotos, which we afterwards discouered, each one holding the Spaniard for a common enemie.

After hee had answered thus farre, he desired leaue to depart,
saying that hee had farre to goe, that hee was olde, and weake,
and was euery day called for by death, which was also his owne
phrase : I desired him to rest with vs that night, but I could not
intreate him, but hee tolde mee that at my returne from the
countrey aboue, hee would againe come to vs, and in the meane
time prouide for vs the best he could, of all that his countrey
yeelded : the same night hee returned to Orocotona his owne
towne, so as hee went that day eight and twentie
miles, the weather being very hot, the countrey being
situate betweene foure and fiue degrees of the
Equinoctial.

Orotona betweene 4. and 5. de-grees of Northerly latitude.

This Topiawari is helde for the prowdest, and
wisest of all the Orenoqueponi, and so hee behaued

himselfe towardes mee in all his answeres at my returne, as I marueiled to finde a man of that grauitie and iudgement, and of so good discourse, that had no helpe of learning nor breede.

The next morning we also left the port, and sailed Westward vp to the Riuer, to view the famous Riuer called Caroli, as well because it was marueilous of it selfe, as also for that I vnderstoode it ledde to the strongest nations of all the frontiers, that were enemies to the Epuremei, which are subiects to Inga, Emporour of Guiana, and Manoa, and that night we ankered at another yland called Caiama, of some fiue or sixe miles in

The yle of Caiama. length, and the next day arriued at the mouth of Caroli. When we were short of it as lowe or

They arriue at the mouth of the riuer Caroli. further downe as the port of Morequito wee heard the great rore and fall of the Riuer, but when wee came to enter with our barge and whirries thinking

to haue gone vp some fourtie miles to the nations of the Cassipagotos, wee were not able with a barge of eight oares to row one stones cast in an houre, and yet the Riuer is as broad as the Thames at Wolwich, and wee tried both sides, and the middle, and euery part of the Riuer, so as we incamped vpon the bankes adioyning, and sent off our Orenequepone (which came with vs from Morequito) to giue knowledge to the nations vpon the Riuer of our being there, and that wee desired to see the Lordes of Canuria, which dwelt within the prouince vpon that Riuer, making them know that we were enemies to the Spaniards, (for it was on this Riuer side that Morequito slewe the Frier, and those nine Spaniards which came from Manoa, the Citie of Inga, and tooke from them fourtie thousand pezos of golde) so as the next day there came downe a Lord or Casique called Wanuretona with many people with him, and brought all store of prouisions to entertaine vs, as the rest had done. And as I had before made my comming knowen to Topiawari, so did I, acquaint this Casique therewith, and howe I was sent by her Maiestie for the purpose aforesaide, and gathered also what I could of him touching the estate of Guiana, and I founde that those also of Caroli were not onely enemies to the Spaniards, but most of all to the Epuremei, which abound in golde, and by this Wanuretona, I had knowledge that on the head of this Riuer were three mighty nations, which were seated on a great lake, from whence this Riuer descended, and were called Cassipagotos, Eparagotos, and Arawagots, and that all those either against the Spaniards, or the Epuremei would ioyne with vs, and that if wee entred the land ouer the mountaines of Curaa, we should satisfie our selues with gold and all other good things : he told vs farther of a nation called Iwarawaqueri before spoken off, that held dayly warre with the Epuremei that inhabited Macureguarai the first ciuill towne of Guiana, of the subiects of Inga the Emperour.

Cassipagotos, Eparagotos, and Arawagotos three mighty nations seated on a lake at the head of the riuer Caroli.

Vpon this riuer one Captaine George, that I tooke with Berreo tolde mee there was a great siluer Mine, and that it was neere the banckes of the saide riuer. But by this time as well Orenoque, Caroli, as all the rest of the riuers were risen foure or fiue foote in height, so as it was not possible by the strength of any men, or with any boat whatsoeuer to rowe into the Riuer against the streame. I therefore sent Captaine Thyn, Captaine Greenuile, my nephew Iohn Gylbert, my cosen Butshead Gorges, Captaine Clarke, and some thirtie shotte more to coast the Riuer by land, and to goe to a towne some twentie miles ouer the valley called Amnatapoi, and they found guides there, to goe farther towards the mountaine foote to another great towne called Capurepana, belonging to a Casique called Haharacoa (that was a nephew to olde Topiawari King of Arromaia our chiefest friend) because this towne and a prouince of Capurepada adioyned to Macureguarai, which was a frontier towne of the Empire : and the meane while my selfe with Captaine Calfield, Edward Hancocke, and some halfe a dosen shotte marched ouer land to viewe the strange ouerfals of the riuer of Caroli which rored so farre off, and also to see the plaines adioyning, and the rest of the prouince of Canuri : I sent also Captaine Whiddon, William Connocke, and some eight shotte with them, to see if they coulde finde any Mineral stone alongst the riuer side. When we were come to the tops of the first hilles of the plaines adioyning to the riuer, we behelde that wonderful breach of waters, which ranne downe Caroli : and might from that mountaine see the riuer howe it ranne in three parts, aboue twentie miles off, and there appeared some tenne or twelue ouerfals in sight, euery one as high ouer the other as a Churchtower, which fell with that fury,

Amnatapoi, a towne.

The strange ouerfals of Caroli.

P

that the rebound of water made it seeme, as if it had bene all couered ouer with a great shower of raine : and in some places wee tooke it at the first for a smoke that had risen ouer some great towne.   For mine owne part I was well perswaded from thence to haue returned, being a very ill footeman, but the rest were all so desirous to goe neere the saide strange thunder of waters, as they drew me on by little and little, till wee A most came into the next valley where we might better dis-
beautifull
country.   cerne the same.   I neuer saw a more beautifull countrey, nor more liuely prospects, hils so raised here and there ouer the valleys, the riuer winding into diuers branches, the plaines adioyning without bush or stubble, all faire greene grasse, the ground of hard sand easie to march on, either for horse or foote, the deere crossing in euery path, the birdes towards the euening singing on euery tree with a thousand seuerall tunes, cranes and herons of white crimson, and carnation pearching in the riuers side, the aire fresh with a gentle Easterly winde, euery stone that we stouped to take vp, promised either golde or siluer by his complexion.   Your Lordship shall see of many sorts, and I hope some of them cannot bee bettered vnder the Sunne, and yet we had no means but our daggers and fingers to teare them out here and there, the rockes being most hard of Abundance that minerall Sparre aforesaid, which is like a flint,
of mineral and is altogether as hard or harder, and besides the
Sparre.   veines lye a fathome or two deepe in the rockes. But we wanted all things requisite saue onely our desires and good will to haue performed more if it had pleased God.   To be short, when both our companies returned, each of them brought also seuerall sorts of stones that appeared very faire, but were such as they found loose on the ground, and were for the most part but coloured, and had not any golde fixed in them, yet such as had no iudge-ment or experience kept al that glistered, and would not be perswaded but it was rich because of the lustre, and brought of those, and of Marquesite with all, from Trinidad, and haue de-liuered of those stones to be tried in many places, and haue thereby bred an opinion that all the rest is of the same : yet some of these stones I shewed afterward to a Spaniard of the Caracas, who tolde mee that it was El Madre del oro, that is the mother of golde, and that the Mine was further in the ground.

But it shall be found a weake policie in me, either to betray my selfe, or my countrey with imaginations, neither am I so farr

in loue with that lodging, watching, care, peril, diseases, ill
sauours, bad fare, and many other mischiefes that accompany
these voyages, as to woo my selfe againe into any of them, were
I not assured that the Sunne couereth not so much riches in any
part of the earth.   Captaine Whiddon, and our Chirurgion
Nicholas Millechap brought mee a kinde of stones like Saphires,
what they may proue I know not.   I shewed them to some of
the Orenoqueponi, and they promised to bring mee to a mountaine, that had of them very large pieces growing Diamond wise :
whether it be Christall of the mountaine, Bristol-Diamond, or
Saphire I doe not yet know, but I hope the best, sure I am that
the place is as likely as those from whence all the rich stones are
brought, and in the same height or very neere.

On the left hand of this riuer Caroli are seated those nations
which are called Iwarawakeri before remembered, which are
enemies to the Epuremei : and on the head of it adioyning to
the great lake Cassipa, are situate those other nations which also
resist Inga, and the Epuremei, called Cassepagotos, Eparegotos,
and Arrawagotos.   I farther vnderstood that this lake
of Cassipa is so large, as it is aboue one dayes iourney Cassipa a
great lake.
for one of their Canoas to crosse, which may bee
some fourtie miles, and that thereinto fall diuers riuers, and that
great store of graines of gold are found in the Summer time when
the lake falleth by the banckes, in those branches.

There is also another goodly riuer beyond Caroli which is
called Arui, which also runneth thorow the lake Cassipa, and
falleth into Orenoque farther West, making all that land betweene Caroli and Arui an yland, which is likewise a most
beautifull countrey.   Next vnto Arui there are two riuers Atoica
and Caora, and on that branch which is called Caora, are a
nation of people, whose heads appeare not aboue their shouldiers ;
which though it may be thought a meere fable, yet for mine
owne part I am resolued it is true, because euery childe in the
prouinces of Arromaia and Canuri affirme the same : Ewaipanoma
they are called Ewaipanoma : they are reported to a strange
haue their eyes in their shoulders, and their mouthes headless
nation.
in the middle of their breasts, and that a long traine
of haire groweth backward betweene their shoulders.   The sonne
of Topiawari, which I brought with me into England told me
that they are the most mighty men of all the land, and vse
bowes, arrowes, and clubbes thrice as big as any of Guiana, or

of the Orenoqueponi, and that one of the Iwarawakeri tooke a prisoner of them the yeere before our arriuall there, and brought him into the borders of Aromaia his fathers countrey. And farther when I seemed to doubt of it, hee told me that it was no wonder among them, but that they were as great a nation, and as common as any other in all the prouinces, and had of late yeeres slaine many hundreds of his fathers people, and of other nations their neighbours, but it was not my chance to heare of them till I was come away, and if I had but spoken one worde of it while I was there, I might haue brought one of them with mee to put the matter out of doubt. Such a nation was written of by Mandeuile, whose reports were holden for fables many yeeres, and yet since the East Indies were discouered. we find his relations true of such things as heretofore were held incredible : whether it be true or 'no, the matter is not great, neither can there bee any profit in the imagination ; for mine owne part I saw them not, but I am resolued that so many people did not all combine, or forthinke to make the report.

When I came to Cumana in the West Indies afterwards by chance I spake with a Spaniard dwelling not farre from thence, a man of great trauell, and after hee knew that I had bene in Guiana, and so farre directly West of Caroli, the first question hee asked me was, whether I had seene any of the Ewaipanoma, which are those without heads : who being esteemed a most honest man of his word, and in all things else, tolde mee that hee had seene many of them : I may not name him, because it may be for his disaduantage, but hee is well knowen to Monsieur Mucherons sonne of London, and to Peter Mucheron merchant of the Flemish shippe that was there in trade, who also heard what he auowed to be true of those people.

The fourth riuer to the West of Caroli is Casnero which falleth into Orenoque on this side of Amapaia, and that riuer *The riuer of Casnero.* is greater then Danubius, or any in Europe : it riseth on the South of Guiana from the mountaines which diuide Guiana from Amazones, and I thinke it to bee nauigable many hundreth miles : but wee had no time, meanes, nor season of the yeere, to search those riuers for the causes aforesayd, the *The Winter of Guiana.* Winter being come vpon vs, although the Winter and Summer as touching colde and heate differ not, neither doe the trees euer sensibly lose their leaues, but haue alwayes fruit either ripe or greene, and most of them both blossome, leaues, ripe fruite, and greene at one time : but their Winter onely consisteth of terrible raines, and ouerflowing of the riuers, with many great stormes and gustes, thunder and lightnings, of which we had our fill, ere we returned.

On the North side, the first riuer that falleth into Orenoque is Cari, beyond it on the same side is the riuer of Limo, betweene these two is a great nation of Canibals, and their chiefe towne beareth the name of the riuer, and is called Acamacari : at this towne is a continuall market of women for three or foure hatchets a piece, they are bought by the Arwacas, and by them sold into the West Indies. To the West of Limo is the riuer Pao, beyond it Caturi, beyond that Voari and Capuri which falleth out of the great riuer of Meta, by which Berreo descended from Nueuo reyno de Granada. To the Westward of Capuri is the prouince of Amapaia, where Berreo wintered, and had so many of his people poysoned with the tawny water of the marshes of the Anebas. Aboue Amapaia toward Nueuo reyno fall in Meta, Pato, and Cassanar. To the West of those towards this prouinces of the Ashaguas and Catetios are the riuers of Beta, Dawney, and Vbarro, and toward the frontier of Peru are the prouinces of Thomebamba, and Caxamalca. Adioyning to Quito in the North side of Peru are the riuers of Guiacar and Goauar : and on the other side of the sayd mountaynes the riuer of Papamene which descendeth into Marannon or Amazones passing thorough the prouince Mutylones where Don Pedro de Osua who was slaine by the traytour Agiri before rehearsed, built his brigandines, when he sought Guiana by the way of Amazones.

Betweene Dawney and Beta lyeth a famous Island in Orenoque now called Baraquan (for aboue Meta it is not knowen by the name of Orenoque) which is called Athule, beyond which, ships of burden cannot passe by reason of a most forcible ouerfall, and current of waters : but in the eddy al smaller vessels may be drawen euen to Peru it selfe : But to speake of more of these riuers without the description were but tedious, and therefore I will leaue the rest to the description. This riuer of Orenoque is nauigable for ships little lesse then 1000 miles, and for lesser vessels neere 2000. By it (as aforesayd) Peru, Nueuo reyno, and Popaian, may be inuaded : it also leadeth to the great empire of Inga, and to the prouinces of Amapaia, and Anebas which abound in

The Isle of Baraquan.

Orenoque a mighty riuer by which Peru, Nueuo reyno, and Popaian may be inuaded.

gold: his branches of Cosnero, Manta, Caora descended
from the middle land and valley, which lieth betweene
the easter prouince of Peru and Guiana ; and it falles into the
sea betweene Marannon and Trinidad in two degrees and a
halfe : all which your Honours shall better perceiue in the
general description of Guiana, Peru, Nueuo reyno, the kingdome
of Popayan, and Roidas, with the prouince of Veneçuela, to the
bay of Vraba, behind Cartagena Westward ; and to Amazones
Southward. While we lay at ankor on the coast of Canuri, and
had taken knowledge of all the nations vpon the head and
branches of this riuer, and had found out so many seuerall
people, which were enemies to the Epuremei, and the new
conquerours : I thought it time lost to linger any longer in that
place, especially for that the fury of Orenoque began dayly to
threaten vs with dangers in our returne : for no halfe day
passed, but the riuer beganne to rage and ouerflowe very fear-
fully, and the raines came downe in terrible showers, and gustes
in great abundance : and withall, our men began to crie out for
want of shift, for no man had place to bestowe any other
apparell then that which he ware on his backe, and that was
throughly washt on his body for the most part tenne times in one
day : and we had now bene wel neere a moneth,
They returne euery day passing to the Westward farther and farther
from our shippes. Wee therefore turned towards the East,
and spent the rest of the time in discouering the riuer towards
the sea, which we had not viewed, and which was not
materiall.

The next day following we left the mouth of Caroli, and
arriued againe at the port of Morequito where we were before :
for passing downe the streame we went without labour, and
against the winde, little lesse then a hundreth miles a day.
Assoone as I came to ankor, I sent away one for olde Topiawari,
with whom I much desired to haue further conference, and also
to deale with him for some one of his countrey, to bring with vs
into England, as well to learne the language, as to conferre
withall by the way, the time being nowe spent of any longer stay
there. Within three houres after my messenger came to him, he
arriued also, and with him such a rabble of all sorts of people,
and euery one loden with somewhat, as if it had beene a great
market or faire in England : and our hungry companies clustered
thicke and threefold among their baskets, euery one

laying hand on what he liked. After he had rested The last conference of Sir Walter
a while in my tent, I shut out all but our selues, and
my interpreter, and told him that I knew that both Ralegh with Topiawari,
the Epuremei and the Spaniards were enemies to whose sonne
him, his countrey and nations: that the one had con- he brought
quered Guiana already, and the other sought to into England.
regaine the same from them both : and therefore I desired him
to instruct me what he could, both of the passage into the golden
parts of Guiana, and to the ciuill townes and apparelled people
of Inga. Hee gaue mee an answere to this effect : first that hee
could not perceiue that I meant to goe onward towards the citie
of Manoa, for neither the time of the yeere serued, neither could
hee perceiue any sufficient numbers for such an enterprize : and
if I did, I was sure with all my company to bee buried there, for
the Emperour was of that strength, as that many times so many
men more were too fewe : besides hee gaue mee this
good counsell and aduised mee to holde it in minde Counsell to be followed
(as for himselfe hee knewe, hee could not liue till my in other
returne) that I should not offer by any meanes here- conquests.
after to inuade the strong parts of Guiana without the helpe of all
those nations which were also their enemies : for that it was impossible without those, either to bee conducted, to be victualled, or to
haue ought caried with vs, our people not being able to indure the
march in so great heate, and trauell, vnlesse the borderers gaue them
helpe, to carie with them both their meate and furniture : For hee
remembred that in the plaines of Macureguarai three hundreth
Spaniards were ouerthrowen, who were tired out, and had none
of the borderers to their friendes : but meeting their enemies as
they passed the frontier, were enuironed on all sides, and the
people setting the long drie grasse on fire, smoothered them, so
as they had no breath to fight, nor could discerne their enemies
for the great smoke. He tolde me farther that 4 daies iourney
from his towne was Macureguarai, and that those
were the next and nearest of the subiects of Inga, Macureguarai ye first towne of Guiana, and of rich and apparelled people.
and of the Epuremei, and the first towne of apparelled
and rich people, and that all those plates of gold
which were scattered among the borderers and
caried to other nations farre and neere, came from
the sayd Macureguarai and were there made, but
that those of the land within were farre finer, and were fashioned
after the images of men, beasts, birds, and fishes. I asked him

whether hee thought that those companies that I had there with me, were sufficient to take that towne or no? He told me that he thought they were.   I then asked him, whether he would assist me with guides, and some companies of his people to ioyne with vs? He answered that he would go himselfe with al the borderers, if the riuers did remaine foordable, vpon this condition that I would leaue with him til my return againe fifty souldiers, which hee vndertooke to victuall: I answered that I had not aboue fiftie good men in all there, the rest were labourers and rowers, and that I had no prouision to leaue with them of powder, shot, apparell, or ought else, and that without those things necessary for their defence, they should bee in danger of the Spaniards in my absence, who I knew would vse the same measure towards mine, that I offered them at Trinidad: And although vpon the motion Captaine Calfield, Captaine Greenuile, my nephew Iohn Gilbert and diuers others were desirous to stay, yet I was resolued that they must needes haue perished, for Berreo expected daylie a supply out of Spaine, and looked also hourely for his sonne to come downe from Nueuo reyno de Granada, with many horse and foote, and had also in Valencia in the Caracas, two hundreth horse ready to march, and I could not haue spared aboue fortie, and had not any store at all of powder, leade, or match to haue left with them, nor any other prouision, either spade, pickeaxe, or ought else to haue fortified withall.

When I had giuen him reason that I could not at· this time leaue him such a companie, he then desired mee to forbeare him and his countrey for that time, for he assured mee that I should bee no sooner three dayes from the coast, but those Epuremei would inuade him, and destroy all the remaine of his people and friendes, if hee should any way either guide vs or assist vs against them.

He further alleaged, that the Spaniards sought his death, and as they had already murthered his Nephew Morequito lord of that prouince, so they had him seuenteene dayes in a chaine before hee was king of the countrey, and ledde him like a dog from place to place, vntill he had payde an hundreth plates of golde, and diuers chaines of Spleen-stones for his ransome : and nowe since he became owner of that prouince, that they had many times layd waite to take him, and that they would bee nowe more vehement, when they should vnderstand of his conference with the English, and because, sayd hee, they would the better displant me, if they cannot lay handes on mee, they haue gotten a Nephew of mine called Eparacano, whom they haue Christened Don Iuan, and his sonne Don Pedro, whom they haue also apparelled and armed, by whom they seeke to make a partie against me in mine owne countrey : hee also had taken to wife one Louiana of a strong familie, which are borderers and neighbours, and my selfe now being olde and in the handes of death am not able to trauell nor to shifte, as when I was of yoonger yeeres : hee therefore prayed vs to deferre it till the next yeere, when he would vndertake to draw in all the borderers to serue vs, and then also it would bee more seasonable to trauell, for at this time of the yeere, wee should not bee able to, passe any riuer, the waters were and would bee so growen ere our returne.

He farther told me, that I could not desire so much to, inuade Macureguarai, and the rest of Guiana, but that the borderers would be more vehement then I, for he yeelded for a chiefe cause that in the warres with the Epuremei, they were spoyled of their women, and that their wiues and daughters were taken from them, so as for their owne parts they desired nothing of the golde or treasure, for their labours, but onely to recouer women from the Epuremei : for hee farther complayned very sadly (as it had beene a matter of great consequence) that whereas they were wont to haue tenne or twelue wiues, they were now inforced to content themselues with three or foure, and that the lords of the Epuremei had fifty or a hundreth : And in truth they war more for women then either for gold or dominion : For the lords of countreys desire many children of their owne bodies, to increase their races and kindreds, for in those consist their greatest trust and strength. Diuers of his followers afterwards desired mee to make haste againe, that they might sacke the Epuremei, and I asked them of what ? They answered, of their women for vs, and their gold for you : for the hope of those women they more desire the war, then either for gold, or for the recouery of their ancient territories. For what betweene the subiects of Inga, and the Spaniards, those frontiers are growen thinne of people, and also great numbers are fled to other nations farther off for feare of the Spaniards.

After I receiued this answere of the old man, we fell into consideration, whether it had bene of better aduice to haue

Q

entred Macureguaria, and to haue begun a warre vpon Inga
at this time, yea or no, if the .time of the yeere, and all things
else had sorted.   For mine owne part (as we were not able to
march it for the riuers, neither had any such strength   as
was requisite, and durst not abide the comming of the Winter,
or to tarie any longer from our ships (I thought it were
euill counsell to haue attempted it at that time, although the
desire of gold will answere many obiections : but it would haue
bin in mine opinion an vtter ouerthrow to the enterprize,
if the same should be hereafter by her Maiesty attempted ;
for then (whereas now they haue heard we were- enemies to
the Spaniards and were sent by her Maiesty to relieue them)
they would as good cheap haue ioyned with the Spaniards
at our returne, as to haue yeelded vnto vs, when they
had proued that we came both for one errant, and that both
sought but to sacke and spoile them, but as yet our desire of
gold, or our purpose of inuasion is not knowen to them of the
empire : and it is likely that if her Maiestie vndertake the enterprize, they will rather submit themselues to her obedience then
to the Spaniards, of whose cruelty both themselues and the
borderers haue already tasted : and therefore till I had knowen
her Maiesties pleasure, I would rather haue lost the sacke of one
or two townes (although they might haue beene very profitable)
then to haue defaced or indangered the future hope of so many
millions, and the great good, and rich trade which England may
be possessed of thereby.   I am assured nowe that they will all
die euen to the last man against the Spaniards in hope of our
succour and 'returne : whereas otherwise if I had either layd
handes on the borderers, or ransomed the lords, as Berreo did,
or inuaded the subiects of Inga, I know all had beene lost for
hereafter.

   After that I had resolued Topiawari lord of Aromaia, that I
could not at this time leaue with him the companies he desired,
and that I was contented to forbeare the enterprize against the
Epuremei till the next yeare, he freely gaue me his onely sonne
to take with me into England, and hoped, that though hee himselfe had but a short time to liue, yet that by our meanes his
sonne should be established after his death : and I left with him
one Francis Sparrow, a seruant of Captaine Gifford, (who was
desirous to tarie, and could describe a countrey with his pen)
and a boy of mine called Hugh Goodwin, to learne the language.

I after asked the maner how the Epuremei wrought those plates of golde, and how they could melt it out of the stone ; hee tolde mee that the most of the golde which they made in plates and images, was not seuered from the stone, but that on the lake of Manoa, and in a multitude of other riuers they gathered it in graines of perfect gold and in peeces as bigge as small stones, and that they put it to a part of copper, otherwise they could not worke it, and that they vsed a great earthern pot with holes round about it, and when they had mingled the gold and copper together, they fastened canes to the holes, and so with the breath of men they increased the fire till the metall ran and they cast it into moulds of stone and clay, and so make those plates and images. I haue sent your Honors of two sortes such as I could by chance recouer, more to shewe the maner of them, then for the value : For I did not in any sort make my desire of gold knowen, because I had neither time, nor power to haue a greater quantity. I gaue among them manie more peeces of gold, then I receiued, of the new money of 20 shillings with her Maiesties picture to weare, with promise that they would become her seruants thencefoorth.

I haue also sent your Honours of the ore, whereof I know some is as rich as the earth yeeldeth any, of which I know there is sufficient, if nothing else were {Most rich gold ore.} to bee hoped for. But besides that we were not able to tarrie and search the hils, so we had neither pioners, barres, ledges, nor wedges of yron to breake the ground, without which there is no working in mines : but wee saw all the hilles with stones of the colour of gold and siluer, and we tried them to be no Marquesite, and therefore such as the Spaniards call El madre del oro, or, The mother of gold, which is an vndoubted assurance of the generall abundance : and my selfe saw the outside of many mines of the Sparre, which I know to be the same that all couet in this world, and of those, more then I will speake of.

Hauing learned what I could in Canuri and Aromaia, and receiued a faithfull promise of the principallest of those prouinces to become seruants to her Maiestie, and to resist the Spaniards, if they made any attempt in our absence, and that they would draw in the nations about the lake of Cassipa, and those Iwarawaqueri, I then parted from olde Topiawari, and receiued his sonne for a pledge betweene vs, and left with him two of ours as aforesayd. To Francis Sparrowe I gaue instructions to trauell

to Macureguarai, with such merchandizes as I left with them,
thereby to learne the place, and if it were possible, to goe on to
the great citie of Manoa: which being done, we weyed ankor,
Guiana on and coasted the riuer on Guiana side, because wee
the South- came vpon the North side, by the launes of the
side.   Saima and Wikiri.

There came with vs from Aromaia a Cassique called Putijma,
that commanded the prouince of Warapana, (which Putijma
slewe the nine Spaniards vpon Caroli before spoken of) who
desired vs to rest in the Porte of his countrey, promising to
bring vs vnto a mountaine adioyning to his towne that had
stones of the colour of golde, which hee perfourmed.   And after
wee had rested there one night, I went my selfe in the morning
with most of the Gentlemen of my company, ouer land towards
the said mountaine, marching by a riuers side called Mana,
leauing on the right hand a towne called Tuteritona, standing in
the Prouince of Tarracoa, of the which Wariaaremagoto is principall.   Beyond it lieth another towne towards the South, in the
valley of Amariocapana, which beareth the name of the sayd
valley, whose plaines stretch themselues some sixtie miles in
length, East and West, as faire ground, and as beautifull fields,
as any man hath euer seene, with diuers copsies scattered here
and there by the riuers side, and all as full of deere as any forrest
or parke in England, and in euerie lake and riuer the like
abundance of fish and foule, of which Irraparragota is lord.

From the riuer of Mana, we crost another riuer in the said
beautifull valley called Oiana, and rested our selues by a cleere
lake, which lay in the middle of the said Oiana, and one of our
guides kindling vs fire with two stickes, wee stayed a while to
drie our shirts, which with the heate hong very wette and heauie
on our sholders.   Afterwards wee sought the ford to passe ouer
towards the mountaine called Iconuri, where Putijma foretold vs
of the mine.   In this lake we saw one of the great fishes, as big
as a wine pipe, which they call Manati, being most excellent and
holsome meate.   But after I perceiued, that to passe the said
riuer would require halfe a dayes march more, I was not able
my selfe to indure it, and therefore I sent Captaine Keymis with
sixe shot to goe on, and gaue him order not to returne to the
port of Putijma, which is called Chiparepare, but to take leisure,
and to march downe the sayd valley, as farre as a riuer called
Cumaca, where I promised to meete him againe, Putijma him-

selfe promising also to bee his guide : and as they marched'
they left the townes of Emparepana and Capurepana, on the
right hand, and marched from Putijmas house downe the sayd
valley of Amariocapana, and wee returning the same day to the
riuers side, saw by the way many rockes, like vnto gold ore, and
on the left hand, a round mountaine which consisted of minerall
stone.

From hence we rowed downe the streame, coasting the prouince of Parino : As for the branches of riuers which I ouerpasse
in this discourse, those shall be better expressed in the description with the mountaines of Aio, Ara, and the rest, which are
situate in the prouinces of Parino and Carricurrina. When we
were come as farre down as the land called Ariacoa, (where
Orenoque deuideth it selfe into three great branches, each of
them being most goodly riuers) I sent away captaine Henrie
Thin, and captaine Greeneuile with the galley, the neerest way,
and tooke with mee captaine Gifford, captaine Calfield, Edward
Porter, and captaine Eynos with mine owne barge, and the two
wherries, and went downe that branch of Orenoque, which is
called Cararoopana, which leadeth towards Emeria the prouince
of Carapana, and towards the East sea, as well to finde out
captaine Keymis, whome I had sent ouer land, as also acquaint
my selfe with Carapana, who is one of the greatest of all the
lords of the Orenoqueponi : and when I came to the riuer of
Cumaca (to which Putijma promised to conduct captaine Keymis)
I left captaine Eynos and master Porter in the sayd riuer to
expect his comming, and the rest of vs rowed downe the
streame towards Emeria.

In this branch called Cararoopana were also many goodly
Islands, some of sixe miles long, some of ten, and some of
twenty. When it grew towards sunne-set, we entred a branch of
a riuer that fell into Orenoque called Winicapora : where I was
enformed of the mountaine of Christall, to which in trueth for
the length of the way, and the euill season of the yeere, I was
not able to march, nor abide any longer vpon the iourney : wee
saw it afarre off and it appeared like a white Church-tower of
an exceeding height. There falleth ouer it a mighty $\quad$ A mighty
riuer which toucheth no part of the side of the $\quad$ cataract or
mountaine, but rusheth ouer the toppe of it, and $\quad$ ouerfall of
falleth to the ground with so terrible a noyse and $\quad$ water.
clamor, as if a thousand great bels were knockt one against

another.   I thinke there is not in the world so strange an ouerfall, nor so wonderfull to behold : Berreo told mee that there
were Diamonds and other precious stones on it, and that they
shined very farre off: but .what it hath I know not, neither durst
he or any of his men ascend to the top of the sayd mountaine,
those people adioyning being his enemies (as they were) and the
way to it so impassable.

Vpon this riuer of Winicapora wee rested a while, and from
thence marched into the countrey to a town called after the
name of the riuer, whereof the captaine was one Timitwara, who
also offered to conduct mee to the top of· the sayd mountaine
called Wacarima : But when wee came in first to the house of
the sayd Timitwara, being vpon one of their sayd feast dayes,
we found them all as drunke as beggers, and the pots walking
from one to another without rest : we that were weary, and hote
with marching, were glad of the plenty though a small quantitie
satisfied vs, their drinke being very strong and headie, and so
rested our selues a while ; after wee had fedde, we drew our
selues backe to our boats, vpon the riuer and there came to vs
all the lordes of the countrey, with all such kinde of victuall as
the place yeelded, and with their delicate wine of. Pinas, and
with abundance of hens, and other prouisions, and of those
stones which we call Spleenestones.

Wee vnderstood by the chiefetaines of Winicapora, that their
lord Carapana was departed from Emeria which was now in
sight, and that he was fled to Cairamo, adioyning to the mountains of Guiana, ouer the valley called Amariocapana, being
perswaded by those tenne Spaniards which lay at his·house,
that we would destroy him, and his countrey.

But after these Cassiques of Winicapora and Saporatona his
followers perceiued our purpose, and saw that we came as
enemies to the Spaniards onely, and had not so much as harmed
any of those nations, no though we found them to be of the
Spaniards owne seruants, they assured vs that Carapana would
be as ready to serue vs, as any of the lords of the prouinces,
which we had passed ; and that he durst doe no other till this
day but entertaine the Spaniards, his countrey lying so directly
in their way, and next of all other to any entrance that should
be made in Guiana on that side.

And they farther assured vs, that it was not for feare of our
comming that he·was remooued, but to be acquited of the·

Spaniards or any other that should come hereafter. For the prouince of Cairoma is situate at the mountaine foote, which deuideth the plaines of Guiana from the countreys of the Orenoqueponi : by meanes whereof if any should come in our absence into his townes, hee would slip ouer the mountaines into the plaines of Guiana among the Epuremei, where the Spaniards durst not follow him without great force.

But in mine opinion, or rather I assure my selfe, that Carapana (being a notable wise and subtil fellow, a man of one hundred yeeres of age, and therefore of great experience) is remooued, to looke on, and if he finde that we returne strong he will be ours, if not, hee will excuse his departure to the Spaniards, and say it was for feare of our comming.

Wee therefore thought it bootlesse to rowe so farre downe the streame, or to seeke any farther of this olde fox : and therefore from the riuer of Waricapana (which lieth at the entrance of Emeria) we returned againe, and left to the Eastward those foure riuers which fall from the mountaines of Emeria into Orenoque, which are Waracayari, Coirama, Akaniri, and Iparoma : below those foure are also these branches and mouthes of Orenoque, which fall into the East sea, whereof the first is Araturi, the next Amacura, the third Barima, the fourth Wana, the fift Morooca, the sixt Paroma, the last Wijmi : beyond them there fall out of the land betweene Orenoque and Amazones 14 riuers which I forbear to name, inhabited by the Arwacas and Canibals.

It is now time to returne towards the North, and wee found it a wearisome way backe from the borders of Emeria, to recouer vp againe to the head of the riuer Carerupana, by which we descended, and where we parted from the galley, which I directed to take the next way to the port of Toparimaca, by which we entred first.

'All the night it was stormie and darke, and full of thunder and great showers, so as wee were driuen to keepe close by the bankes in our small boats, being all heartily afraid both of the billow and terrible curent of the riuer. By the next morning we recouered the mouth of the riuer of Cumaca, where we left captaine Eynos and Edward Porter to attend the comming of captaine Keymis ouer land : but when wee entred the same, they had heard no news of his arriuall, which bred in vs a great doubt what might become of him : I rowed vp a league or two farther into the riuer, shooting off pieces all the way, that hee

might know of our being there.   And the next morning wee heard
them answere vs also with a piece : wee tooke them aboord vs,
and tooke our leaue of Putijma their guide, who of all others
most lamented our departure, and offered to send his sonne
with vs into England, if we could haue stayed till he had sent backe
to his towne : but our hearts were colde to behold the great rage
and increase of Orenoque, and therefore departed, and turned
toward the West, til we had recouered the parting of the three
branches aforesayd, that we might put downe the streame after
the galley.

The next day we landed on the Island of Assapano (which
deuideth the riuer from that branch by which we sent downe to
Emeria) and there feasted our selues with that beast which is
called Armadilla presented vnto vs before at Winicapora, and the
day following we recouered the galley at ankor at the port of
Toparimaca, and the same euening departed with very foule
weather and terrible thunder, and showers, for the Winter was
come on very farre : the best was, we went no lesse then 100
miles a day, downe the riuer : but by the way we entred, it was
impossible to returne, for that the riuer of Amana, being in the
bottome of the bay of Guanipa, cannot be sayled backe by any
meanes, both the brize and current of the sea were so forcible :
and therefore wee followed a branch of Orenoque called Capuri,
which entred into the sea Eastward of our ships, to the end we
might beare with them before the wind, and it was not without
neede, for we had by that way as much to crosse of the maine
sea after we came to the riuers mouth, as betweene Grauelyn, and
Douer, in such boats as your Hon. hath heard.

To speake of what past homeward were tedious, either to
describe or name any of the riuers, Islands, or villages of the
Tiuitivas which dwell on trees : we will leaue all those to the
generall mappe : and to be short, when we were arriued at the
sea side, then grew our greatest doubt, and the bitterest of all our
iourney forepassed, for I protest before God, that we were in a
most desperate estate : for the same night which we ankored in
the riuer of Capuri, where it falleth into the sea, there arose a
mightie storme, and the riuers mouth was at least a league broad,
so as we ranne before night close vnder the land with our small
boates, and brought the Galley as neere as we could, but she had
as much a doe to liue as could be, and there wanted little of her
sinking, and all those in her : for mine owne part I confesse, I

was very doubt full which way to take, either to goe ouer in the Pestred Galley, there being but sixe foote water ouer the sandes, for two leagues together, and that also in the channell, and she drew fiue : or to aduenture in so great a billow, and in so doubt-full weather, to cross the seas in my barge. The longer we taried the worse it was, and therefore I tooke Captaine Gifford, Captaine Calfield, and my cosen Greeneuile into my barge ; and after it cleared vp, about midnight we put our selues to Gods keeping, and thrust out into the sea, leauing the Galley at anker, who durst not aduenture but by day-light : And so being all very sober, and melancholy, one faintly chearing another to shewe courage, it pleased God that the next day about nine of the clocke, wee descried the Ilande of Trinidad, and stearing for the nearest part of it, wee kept the shore till wee came to Curiapan, where wee founde our shippes at ankor, then which there was neuer to vs a more ioyfull sight.

Now that it hath pleased God to send vs safe to our shippes, it is time to leaue Guiana to the Sunne, whom they worshippe, and steare away towardes the North : I will therefore in a fewe wordes finish the discouery thereof. Of the seuerall nations which we found vpon this discouery I will once againe make repetition, and howe they are affected. At our first enterance into Amana, which is one of the outlets of Orenoque, we left on the right hand of vs in the bottome of the bay, lying directly against Trinidad, a nation of inhumaine Canibals, which inhabite the riuers of Guanipa and Berbeese ; in the same bay there is also a third riuer which is called Areo, which riseth on Paria side towards Cumana, and that riuer is inhabited with the Wikiri, whose chiefe towne vpon the sayd riuer is Sayma ; In this bay there are no more riuers, but these three before rehearsed, and the foure branches of Amana, all which in the Winter thrust so great abundance of water into the sea, as the same is taken vp fresh, two or three leagues from the land. In the passages towardes Guiana (that is, in all those landes which the eight branches of Orenoque fashion into Ilands) there are but one sort of people called Tiuitiuas, but of two castes as they tearme them, the one called Ciawani, the other Waraweeti, and those warre one with another.

A rehearsall and descrip-tion of all the nations and riuers found in this discouerie.

On the hithermost part of Orenoque, as at Toparimaca, and Winicapora, those are of a nation called Nepoios, and are of the followers of Carapana, Lord of Emeria. Betweene Winicapora and the port of Morequito which standeth in Aromaia, and all those in the valley of Amariocapana are called Orenoqueponi, and did obey Morequito, and are now followers of Topiawari. Vpon the riuer of Caroli, are the Canuri, which are gouerned by a woman (who is inheritrix of that Prouince) who came farre off to see our Nation, and asked me diuerse questions of her Maiestie, being much delighted with the discourse of her Maiesties greatnesse, and wondering at such reports as we truely made of her Highnesse many vertues : And vpon the head of Caroli, and on the lake of Cassipa, are the three strong Nations of the Cassipagotos. Right South into the land are the Capurepani, and Emparepani, and beyond those adioyning to Macureguarai (the first citie of Inga) are the Iwarawakeri : all these are professed enemies to the Spaniards, and to the rich Epuremei also. To the West of Caroli are diuerse nations of Canibals, and of those Ewaipanoma without heads. Directly West are the Amapaias and Anebas, which are also marueilous rich in gold. The rest towards Peru we wil omit. On the North of Orenoque, betweene it and the West Indies are the Wikiri, Saymi, and the rest before spoken of, all mortall enemies to the Spaniardes. On the South side of the maine mouth of Orenoque, are the Arwacas ; and beyond them the Canibals and to the South of them the Amazones.

To make mention of the seuerall beasts, birds, fishes, fruits, flowers, gummes, sweet woods, and of their seuerall religions and customes, would for the first require as many volumes as those of Gesnerus, and for the rest another bundle of Decades. The religion of the Epuremei is the same which the Ingas, Emperours of Peru vsed, which may be read in Cieça, and other Spanish stories, how they beleeue the immortalitie of the soule, worship the Sunne, and burie with them aliue their best beloued wiues and treasure, as they likewise doe in Pegu in the East Indies, and other places. The Orenoqueponi bury not their wiues with them, but their iewels, hoping to inioy them againe. The Arwacas dry the bones of their Lords, and their wiues and friends drinke them in powder. In the graues of the Peruuians the Spaniards found their greatest abundance of treasure : the like also is to be found among these people in euery Prouince. They haue all many wiues, and the Lords fiue-fould to the common sort : their wiues neuer eate with their husbands, nor among the men, but serue their husbands at meales, and afterwardes feede by themselues. Those that are past their younger yeeres, make all their bread and drinke, and worke their cotten beds, and doe all else of seruice and labour, for the men doe nothing but hunt, fish, play, and drinke, when they are out of the warres.

I will enter no further into discourse of their maners, lawes and customes : and because I haue not my selfe seene the cities of Inga, I cannot auow on my credit what I haue heard, although it be very likely, that the Emperour Inga hath built and erected as magnificent pallaces in Guiana, as his ancestors did in Peru, which were for their riches and rarenesse most maruellous and exceeding all in Europe, and I thinke of the world, China excepted, which also the Spaniards (which I had) assured me to be true, as also the Nations of the borderers, who being but Saluages to those of the in-land, doe cause much treasure to be buried with them : for I was enformed of one of the Cassiques of the valley of Amariocapana which had buried with him a little before our arriuall, a chaire of golde most curiously wrought, which was made either in Macureguaray adioyning, or in Manao : but if we should haue grieued them in their religion at the first, before they had bene taught better, and haue digged vp their graues, we had lost them all : and therefore I helde my first resolution, that her Maiestie should either accept or refuse the enterprise, ere any thing should be done that might in any sort hinder the same. And if Peru had so many heapes of golde, whereof those Ingas were Princes, and that they delighted so much therein; no doubt but this which now liueth and reigneth in Manao, hath the same honour, and I am assured hath more abundance of golde, within his territorie, then all Peru and the West Indies.

For the rest, which my selfe haue scene, I will promise these things that follow, which I know to be true. Those that are desirous to discouer and to see many nations, may be satisfied within this riuer, which bringeth foorth so many armes and branches leading to seuerall countries and prouinces, aboue 2000 miles East and West, and 800 miles South and North, and of these, *Exceeding commendation of the riuer of Orenoque.* the most eyther rich in golde, or in other marchandizes. The common souldier shall here fight for golde, and pay himselfe in steede of pence, with plates of halfe a foote broad, whereas he

breaketh his bones in other warres for prouant and penury
Those commanders and chieftaines that shoot at honour and
abundance, shall finde there more rich and beautifull cities, more
temples adorned with golden images, more sepulchres filled with
treasure, then either Cortez found in Mexico, or Piçarro in
Peru : and the shining glory of this conquest will eclipse all those
so farre extended beames of the Spanish nation.   There is no
countrey which yeeldeth more pleasure to the inhabitants, either
for those common delights of hunting, hawking, fishing, fowling,
or the rest, then Guiana doth.   It hath so many plaines, cleere
riuers, abundance of Phesants, Partridges, Quailes, Railes, Granes,
Herons, and all other fowle : Deere of all sorts, Porkes, Hares,
Lions, Tygers, Leopards, and diuers other sortes of beastes,
either for chase, or food.   It hath a kind of beast called Cama,
or Anta, as bigge as an English beefe, and in great plentie.

To speake of the seuerall sorts of euery kind, I feare would be
troublesome to the Reader, and therefore I will omit them, and
conclude that both for health, good ayre, pleasure, and riches I
am resolued it cannot bee equalled by any region either in the
The holsome- East or West.   Moreouer the countrey is so healthfull,
nesse of the as of an hundred persons and more (which lay with-
countrey. out shift most sluttishly, and were euery day almost
melted with heate in rowing and marching, and suddenly wet
againe with great showers, and did eate of all sorts of corrupt
fruits, and made meales of fresh fish without seasoning, of
Tortugas, of Lagartos or Crocodiles, and of all sorts good and
bad, without either order or measure, and besides lodged in the
open aire euery night) we lost not any one, nor had one ill disposed to my knowledge, nor found any Calentura, or other of
those pestilent diseases which dwell in all hot regions, and so
neere the Equinoctiall line.

Where there is store of gold, it is in effect needlesse to
remember other commodities for trade : but it hath towards the
South part of the riuer, great quantities of Brasil-wood, and
Excellent diuerse berries that die a most perfect crimson and
dyes. carnation : And for painting, all France, Italy, or the
East Indies yeelde none such : For the more the
skin is washed, the fairer the colour appeareth, and with which,
euen those browne and tawnie women spot themselues, and
colour their cheekes.   All places yeeld abundance of cotton, of
silke, of balsamum, and of those kindes most excellent, and

neuer knowen in Europe, of all sortes of gummes of Indian pepper : and what else the countries may afford within the land we knowe not, neither had we time to abide the triall, and search. The soile besides is so excellent and so full of riuers, as it will carrie sugar, ginger, and all those other commodities, which the West Indies haue.

The nauigation is short, for it may be sayled with an ordinarie winde in sixe weekes, and in the like time backe againe, and by the way neither lee shore, enemies coast, rockes, nor sandes, all which in the voyages to the West Indies, and all other places we are subiect vnto, as the chanell of Bahama, comming from the West Indies, cannot well be passed in the Winter, and when it is at the best, it is a perilous and a fearefull place. The rest of the Indies for calmes, and diseases very troublesome, and the sea about the Bermudas a hellish séa for thunder, lightning, and stormes. *The short, easie, and commodious nauigation to Guiana.*

This very yeere there were seuenteene sayle of Spanish ships lost in the chanell of Bahama, and the great Philip like to haue sunke at the Bermudas was put backe to Saint Iuan de Puerto rico. And so it falleth out in that Nauigation euery yeere for the most part, which in this voyage are not to be feared : for the time of yeere to leaue England is best in Iuly, and the Summer in Guiana is in October, Nouember, December, Ianuarie, Februarie, and March, and then the ships may depart thence in Aprill, and so returne againe into England in Iune, so as they shall neuer be subiect to Winter-weather, either comming, going, or staying there : which for my part, I take to be one of the greatest comforts and incouragements that can be thought on, hauing (as I haue done) tasted in this voyage by the West Indies so many calmes, so much heat, such outragious gustes, foule weather, and contrarie windes. *1595.*

To conclude, Guiana is a countrey that hath yet her maydenhead, neuer sackt, turned, nor wrought, the face of the earth hath not bene torne, nor the vertue and salt of the soyle spent by manurance, the graues haue not bene opened for golde, the mines not broken with sledges, nor their Images puld downe out of their temples. It hath neuer bene entered by any armie of strength, and neuer conquered or possessed by any christian Prince. It is besides so defensible, that if two forts be builded in one of the Prouinces which I haue seene, the flood setteth in so neere the banke, where the channell also lyeth, that no ship can passe vp but within a Pikes length of the artillerie, first of the one, and afterwards of the other : Which two Forts will be a sufficient guarde both to the Empire of Inga, and to an hundred other seuerall kingdomes, lying within the said riuer, euen to the citie of Quito in Peru.

There is therefore great difference betweene the easiness of the conquest of Guiana, and the defence of it being conquered, and the West or East Indies : Guiana hath but one entrance by the sea (if it hath that) for any vessels of burden : so as whosoeuer shall first possesse it, it shall be found vnaccessible for any enemie, except he come in Wherries, Barges, or Canoas, or else in flat bottomed boates, and if he doe offer to enter it in that manner, the woods are so thicke two hundred miles together vpon the riuers of such entrance, as a mouse cannot sit in a boat vnhit from the banke. By lande it is more impossible to approch, for it hath the strongest situation of any region vnder the sunne, and is so enuironed with impassable mountaines on euery side, as it is impossible to victuall any company in the passage : which hath bene well prooued by the Spanish nation, who since the conquest of Peru haue neuer left fiue yeeres free from attempting this Empire, or discouering some way into it, and yet of three and twentie seuerall Gentlemen, Knights, and Noble men, there was neuer any that knewe which way to leade an army by land, or to conduct shippes by sea, any thing neere the saide countrie. Orellana, of whom the riuer of Amazones taketh name, was the first, and Don Antonio de Berreo (whom we displanted) the last : and I doubt much, whether he himselfe or any of his yet know the best way into the sayde Empire. It can therefore hardly be regained, if any strength be formerly set downe, but in one or two places, and but two or three crumsters or gallies built, and furnished vpon the riuer within : The West Indies haue many portes, watering places, and landings, and nearer then three hundred miles to Guiana, no man can harbour a shippe, except he know one onely place, which is not learned in haste, and which I will vndertake there is not any one of my companies that knoweth, whosoeuer hearkened most after it.

Besides by keeping one good Fort, or building one towne of strength, the whole Empire is guarded, and whatsoeuer companies shall be afterwardes planted within the land, although in twentie seuerall Prouinces, those shall be able all to reunite themselues vpon any occasion eyther by the way of one riuer, or be able to march by land without either wood, bogge, or mountaine: whereas in the West Indies there are fewe townes or Prouinces that can succour or relieue one the other, eyther by land or sea: By land the countries are either desert, mountaynous, or strong enemies: by sea, if any man inuade to the Eastward, those to the West cannot in many moneths turne against the brize and Eastern wind, besides the Spaniards are therein so dispersed, as they are no where strong, but in Nueua Espanna onely: the sharpe mountaines, the thornes, and poysoned prickles, the sandie and deepe wayes in the valleys, the smothering heate and aire, and want of water in other places are their onely and best defence, which (because those nations that inuade them are not victualled or prouided to stay, neither haue any place to friend adioyning) doe serue them in steede of good armes and great multitudes.

The West Indies were first offered her Maiesties grandfather by Columbus a stranger, in whom there might be doubt of deceipt, and besides it was then thought incredible that there were such and so many lands and regions neuer written of before. This Empire is made knowen to her Maiestie by her owne vassall, and by him that oweth to her more duetie then an ordinary subiect, so that it shall ill sort with the many graces and benefites which I haue receiued to abuse her Highnesse, either with fables or imaginations. The countrie is alreadie discouered, many nations wonne to her Maiesties loue and obedience, and those Spaniardes which haue latest and longest laboured about the conquest, beaten out, discouraged and disgraced, which among these nations were thought invincible. Her Maiestie may in this enterprize employ all those souldiers and gentlemen that are yongér brethren, and all captaines and chieftaines that want employment, and the charge will be onely the first setting out in victualling and arming them: for after the first or second yeere I doubt not but to see in London a Contractation house of more receipt for Guiana, then there is now in Siuill for the West Indies.

And I am resolued that if there were but a small army a foote in Guiana, marching towards Manoa the chiefe citie of Inga, he would yeeld to her Maiestie by composition so many hundred thousand pounds yeerely, as should both defend all enemies abroad, and defray all expences at home, and that he would

besides pay a garrison of three or foure thousand souldiers very
royally to defend him against other nations : for he cannot but
knowe, how his predecessors, yea how his owne great vncles
Guascar and Atabalipa sonnes to Guainacapa Emperour of Peru,
were (while they contended for the Empire) beaten out by the
Spaniards, and that both of late yeres and euer since the said
conquest, the Spaniards haue sought the passages and entrey of
his countey : and of their cruelties vsed to the borderers he
cannot be ignorant.   In which respects no doubt but he will be
brought to tribute with great gladnesse, if not, he hath neither
shot nor yron weapon in all his Empire, and therefore may easily
be conquered.

And I farther remember that Berreo confessed to me and
others (which I protest before the Maiestie of God to be true)
that there was found among prophesies in Peru (at such time as
the Empire was reduced to the Spanish obedience) in their
chiefest temples, amongst diuers others which foreshewed the
losse of the said Empire, that from Inglatierra those Ingas should
be againe in time to come restored, and deliuered from the
seruitude of the said Conquerors.   And I hope, as we with these
few hands haue displanted the first garrison, and driuen them
out of the said countrey, so her Maiestie will giue order for the
rest, and either defend it, and hold it as tributary, or conquere
and keepe it as Empresse of the same.   For whatsoeuer Prince
shall possesse it, shall be greatest, and if the King of Spaine
enioy it, he will become vnresistable.   Her Maiestie hereby
shall confirme and strengthen the opinions of all nations, as
touching her great and princely actions.   And where the South
border of Guiana reacheth to the Dominion and Empire of the
Amazones, those women shall hereby heare the name of a virgin,
which is not onely able to defend her owne territories and her
neighbours, but also to inuade and conquer so great Empires
and so farre remooued.

To speake more at this time, I feare would be but troublesome : I trust in God, this being true, will suffice, and that he
which is King of all Kings, and Lord of Lords, will put it into
her heart which is Ladie of Ladies to possesse it, if not, I will
iudge those men worthy to be kings thereof, that by her grace
and leaue will vndertake it of themselues.

An abstract taken out of certaine Spaniards letters concerning Guiana and the countries lying vpon the great riuer Orenoque : with certaine reports also touching the same.

An aduertisement to the Reader.

THose letters out of which the abstracts following are taken, were surprised at sea as they were passing for Spaine in the yeere 1594. by Captaine George Popham : who the next yeere, and the same that Sir Walter Ralegh discouered Guiana, as he was in a voyage for the West Indies, learned also the reports annexed. All which, at his returne, being two moneths after Sir Walter, as also so long after the writing of the former discourse, hearing also of his discouerie : he made knowen and deliuered to some of her Maiesties most honourable priuie Councell and others. The which seeing they confirme in some part the substance, I meane, the riches of that countrey : it hath bene thought fit that they should be thereunto adioyned. Wherein the Reader is to be aduertised, that although the Spaniards seeme to glorie much of their formall possession taken before Morequito the Lord of Aromaya, and others thereabouts, which throughly vnderstood them not at that time, whatsoeuer the Spaniards otherwise pretend : yet, according to the former discourse, and as also it is related by Cayworaco, the sonne of Topiawary now chiefe Lord of the said Aromaya, who was brought into England by Sir Walter Ralegh, and was present at the same possession and discoucrie of the Spaniards mentioned in these letters ; it appeareth that after they were gone out of their countrey, the Indians then hauing farther consideration of the matter, and more then coniecture of their intent, hauing knowen and heard of their former cruelties vpon their borderers and others of the Indians elsewhere : At their next comming, there being ten of them sent and imployed for a farther discouery, they were prouided to receiue and enter-taine them in an other maner of sort then they had done before ; that is to say, they slew them and buried them in the countrey so much sought. They gaue them by that meanes a full and complete possession, the which before they had but begunne. And so they are minded to doe, to as many Spaniards as come after. Other possession they haue had none since. Neither doe the Indians meane, as they protest, to giue them any other. One other thing to be remembred is that in these letters the Spaniards

S

seeme to call Guiana and other countries neere it, bordering
vpon the riuer of Orenoque, by the name of Nueua Dorado,
because of the great plentie of golde there in most places to be
found.   Alluding also to the name of El Dorado which was giuen
by Martinez to the great citie of Manoa, as is in the former
treatise specified.   This is all I thought good to aduertise.   As
for some other matters, I leaue them to the consideration and
iudgement of the indifferent Reader.

                                                                    W. R.

Letters taken at sea by Captaine George Popham. 1594.

Alonso his letter from the Gran Canaria to his brother being commander of S. Lucar, concerning El Dorado.

THere haue bene certaine letters receiued here of late, of a
land newly discouered called Nueuo Dorado, from the sonnes of
certaine inhabitants of this citie, who were in the discouery :
they write of wonderfull riches to be found in the said Dorado,
and that golde there is in great abundance : the course to fall
with it is fiftie leagues to the windeward of Margarita.

Alonsos letter from thence to certaine Marchantes of Sant Lucar concerning El Dorado.

SIrs, we haue no newes worth the writing, sauing of a discouery
lately made by the Spaniardes in a new land called Nueuo Dorado,
which is two dayes sayling to the windward of Margarita : there
is golde in such abundance, as the like hath not bene heard of.
Wee haue it for certaine in letters written from thence by some
that were in the discouerie, vnto their parents here in this citie.
I purpose (God willing) to bestow tenne or twelue dayes in search
of the said Dorado, as I passe in my voyage towards Carthagena,
hoping there to make some good sale of our commodities.   I haue
sent you therewith part of the information of the said discouerie,
that was sent to his Maiestie.

Part of the Copie that was sent to his Maiestie, of the discouery of Nueuo Dorado.

IN the riuer of Pato otherwise called Orenoque, in the
principall part thereof called Warismero, the 23 of April 1593

Domingo de Vera master of the campe, and Generall for Antonio
de Berreo Gouernour and Captaine generall for our lord the king,
betwixt the riuers of Pato and Papamene alias Orenoque, and
Marrannon, and of the Iland of Trinidad, in presence of me
Rodrigo de Carança Register for the sea, commanded all the
souldiers to be drawen together and put in order of battaile, the
Captaines and souldiers, and Master of the campe standing in the
middest of them, said vnto them : Sirs, Souldiers, and Captaines,
you vnderstand long since that our General Antonio de Berreo,
with the trauell of eleuen yeeres, and expence of more then an
hundred thousand pezos of golde, discouered the royall Prouinces
of Guiana and Dorado : of the which he tooke possession . to
gouerne the same, but through want of his peoples health, and
necessarie munition, he issued out at the Iland Margarita, and
from thence peopled Trinidad. But now they haue sent me to
learne out and discouer the wayes most easily to enter, and to
people the said Prouinces, and where the campes and armies may
best enter the same. By reason whereof I intend so to doe in
the name of his Maiestie, and the saide gouernour Antonio de
Berreo, and in token thereof I require you Francis Carillo, that
you aide mee to aduance this crosse that lieth here on the ground,
which they set on end towardes the East, and the said Master of
the campe, the captaines and souldiers kneeled downe, and did
due reuerence vnto the saide crosse, and thereupon the master of
the campe tooke a bowle of water and dranke it off, and tooke
more and threw abroad on the gronnd : he also drewe out his
sworde and cut the grasse off the ground, and the boughes off the
trees saying, I take this possession in the name of the king Don
Philip our master, and of his Gouernour Antonio de Berreo : and
because some make question of this possession, to them I answere,
that in these our actions was present the Cassique or principall
Don Antonio, otherwise called Morequito, whose land this was,
who yeelded consent to the said possession, was glad thereof, and
gaue his obedience to our lord the king, and in his name to the
said Gouernour Antonio de Berreo. And the said master of the
campe kneeled downe being in his libertie, and all the Captaines
and souldiers said, that the possession was well taken, and that
they would defend it with their liues, vpon whosoeuer would say
the contrary. And the said master of the campe hauing his
sword drawen in his hand saide vnto me : Register, that art here
present, giue me an instrument or testimoniall to confirme me in

this possession, which I haue taken of this land, for the Gouernour Antonio de Berreo, and if it be needefull I will take it a newe. And I require you all that are present to witnesse the same, and do further declare that I will goe on, taking the possession of all these landes wheresoeuer I shall enter.   Signed thus.

> Domingo de Vera,
>> and vnderneath,
>>> Before me Rodrigo de Carança,
>>>> Register of the armie.

ANd in prosecution of the said possession, and the discouerie of the way and Prouinces, the 27 of April of the said yeere, the master of the campe entred by little and little with all the campe and men of warre, more then two leagues into the in-land, and came to a towne of a principall, and conferring with him did let him vnderstand by meanes of Antonio Bisante the Interpreter, that his Maiestie and Antonio de Berreo had sent him to take the said possession.   And the said frier Francis Carillo by the Interpretor, deliuered him certain things of our holy Catholique faith, to all which he answered, that they vnderstood him well and would become Christians, and that with a very good will they should aduance the crosse, in what part or place of the towne it pleased them, for he was for the Gouernour Antonio de Berreo, who was his master.   Thereupon the said master of the campe tooke a great crosse, and set it on ende towarde the East, and requested the whole campe to witnesse it, and Domingo de Vera firmed it thus.

> It is well and firmely done.
>> And vnderneath.
>>> Before me Rodrigo Carança,
>>>> Register of the armie.

THe first of May they prosecuted the said possession and discouerie to the towne on Carapana. From thence the said Master of the Campe passed to the towne of Toroco whose principall is called Topiawary being fiue leagues farther within the land then the first Nation, and well inhabited. And to this principall by meane of the Interpretor they gaue to vnderstand that his Maiestie and the said Corrigidor commanded them to take the possession of that lande, and that they should yeelde their obedience to his Maiestie, and to his Corrigidor, and to the master of the campe in his name, and that in token thereof he would place a crosse in the middle of his towne. Whereunto the said Cassique answered they should aduance it with a very good will, and that he remained in the obedience of our lord the king, and of the said Gouernour Antonio de Berreo whose vassall he would be.

The fourth of May we came to a Prouince aboue fiue leagues thence, of all sides inhabited with much people, the principall of this people came and met vs in peaceable maner : and he is called Reuato, he brought vs to a very large house where he entertained vs well, and gaue vs much Golde, and the interpreter asking him from whence that golde was, he answered, From a Prouince not passing a dayes iourney off, where there are so many Indians as would shadowe the sunne, and so much Golde as all yonder plaine will not conteine it. In which Countrey (when they enter into the Borracheras or their drunken feasts) they take of the said Golde in dust and anoynt themselues all ouer therewith to make the brauer shew ; and to the end the Golde may couer them, they anoynt their bodies with stamped herbes of a glewy substance: and they haue warre with those Indians. They promised vs that if we would goe vnto them, they would ayde vs ; but they were such infinite numbers, as no doubt they would kill vs. And being asked how they gat ye same Gold, they told vs they went to a certaine Downe or playne, and pulled or digged vp the grasse by the roote : which done, they tooke of the earth, putting it in great buckets, which they caried to wash at the riuer, and that which came in powder they kept for their Borracceras or drunken feasts: and that which was in peeces they wrought into Eagles.

The eight of May wee went from thence, and marched about fiue leagues : at the foote of a Hill wee found a principall called Arataco with three thousand Indians, men and women all in peace and with much victuall, as Hennes and Venison in great abundance, and many sortes of wine. Hee intreated vs to goe to his house, and to rest that night in his Towne, being of fiue hundred houses. The interpreter asked whence hee had those Hennes : he sayde they were brought from a mountaine not passing a quarter of a league thence, where were many Indians, yea so many as grasse on the ground, and that these men had the points of their shoulders higher then the Crownes of their heads,

and had so many Hennes as was wonderfull ; and if wee would
haue any, wee should send them Iewes harpes, for they would
giue for euery one two Hennes.   Wee tooke an Indian, and gaue
him fiue hundred Harpes ; the Hennes were so many that hee
brought vs, as were not to be numbered.   Wee sayde wee would
goe thither ; they tolde vs they were now in their Borracheras or
drunken feasts, and would kill vs.   Wee asked the Indian that
brought the Hennes, if it were true ; hee sayde it was most true.
Wee asked him how they made their Borracheras or drunken
feasts ; he sayde, they had many Eagles of golde hanging on their
breasts, and Pearles in their eares, and that they daunced being
all couered with Golde.   The Indian sayde vnto vs, if wee would
see them, wee should giue him some Hatchets, and he would
bring vs of those Eagles   The Master of the Campe gaue him one
Hatchet (hee would giue him no more because they should not
vnderstand we went to seeke golde) he brought vs an Eagle that
weighed 27. pounds of good Golde.   The Master of the Campe
took it, and shewed it to the souldiers, and then threw it from
him, making shewe not to regard it.   About midnight came an
Indian and sayd vnto him, Giue mee a Pickeaxe, and I will tell
thee what the Indians with the high shoulders meane to doe.   The
Interpreter tolde the Master of the Campe, who commanded one
to be giuen him : hee then told vs, those Indians were comming to
kil vs for our marchandize.   Hereupon the Master of the Campe
caused his company to bee set in order, and beganne to march.
The eleuenth day of May wee went about seuen leagues from
thence to a prouince, where wee found a great company of
Indians apparelled : they tolde vs that if wee came to fight, they
would fill up those Plaines with Indians to fight with vs ; but if
we came in peace, we should enter and bee well entertained of
them, because they had a great desire to see Christians : and there
they told vs of all the riches that was.   I doe not heere set it
downe, because there is no place for it, but it shall appeare by
the information that goeth to his Maiestie : for if it should heere
bee set downe, foure leaues of paper would not containe it.

The Letter of George Burien Britton from the sayde Canaries vnto his cousin a Frenchman dwelling in S. Lucar, concerning El Dorado.

SIr, and my very good cousin, there came of late certaine

Letters from a new discouered countrey not farre from Trinidad, which they write, hath Golde in great abundance : the newes seemeth to bee very certaine, because it passeth for good amongst the best of this Citie.   Part of the information of the Discouery that went to his Maiestie, goeth inclosed in Alonsos letters ; it is a thing worth the seeing.

The report of Domingo Martinez of Iamaica concerning El Dorado.

HE sayth that in 1593. being at Carthagena, there was a generall report of a late discouery called Nueuo Dorado, and that a litle before his comming thither, there came a Frigat from the said Dorado, bringing in it the portrature of a Giant all of Gold, of weight 47. kintals, which the Indians there held for their Idoll. But now admitting of Christianitie and obedience to the King of Spaine, they sent their sayd Idol vnto him in token they were become Christians, and held him for their King.   The company comming in the said Frigat, reported Golde to be there in most abundance, Diamonds of inestimable value, with great store of pearle.

The report of a French man called Bountillier of Sherbrouke,* concerning Trinidad and Dorado.

HE sayth that beeing at Trinidad in 1591. he had of an Indian there a piece of Golde of a quarter of a pound in exchange of a knife ; the sayde Indian tolde him hee had it at the head of that riuer which commeth to Paracoa in Trinidad : and that within the Riuer of Orenoque, it was in great abundance.   Also in 1593. beeing taken by the Spanyardes, and brought prisoner into the Iland of Madera (the place for his prison) there came in this meane time a Barke of fortie Tunnes from a new Discouery, with two millions of Golde ; the company whereof reported Golde in that place to bee in great abundance, and called it El Nueuo Dorado.   This Frenchman passed from Spaine in the Barke, and hauing a cabben neere a gentlemsn, one of the Discouerers that came from that place in the sayde Barke, had diuers times conference with him, and amongst other things, of the great abund-

---

* Probably *Cherbourg.*

ance of Golde in the sayd Dorado, being as they sayd within the
riuer of Orenoque.

Reportes of certaine Merchants of Rio de Hacha, concerning El Nueuo Dorado.

THey sayd (aduancing the kings great treasure in the Indies)
that Nueua Reyno yeelded very many Golde mines, and wonderfull rich ; but lately was discouered a certaine Prouince so rich in
Golde, as the report thereof may seeme incredible, it is there in
such abundance, and is called El Nueuo Dorado : Antonio de
Berreo made the said discouerie.

The report of a Spanyard, Captaine with Berreo in the discouerie of El Nueuo Dorado.

THat the information sent to the king was in euery poynt
truely sayde, that the riuer Orenoque hath seuen mouths, or outlets into the sea, called Las Siete bocas de dragon, that the sayd
riuer runneth farre into the land, in many places very broad, and
that Anth. de Berreo lay at Trinidad, making head to goe to con-
quere and people the sayd Dorado.

A Relation of the second Voyage to Guiana, performed and written in the yeeere 1596. by Laurence Keymis Gent.

To the approved, Right Valorous, and worthy Knight, Sir Walter Ralegh, Lord warden of the Stanneries, Captaine of her Maiesties Guard, and her Highnesse Lieutenant generall of the Countie of Cornewall.

I Haue here briefly set downe the effect of this your second
Discouerie without any enlargement of made wordes : for in this
argument, single speech best beseemeth a simple trueth.   Where
the affinitie of the matter with your person, leadeth mee to write
of your self, vnto your selfe, the small libertie which I haue
therein vsed, shall, 1 doubt not, without offence or sinister construction, be giuen to the cause in hand : which, whether it suffer
not detriment, by attributing lesse then of right belongeth ; the
iudgement bee theirs, that vprightly and indifferently shall weigh
the consequents of their euill purpose, who in seeking to detract
from the Author of these Discoueries, doe so much as in them

lieth, wound, deface, and tread vnder foot the thing it selfe. But
this is no nouelty, nor proper only to these our dayes.
For long since it hath bin said, Laudes eo vsque sunt   Pericles.
tolerabiles, donec ea dicuntur, quæ auditores se quoque facere
posse existimant : si maiora proserantur, inuident, non credunt.
The feruent zeale and loyalty of your minde in labour with this
birth of so honorable expectation, as it hath deserued a recompence farre different, so needeth it not my poore suffrage to
endeare the toyle, care and danger that you haue willingly vndergone for the good and aduancement of our weale publique. The
praise-worthinesse thereof doeth approue it selfe, and is better
read in your liuing doings, then in my dead vnregarded papers.
All that I can wish, is that my life were a sufficient pledge, to
iustifie, how more easie, and more materiall, the course for
Guiana would be then others, which requiring greater charge,
yeelde not so large benefit, and are subject to more doubtfull
euents. If vnto their wisdomes who sit in place and
authority, it shall appear otherwise, and that in following of other attempts there is lesse difficultie,
certainer profit, and needfuller offence vnto the enemie : the cost
and trauaile which you haue bestowed, shall not, I hope, be
altogether lost, if vnto your Honour I can proue how, and where
the amend is to be had, maugre the force and preuention of all
Spaniards.

Your Lordships to be commanded in all seruice,

LAVRENCE KEYMIS.

To the Fauourers of the Voyage for Guiana.

IN things earnestly desired, though neuer so likely, we are
still suspicious : thinking it more credite to our common wisedome,
to discredite most noble and profitable indeuours with distrust,
then touch to our valours and safeties, to lie wilfully idle. So
that howsoeuer an action well and iudicially attempted, bee
esteemed halfe performed ; yet is this my iealous conceite concerning Guiana, that nothing is begun, before all be ended. In
this regarde (gentle Reader) I haue presumed to burthen thine
eares with the weake plea of a good cause, and in stead of
opening it throughly to thy prudent consideration, to note only

T

mine owne vnsatisfied affection : hoping that because I doe name
Guiana vnto thee, thou wilt vouchsafe hoc nomine, to uaile and
couer all other my defects in the desert of a good meaning. In
publishing this Treatise, my labor principally tendeth to this end ;
to remoue all fig-leaues from our vnbeliefe, that either it may
haue cause to shake off the colourable pretences of ignorance :
or if we will not be perswaded ; that our selfe-will may rest
inexcusable. They that shall apply, and construe this my doing,
to serue the Spaniard his turne so wel as our owne ; in so much
as it may seeme to instruct, warne, and arme him : for their
satisfaction herein, they must not be ignorant, that his eyes, in
seeing our shipping there, doe as effectually informe him, that
many of our hearts are toward that place, as if it should be
credibly aduertised by some corrupt hireling, that we thinke,
write, and discourse of nothing els. Neither can I imagine,
that to conceale our knowledge herein (which to conceale may
perhaps proue, and be hereafter taken for worse the paricide)
would be of better purpose, then to hood winke our
selues, as who would say, No man shall see vs. Besides if the
action were wholy to bee effected at her Maiesties charge ;
then might it at her Highnesse pleasure be shadowed with some
other drift, and neuer be discouered, vntill it were acted. But
since it craueth the approbation and purses of many Adventurers,
who cannot be so prodigall both of their possessions and liues, as
voluntarily to run themselues out of breath, in pursuing they
know not what ; great reason it is, that where assistance is to be
asked, due causes be yeelded to perswade and induce them vnto
it. The Spaniard is not so simple, vnsetled, and vncertaine in
his determinations, as to build them on our breath, or to make
our papers his Bulwarks ; nor so slow as to expect a precedent of
our forwardnes. His proceedings are sufficiently strengthened
with the trauailes, reports, and substantial proofes of his own
men, that haue aboue 60. yeeres beaten round about this bush.
And to say a trueth, the expedition that he hath vsed in sending
so many ships in February last to people this country, and
disappoint vs ; as it doth consequently shew, that he findeth his
chiefest force and sinewes to consist in golde : so doeth he
thereby plainly to our faces exprobrate our remisnesse and long
deliberations, that in 12. moneths space haue done, or sought to
doe nothing worthy the ancient fame and reputation of our
English nation, interested in so weighty businesse. His late

prouision of a new supply of whole families to the
number of 6oo. persons, bound for Guiana, but that it
pleased God, that by meanes of that right honourable
seruice most resolutely performed in the sea-fight, and sacking
of Cadiz, the ships wherein they should haue bin conueyed,
were conuerted into ashes : what might it signifie ? Certes, as it
doth euidently proue, that El Dorado hath vndoubted credit and
account in their iudgements : so pointeth it at vs, whilst we only
to entertain idle time, sit listening for Guiana newes, and in-
stantly forget it, as if we were nought els, but a pleasing dreame
of a golden fancy.   If we with our selues shall expostulate, how
this commeth to passe, that the aduantage wholy resting on our
side, in respect that Berreo was this last yere beaten out, the
countrey thoroughly discouered, and the Inhabitants made desirous of her sacred Maiesties happy gouernment ; they notwithstanding by entring before vs, haue now gotten y^c start of vs :
what may we thinke ?   Shal wee iudge that their natiue countrey
is lesse deare, or more wearisome vnto them, then ours is vnto
vs ?   Their Peruleri, who going bare and empty out of Spaine,
do againe within 3. or 4. yeres returne from Peru, rich and in
good estate, doe apparently disproue all such conceits of them.
Shall wee say that they haue more spare men to be imployed in
such actions ?   It is no secret to know the contrary.   Are they
subiect to penury ?   In all parts of Christendom, where money is
not scant, all other things are plentifull.   Or is their land not
able to sustain their numbers of people ?   They buy many slaues
to follow their husbandry, and themselues disdaining base idle-
nes and beggery, do all honour military profession, highly
esteeming it in their mercenaries and strangers.   Is it then want
of ability, in those that are willing, lacke of incouragement, or
default of speedy order and direction for those that doe voluntarily offer themselues, their substance, and best indeuour to
further this cause ; that maketh vs to be thus coated of the
Spaniard ?   The first is no question.   The later needeth no
answere.   The profit then by their example to be gathered, is,
not to lose opportunitie by delay, or to seeme feareful and dismayed, where there is no cause of doubt.   For as yet their post-
haste doeth no way preiudice our aduised leisure in setting forward, since their preparations of Negroes to worke in the mynes,
their horses, cattell, and other necessaries may (by the fauour of
God) at our first comming, both store vs w^t quantities of gold

In Iune
1596.

oare, and ease vs of much trouble, paines, and trauaile. If we
should suppose our selues now to liue in the dayes of King
Henry the seuenth of famous memory, and the strange report of a
West Indies, or new world abounding with great treasure should
entice vs to beleeue it : perhaps it might be imputed for some
blame to the grauity of wise men, lightly to bee carried with the
perswasion and hope of a new found Vtopia, by such a one as
Columbus was, being an alien, and many wayes, subiect to suspition.   But since the penance of that incredulity lieth euen now
heauy on our shoulders ; the example forethreatning, I know
not what repentance : and that we haue the personal triall of
so honourable and sufficient a Reporter, our own Countriman :
let it be farre from vs to condemne our selues in that, which so
worthily we reproue in our predecessors ; and to let our idle
knowledge content it selfe with naked contemplation, like a
barren wombe in a Monastery.   We cannot denie that the chiefe
commendation of vertue doth consist in action : we truely say,
that Otium is animæ viuæ sepultura : we beleeue, that perfect
wisedome in this mobility of all humaine affaires, refuseth not
with any price to purchase safetie : and we iustly do acknowledge that the Castilians from bare legged mountainers haue
atteined to their greatnesse by labour and industrie.   To sleepe
then, because it costeth nothing ; to imbrace the present time,
because it flattereth vs with deceitfull contentment ; and to kisse
security, saying, What euill happeneth vnto vs ? is the plaine
high way to a fearefull downfall : from which the Lord in his
mercy deliuer vs, and giue vs an vnderstanding heart, in time to
see, and to seeke that, which belongeth vnto our peace.

De Guiana carmen Epicum.

WHat worke of honour and eternall name,
For all the world t'enuie and vs t'atchieue,
Filles me with furie, and giues armed hands
To my hearts peace, that els would gladly turne
My limmes and euery sense into my thoughts
Rapt with the thirsted action of my mind ?
O Clio, Honors Muse, sing in my voyce,
Tell the attempt, and prophecie th'exploit
Of his Eliza-consecrated sworde,
That in this peacefull charme of Englands sleepe,

Opens most tenderly her aged throte,
Offring to powre fresh youth through all her vaines,
That flesh of brasse and ribs of steele retaines.
Riches, and Conquest, and Renowme I sing,
Riches with honour, Conquest, without blood,
Enough to seat the Monarchie of earth,
Like to Ioues Eagle on Elizas hand.
Guiana, whose rich feete are mines of golde,
Whose forehead knockes against the roofe of Starres,
Stands on her tip-toes at faire England looking,
Kissing her hand, bowing her mightie breast,
And euery signe of all submission making,
To be her sister, and the daughter both
Of our most sacred Maide : whose barrennesse
Is the true fruite of vertue, that may get,
Beare and bring forth anew in all perfection,
What heretofore sauage corruption held
In barbarous Chaos ; and in this affaire
Become her father, mother, and her heire.

Then most admired Soueraigne, let your breath
Goe foorth vpon the waters, and create
A golden world in this our yron age,
And be the prosperous forewind to a Fleete,
That seconding your last, may goe before it
In all successe of profite and renowme :
Doubt not but your election was diuine,
(Aswell by Fate as your high iudgement ordred)
To raise him with choise Bounties, that could adde
Height to his height ; and like a liberall vine,
Not onely beare his vertuous fruite aloft,
Free from the Presse of squint-eyd Enuies feete,
But decke his gracious Proppe with golden bunches,
And shroude it with broad leaues of Rule oregrowne
From all blacke tempests of inuasion.

Those Conquests that like generall earthquakes shooke
The solid world, and made it fall before them,
Built all their braue attempts on weaker grounds,
And lesse perswasiue likelihoods then this ;
Nor was there euer princely Fount so long

Powr'd forth a sea of Rule with so free course,
And such ascending Maiestie as you :
Then be not like a rough and violent wind,
That in the morning rends the Forrests downe,
Shoues vp the seas to heauen, makes earth to tremble,
And toombes his wastfull brauery in the Euen :
But as a riuer from a mountaine running,
The further he extends, the greater growes,
And by his thriftie race strengthens his streame,
Euen to ioyne battell with th'imperious sea
Disdayning his repulse, and in despight
Of his proud furie, mixeth with his maine,
Taking on him his titles and commandes :
So let thy soueraigne Empire be encreast,
And with Iberian Neptune part the stake,
Whose Trident he the triple world would make.

You then that would be wise in Wisdomes spight,
Directing with discredite of direction,
And hunt for honour, hunting him to death.
With whom before you will inherite gold,
You will loose golde, for which you loose your soules ;
You that chuse nought for right, but certaintie,
And feare that valour will get onely blowes,
Placing your faith in Incredulitie.
Sit till you see a wonder, Vertue rich :
Till Honour hauing golde, rob golde of honour,
Till as men hate desert that getteth nought,
They loath all getting that deserues not ought ;
And vse you gold-made men as dregges of men ;
And till your poysoned soules, like Spiders lurking
In sluttish chinckes, in mystes of Cobwebs hide
Your foggie bodies, and your dunghill pride

O Incredulitie, the wit of Fooles,
That slouenly will spit on all things faire,
The Cowards castle, and the Sluggards cradle
How easie t'is to be an Infidel ?

But you Patrician Spirites that refine
Your flesh to fire, and issue like a flame

On braue indeuours, knowing that in them
The tract of heauen in morne-like glory opens,
That know you cannot be the Kings of earth,
(Claiming the rights of your creation)
And let the Mynes of earth be Kings of you ;
That are so farre from doubting likely drifts,
That in things hardest y'are most confident :
You that know death liues, where power liues vnusde,
Ioying to shine in waues that burie you,
And so make way for life euen through your graues ;
That will not be content like horse to hold
A thread-bare beaten way to home affaires :
But where the sea in enuie of your reigne,
Closeth her wombe, as fast as t'is disclosede,
That she like Auarice might swallow all,
And let none find right passage through her rage :
There your wise soules as swift as Eurus lead
Your Bodies through, to profit and renowne,
And skorne to let your bodies choke your soules,
In the rude breath and prisoned life of beastes :
You that herein renounce the course of earth,
And lift your eyes for guidance to the starres,
That liue not for yourselues, but to possesse
Your honour'd countrey of a generall store ;
In pitie of the spoyle rude selfe-loue makes,
Of them whose liues and yours one ayre doth feede,
One soile doeth nourish, and one strength combine ;
You that are blest with sence of all things noble,
In this attempt your compleat woorthes redouble.

But how is Nature at her heart corrupted,
(I meane euen in her most ennobled birth)
How in excesse of Sence is Sence bereft her !
That her most lightening-like effects of lust
Wound through her flesh, her soule, her flesh vnwounded ;
And she must neede incitements to her good,
Euen from that part she hurtes ! O how most like
Art thou (heroike Autor of this Act)
To this wrong'd soule of Nature, that sustainst
Paine, charge, and perill for thy countreys good,
And she must like a bodie numb'd with surfeits,

Feeles not thy gentle applications
For the health, vse, and honour of her powers !
Yet shall my verse through all her ease-lockt eares
Trumpet the Noblesse of thy high intent :
And if it cannot into act proceed,
The fault and bitter penance of the fault
Make red some others eyes with penitence,
For thine are cleare ; and what more nimble spirits,
Apter to byte at such vnhooked baytes,
Gaine by our losse ; that must we needs confesse
Thy princely valure would haue purchast vs.
Which shall be fame eternall to thy name,
Though thy contentment in thy graue desires,
Of our aduancement, faile deseru'd effect.
O how I feare thy glory which I loue,
Least it should dearely grow by our decrease.
Natures that sticke in golden-graueld springs,
In mucke-pits cannot scape their swallowings.

But we shall foorth I know ; Golde is our Fate,
Which all our actes doth fashion and create.

Then in the Thespiads bright Propheticke Fount,
Me thinkes I see our Liege rise from her throne,
Her eares and thoughts in steepe amaze erected,
At the most rare endeuour of her power.
And now she blesseth with her woonted Graces
Th' industrious Knight, the soule of this exploit,
Dismissing him to conuoy of his starres.
And now for loue and honour of his woorth,
Our twise-borne Nobles bring him Bridegroome-like,
That is espousde for vertue to his loue
With feasts and musicke, rauishing the aire,
To his Argolian Fleet, where round about
His bating Colours English valure swarmes
In haste, as if Guianian Orenoque
With his Fell waters fell vpon our shore.
And now a wind as forward as their spirits,
Sets their glad feet on smooth Guianas breast,
Where (as if ech man were an Orpheus)
A world of Sauages fall tame before them,

Storing their theft-free treasuries with golde,
And there doth plentie crowne their wealthie fields,
There Learning eates no more his thriftlesse bookes,
Nor Valure Estridge-like* his yron armes.
There Beautie is no strumpet for her wants,
Nor Galique humours putrifie her blood :
But all our Youth take Hymens lights in hand,
And fill eche roofe with honor'd progenie.
There makes Societie Adamantine chaines,
And ioyns their hearts with wealth, whom wealth disioin'd.
There healthfull Recreations strow their meades,
And make their mansions daunce with neighbourhood,
That here were down'd in churlish Auarice.
And there do Pallaces and temples rise
Out of the earth, and kisse th' enamored skies,
Where new Britannia humblie kneeles to heauen,
The world to her, and, both at her blest feet,
In whom the circles of all Empire meete.

G. C.

Ad Thomam Hariotum Matheseos, et vniuersæ Philosophiæ
  peritissimum, de Guiana Carmen.   Dat. Anno. 1595.

MOntibus est Regio, quasi muris, obsita, multis :
   Circumsepit aquis quos Raleana suis.
Intus habet largos Guaiana recessus :
   Hostili gestans libera colla iugo.
Hispanus cliuis illis sudauit, et alsit
   Septem annos, nouies : nec tamen inualuit.
Numen, et omen inest numeris.   Fatale sit illi :
   Et nobis virtus sit recidiua, precor.
Gualtero patefacta via est duce et auspice Ralegh
   Mense vno : ô factum hoc nomine quo celebrem ?
Nocte diéq ; datis velis, remisque laborans,
   Exegit summæ dexteritatis opus.
Scilicet expensis magnis non ille pepercit,
   Communi natus consuluisse bono.
Prouidus excubuit simili discrimine Ioseph :
   Sic fratres, fratrem deseruêre suum :

---

* Ostrich-like.
V

Fama coloratam designet sibona, vestem :
  Vestis Scissa malis sic fuit illa modis.
Mira leges.   Auresque animumque tuum arrige.   Tellus
  Hæc aurum, et gemmas graminis instar, habet.
Ver ibi perpetuum est : ibi prodiga terra quotannis
  Luxuriat, sola fertilitate nocens.
Anglia nostra licet diues sit, et vndique fœlix :
  Anglia, si confers, indigna frugis erit.
Expertes capitum, volucres piscesque ferásq ;
  Prætereo : haud prosunt, quæ nouitate, placent.
Est ibi, vel nusquam, quod quærimus.   Ergo petamus :
  Det Deus, hanc Canaan possideamus.   Amen.
                                   Tui Amantiss.   L. K.

The second voyage to Guiana.

MVnday the 26. of January, in the yeere of our Lord 1596. we departed from Portland road, in the Darling of London, hauing in company the Discouerer, a small pinnesse, whom we lost at sea, in foule weather, the Thursday next following. Friday the 13. of February, wee fell with the Canarie Islands, where we expected our pinnesse, according to our appoyntment, seuen or eight dayes.   Here we tooke two boats, the one a passenger, we bulged, the other wee towed at our shippe sterne, steering Southsouthwest for the Islands of Cape Verde.   Therehence we set saile the 28. of Februarie, keeping a Westsouthwest course.   In this passage wee found very smooth seas, faire weather, and steddie winds, blowing ordinarily betweene the East and Northeast poynts.   Neere 30. leagues from these Islands, wee came into a growne sea, the swollen waters making a strange noise and hurtling together, as if it might be two strong currents encountring ech other.   The 12 of March wee sounded, and had sandie ground in 47. fathome.   At midnight in twelue fathom wee came to an anker, the ground sandie oaze. Sunday the 14. towards night, about some sixe leagues from the shore, wee descried a low land in the bottome of a bay.   From the 9. of March vntill this time, we kept for the most part a Southsouthwest course.   The water in this place is smooth, but muddie, and the colour red or tawny.   From the Westermost of the CapeVerde-Islands vnto this Bay I doe estimate the distance to be neere 550. leagues.   It seemed to most of our sea-men, to be the very banke of a shoald vpon a lee-shore : the rather because without it, in the cleane greene sea wee had but 7. fathome depth : but after by proofe finding that there is no sudden alteration in any part of the coast, and that the sea is smoothest neere the land, we alwayes at night sought to anker in three or four fathome. And doubtlesse as the hand of God is woonderfull in all his workes : so herein his mercifull prouidence is most admirable, that vpon a A notable
obseruation. lee-shore subiect vnto a perpetuall Easterly gale, neither much wind can endanger shipping, by reason that the foule heauie water is not capable of vehement motion, and the soft light oaze, if they touch, cannot bruise them : nor is there any ieopardie in beeing wind-bound, or imbyed :* for the most forcible windes make the greatest flood-tides, whereby the freshets when they take their ordinarie course of ebbe, doe grow strong and swift, setting directly off to sea against the wind. Wee by turning went cleere of all Bayes : howbeit in this case, as also in the riuers, the vse of a droue sayle seemeth a good and readie helpe. The first place wherein wee ankered, was in the mouth of Arrowari, a faire great riuer. It standeth in one degree and fourtie minutes : for we fell so farre to the Southwardes by your lordships direction. The barre without hath at the least three fathome, at the shoaldest place, when it is lowe ebbe. The depth within is eight and tenne fathome. The water alwayes brackish. We found not any inhabitants in this place neere the sea coast. I omit here to recite the names of the nations that are borderers, their townes, Captaines and commodities that their countreyes doe yeelde, as also the soundings, tydes, and how the coast lyeth etc. thinking it fittest to reduce these disioyned and scattering remembrances to one place. As wee passed we alwayes kept the shore within viewe and stopped the floods, still ankering at night in three or foure fathome. When we came to the North headland of this Bay (which wee named Cape Cecyl) we sawe two high mountaines like two islands, but they ioyne with the mayne. In this tract lying Northnorthwest neere 60. leagues, there fall into the sea these seuerall great riuers, Arrowari, Iwaripoco, Maipari, Coanawini, Caipurogh. Wee ankered in two fathome not farre from these hilles, and filled all our caske with fresh water by the shippe side, for in the sea

* Embayed.

thirtie miles from the mouth of any riuer it is fresh and good. This second Bay extendeth it selfe about thirtie leagues to the Westward, and containeth within it these riuers Arcooa, Wiapoco, Wanari, Caparwacka, Cawo, Caian, Wia, Macuria, Cawroor, Curassawini.   Here leauing the ship at anker, I tooke into the boate Iohn Prouost, my Indian Interpreter, Iohn Linsey, and eight or nine others, intending to search some of these riuers, and to seeke speech with the Indians.   In Wiapoco, at the foote of the Eastermost mountaine, where the riuer falleth into the sea, wee found twentie or thirtie houses, but not inhabited.   Wee stayed there but one night.   Wanari we ouerpassed, because the entrance is rockie and not deepe.   In Caperwacka we sailed some fourtie miles, but could see no Indian.   At one of their portes vnder the side of a hill, wee tooke in so much Brasill wood as our boate could carrie.   Amongst other trees we cut downe one for an example, which I doe verily beleeue to be the same sort of sinamon, which is found in the streights of Magellan. From Caperwacka wee passed to Cawo, and there met with a Canoa, wherein were two Indians.   It was long time before wee could procure them to come neere vs, for they doubted least wee were Spanish.   When my interpreter had perswaded them the contrarie, and that wee came from England, they without farther speech or delay, brought vs to Wareo their Captaine, who entertained vs most friendly, and then at large declared vnto vs, that hee was lately chased by the Spaniards from Moruga, one of the neighbour riuers to Raleana, or Orenoque : and that hauing burnt his owne houses, and destroyed his fruites and gardens, hee had left his countrey and townes to bee possessed by the Arwacas, who are a vagabound nation of Indians, which finding no certaine place of abode of their owne, doe for the most part serue and follow the Spanyards.   Hee shewed mee that he was of the nation of the Ioas, who are a mightie people, and of a late time were Lords of all the sea coast so farre as Trinidad, which they likewise possessed.   Howbeit, that with a generall consent, when the Spaniards first began to borrow some of their wiues, they all agreed to change their habitation, and doe now liue vnited for the most part towards the riuer of Amazones. But the especial cause of his present remooue was, because two or three yeeres past, twentie Spaniards came to his towne, and sought to take his best wife from him : but before they carried her away, hee at time and place of aduantage killed halfe of them: the rest fledde, most of them sore hurt. Now in this case hee thought it best to dwell farre ynough from them. Your Indian pilot Ferdinando, who conducted you by Amana, and now abideth neere the head of Dessekebe, is one of this mans subiects: By whom (as it may seeme) hee hath taken good notice of our princesse and countrey. For hee descended more particularly to inquire what forces were come with vs, assuring me of the Spaniards beeing in Trinidad, and that the Indians our friendes betwixt hope and feare, haue earnestly expected our returne from England these foure or fiue moneths. When I had answered him, that at our departure we left no Spaniards aliue to annoy them; that we now came only to discouer, and trade with them; and that if her Maiestie should haue sent a power of men, where no enemie was to resist, the Indians might perhaps imagine, that wee came rather to inuade, then to defend them: He replied, that this course very wel sorted with the report which they had heard of our Princesse iustice, rare graces, and vertues: the fame of whose power in beeing able to vanquish the Spaniards, and singular goodnesse in vndertaking to succour and defend the afflicted Indians, was now so generall, that the nations farre and neere were all agreed to ioyne with vs, and by all meanes possible to assist vs in expelling and rooting out the Spaniards from all parts of the land: and that we were deceiued, if wee thought this countrey not large ynough to receiue vs, without molestation or intrusion vpon the Indians, who wanted not choise of dwelling places, if they forsooke one to liue in another: but stoode in neede of our presence at all times to ayde them, and maintaine their libertie, which to them is deerer then land or liuing. He then farther desired, that he with his people might haue our fauour against the Arwaccas, who not being content to enioy their groundes and houses, had taken from them many of their wiues and children, the best of whose fortune was, if they liued, to liue in perpetuall slauerie vnder the Spaniards. Wee put him in good hope and comfort thereof. And hee to deserue some part of this friendship, commended vnto vs an elderly man to be our Pilote in bringing vs to Raleana. When we were ready to depart, he demanded whether we wanted any Vrapo; which is the wood, that is vsually carried from these parts to Trinidad in Canoas, and is there sold to the French for trade:

[marginal note:] Ferdinando the Indian pilote of sir Walter Ralegh.

he offered, if we would bring our ship neere his port, to put in
her lading thereof.   But because most of our caske was not
yron bound, and in making stowage way to remoue it, would
haue bene the losse of our Sider and other drinke ; I therefore
referred the taking of any quantity to fitter opportunitie ;
thinking it sufficient at this time, to haue only my boats lading
thereof : which afterwards in extremitie of foule weather, before
we could get aboord our ship, wee were inforced in a darke
night to heaue all ouerboord : thinking our selues happy, to
haue recouered thither at seuen dayes ende, with safetie of life
onely.   All which time we could no where set foote on shore,
but rested day and night wet and weatherbeaten in our couert-
lesse boate, which was sometimes ready to sinke vnder vs.   For
wee had in this place without comparison more raine, wind, and
gustes, then elsewhere at any time.   To be briefe, my men
became weake and sicke, and if wee had stayed any longer time
out, I doubt whether the greatest part of vs had euer come
aboord againe.   I afterwards vnderstood by my Indian pilot,
that this weather is for most part of the yeere vsuall, neere the
Island Oncaiarie, which lyeth North from the riuer Capurwacka
some sixe leagues into the sea : and that they hold opinion how
Vnseasonable this Island is kept by some euill spirit : for they
weather about verily beleeue, that to sleepe in the day time neere
the Isle of it (except it be after much drinke) is present death.
Oncaiarie.   The only season wherein little raine doth fal there, is
(as I gathered by their speech, they diuiding all times by their
Moones) at our Winter Solstice.   The mother-wind of this coast
is for the most part to the Northward of the East, except when
the Sunne is on this side of the Equinoctiall, for then it often
veares Southerly, but most in the night.   This our guid is of the
Iaos, who doe al marke themselues, thereby to bee knowen from
other nations after this maner.   With the tooth of a small beast
like a Rat, they race some their faces, some their bodies, after
diuers formes, as if it were with the scratch of a pin, the print of
which rasure can neuer bee done away againe during life.   When
he had sometime conuersed with our Indians, that went from
England with vs, hee became willing to see our countrey.   His
sufficience, trustinesse, and knowledge is such, that if the pretended voyage for Guiana doe take place, you shall (I doubt not)
find him many wayes able to steed your Lordship in your
designes and purposes.   For besides his precise knowledge of all

the coast, and of the Indian townes and dwellings, he speaketh all their languages, was bred in Guiana, is a sworne brother to Putima, who slewe the Spaniards in their returne from Manao, can direct vs to many golde mines, and in nothing will vndertake more, then hee assuredly will performe.

To the Westward this Bay hath many good roads vnder small Islands, whereof the greatest named Gowateri, is inhabited by the Shebaios : and besides the plenty of foule, fish, fruits, wilde porks and deere, which are there to be had, where Caiane* falles into the sea, (for it standeth in the mouthes of Wia and Caiane) it yeeldes safe and good harbour in foure and fiue fathome for ships of great burthen.   On all that coast we found not any like it : wee therefore honoured this place by the name of Port Howard.   The road vnder Triangle Islands, which are the Westermost from the rest and stand in fiue degrees, which haue also store of fish, foule, deere

Port Howard otherwise called Gowateri.

and Iwanas, is good, but not comparable with this other, where in all windes and weather, shippes, though they be many, may all ride securely.   The hils and high lands are limits to this bay on ech side : for to the Eastward beyond it appeare none at all, and to the Westward of mount Hobbeigh very few.   Where the mountaines faile, there Brasill wood is no farther to bee sought for : but in all parts cotton, pepper, silke, and Balsamum trees doe grow in abundance.   The rootes of the herbe Wiapassa are here most plentifull : I finde them in taste nothing different from good ginger, and in operation very medicinable against the flixe and headach.   These riuers, as also others neerer Raleana, doe all fall out of the plaines of this empire ouer rocks, as the riuer Caroli doeth into Raleana : and in most places within the vtmost hedge of woods, the land within is plaine, voyd of trees, and beareth short grasse like Arromaiaries countrey.

Next adioining vnto these, are the riuers Cunanamma, Vracco, Mawara, Mawarparo, Amonna, Marawini, Oncowi, Wiawiami, Aramatappo, Camaiwini, Shurinama, Shurama, Cupanamma, Inana, Guritini, Winitwara, Berbice, Wapari, Maicaiwini, Maha-waica, Wappari, Lemdrare, Dessekebe, Caopui, Pawrooma, Moruga, Waini, Barima, Amacur, Aratoori, Raleana.†   From Cape Cecyl :o Raleana, the coast trendeth two hundred leagues

* This is the Cayenne River, and the Island referred to below would then be Wakenaam.
† The Orenoque.

next hand Westnorthwest.   In this varietie of goodly riuers,
Amonna among the rest powreth himselfe into the sea in a large
and deepe chanell: his swiftnesse suffereth no barre, nor refuseth any shipping of what burthen soeuer they be: within his
mouth for good and hopefull respectes is port Burley placed.
The inhabitants that dwell Eastward, doe neuer passe lower then
Berbice to trade.   Aboue Curitini in the woods they gather great
quantities of hony.   Farther to the Eastward then Dessekebe,
no Spaniard euer trauelled.   In which respect, and that no sea
card that I haue seene at any time, doth in any sort neere a trueth,
describe this coast: I thought the libertie of imposing English
names to certaine places of note, of right to belong vnto our
labours ; the rather because occasion thereby offereth it selfe grate-
fully to acknowledge the honour due vnto them that haue beene, and
I hope will still continue fauourers of this enterprize.   The Indians
to shew the worthinesse of Dessekebe (for it is very large and
full of Islands in the mouth) doe call it the brother of Orenoque.
It lyeth Southerly into the land, and from the mouth of it vnto
the head, they passe in twentie dayes iourney: then taking
their prouision they carrie it on their shoulders one dayes
iourney: afterwards they returne for their Canoas, and beare
them likewise to the side of a lake, which the Iaos call Ropono-
wini, the Charibes, Parime: which is of such bignesse, that they
know no difference betweene it and the maine sea.
The great There be infinite numbers of Canoas in this lake,
lake whereon
Manoa or and (as I suppose) it is no other then that, whereon
El Dorado Manoa standeth: In this riuer, which we now call
standeth.
Deuoritia, the Spaniards doe intend to build them a
towne.   In Moruga it was, that they hunted Wareo and his
In September. people, about halfe a yere since.   Arromaiarie, who
wan so great credit by ouerthrowing the Tiuitiuas of
Amana, and making free the passage of that riuer (but now
againe liueth in disgrace, by reason that the Charibes of Guanipa
haue killed most of his followers, and burnt his townes) was
present with them, and tooke away many of the women of that
This Spaniard place.   Arracurri, another Indian of the nation of
vnderstandeth the Arwaccas inhabiting in Barima, was likewise
the Guianian present, and conducted the Spaniards to all the
language,
and is Indian dwellings.   They were not of Anthonie de
reputed a Berreo his companie, that followed this chase, but
very sufficient
man. were the Spaniards of Margarita, and the Caraccas,

with whom Santiago forsaking his gouernour Berreo, ioyned himselfe. For which ·fact he now lyeth in fetters at Trinidad, euery day expecting sentence of death. The occasion hereof grew as followeth.

When Berreo, hauing lost his men, was left with Fasshardo at Cumana all alone, as forlorne, and neuer likely to compasse his intended conquest of Guiana: the gouernours of the Caraccas and Margarita consulting together, sent with all speede into Spaine, to aduertise their king, that Berreo was vtterly vnable to follow this enterprise, that he had giuen it ouer, and did now soiorne in his old dayes at Fasshardo his house, minding nothing else but his solace, and recreation. They farther declared, of how great importance this matter was : and that an English gentleman of such reckoning, as they named your lordship to be, hauing bene in Guiana, and vnderstanding so much of the state thereof, and the nations thereunto .adioyning, as Topiawarie,. being both olde and wise, could informe you of, who also in confirmation of friendship, had giuen you his onely sonne, to whome the inheritance of the countrey did belong after him : there was no other likelihood, but that you, who aduentured so farre, and in such sort as you did, onely to see, and knowe a certainty, would leaue nothing vnattempted to possesse so rich a countrey, and without all doubt would returne presently. That meane time, you had left this aged Sire aliue, to bee a blocke in their way, to whom after his decease, this enterprise by patent did belong, and to bee a weake aduersarie against your selfe, whom at all times you knew easily how to distresse : and that therefore it might bee behoouefull for his maiestie to reuoke Berreo his grant, and to vse their seruice, who were readie and willing without any delay to vndertake the charge. These newes being at large amplified and deliuered to the king : Domingo de Vera, Berreo his Camp-master, who was sent into Spaine, fiue moneths before your arriuall at Trinidad, with a sufficient quantitie of gold gotten out of Guiana, to leuie and furnish 500. men, hauing gotten knowledge of this practise, so solicited this cause in Berreo his behalfe, that present order was giuen for the victualling and manning of tenne ships to be sent to Berreo : and farther, this gold bore such waight, that the king commanded other 18 of his ships to stop at Trinidad, and not to follow their other directions, before they saw that place secured from enemies.

W

Berreo supposing that these gouernours in sending with such speede into Spaine, meant him no good ; to approue his care and constancie, and that he neuer would yeelde vnder the burthen of his aduerse fortune ; giuing no time or breath to his aduersaries nor himselfe ; returned foorthwith to Carapana his port, onely with fifteene men, being the scattered remnant of those whom you lately dispossessed of Trinidad. These gouernours followed him, and assuring themselues of present imployment from their king, preoccupating the time of their directions to bee returned from Spaine, entered Guiana with their men, with full determination to murther Berreo, and to dispatch all his company. They indeed killed two or three, but Berreo fledde towards Caroli, where hee stayed hoping for succour from his sonne Antonie de Ximenes, to come downe the riuer from Nueuo Reyno de Granada. The Margaritanes with their accomplices busied themselues, some in searching the countrey, others in purueying of victuals out of the riuers that doe lie Eastward, of which number these were, that entred into Moruga with twentie Canoas.   Santiago passed vp into Topiawaries countrey, and there tooke Francis Sparrowe sir George Gifford his man prisoner, who with plentie of gold ransomed his life, and is now abiding in Cumana.   This done, they all returned to Trinidad, and beganne to builde their towne there, when vnhappily to their small comfort the eight and twentie sayles arriued, and tooke Santiago prisoner. The other Actors in this Enterlude vanished, and in Canoas recouered Margarita and Cumana againe.   Eighteene of the said ships leauing all things in good order, departed from Trinidad to follow their other directions : ten doe yet remaine fortifying at Conquerabia, and expecting our comming.

[marginal note: Francis Sparrow taken prisoner.]

This particular relation I had from an Indian, seruant to Berreo, that could speake Spanish, whom I tooke in the riuer.   He is of the nation of the Iaos, and from a child bred vp with Berreo.   I gaue him trade to buy him a Canoa to returne into his countrey, and so left him glad, that hee had met with vs.

Now the Indians of Moruga being chased from their dwellings, doe seeke by all meanes possible to accord all the nations in one, so to inuade the Arwaccas who were guides to the Spaniards, in showing their townes, and betraying them.   For they are fully perswaded, that by driuing these Arwaccas, who serue the Spaniards (for a great part of this nation doth also hate, or not know them) out of their territories, and Trinidad, the Spaniards for want of bread, will bee inforced to seeke habitation farther off, or at the least in time consume and be wasted.

The 6. day of Aprill we came to an anker within the mouth of the riuer Raleana, hauing spent twentie and three dayes in discouerie vpon this coast. The channell of this riuer hath sixe or seuen fathome They anker within Raleana or Orenoque. depth, nine or ten miles off at sea, the barre lyeth farther out, and at low water hath not full two fathome. It highes not aboue fiue foote, except at a spring tyde. Wee ankered in ten fathome the first night: the next morning twelue Canoas came vnto vs, furnished and prouided of victuals after their maner for the warres. Their Captaines names were Anwara, and Aparwa. These Cassiques, when the Spaniards made the last inrode in those parts, were in the inland amonst the Iwarawakeri their neighbours, by which occasion hauing lost some of their wiues (for notwithstanding their profession of Christianitie, some of these Spaniards keepe ten or twelue women, Spanish Paganisme. thinking themselues wel and surely blessed, howsoeuer they liue, if their towne and houses be religiously crossed) they kept together 30. Canoas, hoping at our comming which they had now long expected to recouer this losse vpon them and the Arwaccas, who in their absence had done this wrong. They shewed me of this their purpose, and required to be ioyned in league of friendship with vs against our enemies. When of them I had learned so much of the present estate of the countrey, as they did know: they demanded whether we had brought no more forces with vs, but onely one ship? I answered them as before I did the others, that wee now came only to trade, not knowing vntil this present that any Spaniards were in Guiana; that vpon our returne our whole fleete will hasten to set forwardes, and that in the meane time, wee would now visite our friendes, and helpe them so farre as wee could in any thing that wee should finde needefull presently to bee done. After long discourse (for their chiefe man stayed with mee all night) when hee had caused mee to spit in my right hand, with many other ceremonies which they vse in confirming friendshippe, hee went to the shoare, and one of his Canoas hee sent to bring forwardes the other twentie: one other hee caused to goe vp the riuer before vs, to bring intelligence. Then calling together the chiefe of his companie, they made small fyers, and sitting in their Hamacas, or Indian beddes, each one sorted himselfe with his companion, recounting amongst themselues the worthiest deedes, and deaths of their Ancestours, execrating their enemies most despitefully, and magnifying their friendes with all titles of prayses and honour, that may bee deuised. Thus they sitte talking, and taking Tobacco some two houres, and vntill their pipes bee all spent (for by them they measure the time of this their solemne conference) no man must interrupt, or disturbe them in any sort: for this is their religion, and prayers, which Her Maiestie. they now celebrated, keeping a precise fast one whole day, in honour of the great Princess of the North, their Patronesse and defender. Their Canoas being made ready, they accompanyed vs, and in their way shewed vs, where the shoaldes of the riuer doe lye. By this Captaine I learned that Muchikeri is the name of the Countrey where Macureguerai the first towne of the Empire of Guiana, that lyeth towardes Raleana, is seated in a fayre and exceeding large plaine, belowe the high mountaines, that beare Northwesterly from it, that it is but three dayes iourney distant from Carapana his Porte, and that Manoa is but six dayes farther. That they themselues doe passe in three dayes into the Countrey of the Iwarewakeri by the Riuer Amacur, which though it bee not the directest, yet it is the readiest way to Macureguarai, for that which leadeth to Carapana his dwelling, is in some places difficult, and mountainous. That a nation of clothed people, called Cassanari, doe dwell not farre from the place, where the Riuer doeth first take the name of Orenoque, and that farre within, they border vpon a Sea of salt water, named Parime. That a great Riuer, called Macurwini, passeth through their Countrey into Orenoque. That Manao standeth twentie dayes iourney from the mouth Wiapoco: sixeteene dayes from Barima, thirteene dayes from Amacur, and tenne dayes from Aratoori. That the best way vnto it, is not by Macureguerai. That of all others the Charibes that dwell high vp in Orenoque, knowe most the inlande, and of those nations, and they speake no other language, then such as Iohn your Interpreter doeth well vnderstand. Hee certified mee of the headlesse men, and that their mouthes in their breastes are exceeding wide. The name of their nation in the Charibes language is Chiparemai, and the Guianians call them Ewiapanomos. What I haue heard of a sorte of people more monstrous,

I omit to mention, because it is no matter of difficultie to get one of them, and the report otherwise will appeare fabulous. Lastly hee tolde mee of an Inland Riuer, named Cawrooma, adioyning to Aratoori, and that the Quepyn mountaines, where Carapana dwelleth, are hardly accessible. That the Amapagotos haue images of gold of incredible bignesse, and great store of vnmanned horses of the Caracas breed: and they dwell fiue dayes iourney vp the Riuer about Caroli. *They haue eminent heads like dogs, and liue all the day time in the sea, they speake the Charibes language.* Wee with our fleete of Canoas were now not farre from Carapanas Port, when our intelligencer returned and informed vs that tenne Spaniardes were lately gone with much trade to Barima, where these Indians dwelt, to buy Gassaui bread; and that within one day two other Canoas of Spaniards were appointed to come by the Riuer Amana, to Carapana his Port.

Vpon this occasion they tooke counsell, and in the ende desired to returne to their houses, least the Spaniardes finding them from home, and imagining that they did purposely absent themselues, shoulde take away their wiues and spoyle their dwellings. They farther resolued if it were possible to cut them off: which afterwardes they did perfourme. For when they were dispersed in their houses seeking Cassaui, suddenly at one time, in all places they were assaulted, and not one of them escaped. Carapana, whose hand was in laying this plot, sent vs this newes, as wee returned downe the Riuer. The two other Canoas that came from Trinidad by Amana, notwithstanding that wee kept a league before the shippe with our boates, sawe the shippe before wee had sight of them, and presently with all speede went to Berreo to aduertize him of our comming. Hee foorthwith dispatched two or three messengers to Trinidad. One of his Canoas mette with our spie, whome the Indians of Barima had left to goe with vs: they rifled him of his victuals, gaue him kniues, and dismissed him.

In eight dayes sayling still before a winde, wee arriued at Topiawaries Porte, in all which time no Indian that wee knew came abourd vs. For the time of our returne promised at your Lordshippes departure from thence being expired; they in dispaire seuered themselues amongst the other nations. Here the Spaniardes haue seated their Rancheria of some twentie or thirtie houses. The high rockie Island, that lyeth in the middest of the Riuer, against the mouth of Caroli, is their Forte or refuge, when they misdoubt safetie in their towne, or hauing notice of any practise against them : but now leauing both towne and Island, they ioyned themselues together, and returning to the mouth of Riuer Caroli, placed there a secret ambush, to defend the passage to those mines, from whence your Oare and white stones were taken the last yeere : Wee all not without griefe to see ourselues thus defeated, and our hungry hopes made voyde, were witnesses of this their remooue. As we road at ancor within musket shot of their Towne, an Indian came vnto vs with lean cheeks, thinne haire, and a squint eye, to informe vs that they were very strong, that Berreo his sonne was with him, that they had but two small Pinnisses at Trinidad, which they dayly looked for to come vp the Riuer, and lastly to viewe our shippe well, and our prouisions, but especially to learne whether Gualtero, Topiawarie his sonne were with vs.

This informers very countenance gaue him to bee suspected, and therefore partlie by threatning, partlie by promise of rewarde wee wonne him to confesse the trueth. Which hee did, assuring vs that Berreo had not full fiftie fiue men with him, whereof twentie came lately from Triuidad, twentie from Nueuo Reyno, and the rest hee brought with him about fiue moneths since, when hee fledde from Carapana his Porte, and was driuen with his small companie to keepe the aforesaide Island neere Caroli. And that though nowe his number is thus increased yet dareth hee not aduenture at any time to leaue the fast woodes, and to goe but halfe a league from his holde into the plaines. That some fewe of the Arwaccas are abiding with him. That hee dayly looketh for his sonne from Nueuo Reyno, for his Campe-master from Trinidad, and for horses from the Caraccas. That Topiawarie is dead : the Indians of that coast all fledde, and dispersed, excepting the sonne of one Curmatoi, and another woman of account, whome the Spaniardes holde prisoners, for consenting to the death of their nine men, and the holy Fryer in Morekito his time. This Curmatoi is fledde towardes Guanipa, and is a man of speciall note amongst the Indians. That Iwiakanarie Gualtero his neere kinsman, hath helde the Countrey to his vse, by his fathers appointment, euer since your being in the Riuer. That there are tenne ships, and many Spaniardes at Trinidad. That the Indians our friendes did feare, least you with your company were all slaine, and your shippes sunke at Cumanà (for so the Spaniardes noysed

Topiawarie his sonne.

it amongst them,) that some of Gualtero his friendes
with Putijma, were in the mountaines not farre from
the hill Aio.   And that Berreo had sent for sixe
peeces of ordinance, which he meant to plant, where they might
best command the Riuer.

When wee had stayed here two dayes, considering that where
no hope was left of doing good, to abide there in harmes way
doing nothing, would be bootlesse : I resolued to seeke Putijma
in the mountaines : and turning downe the Riuer with the force
of the streame some twentie miles in sixe houres : the next
morning with ten shot I went ashoare, intending if the Indians
should thinke themselues too weake, with our helpe to displant
the Spaniards : to set some of them on worke, for hatchets and
kniues to returne vs golde graines, and white stones from such
places, as they should be directed vnto.   When wee came to
the place of their vsuall abode ; wee sawe that they lately had
bene there, but could speake with none of them.   It may be that
feare (which is easie of beliefe) perswaded them that we were
Spaniards.   Gilbert my Pilot here offered to bring vs either to
the myne of white stones neere Winicapora, or else to a gold
myne, which Putijma had shewed him, being but one dayes
iourney ouerland, from the place where we now stayed at an
ancor.   I sawe farre off the mountaine adioyning to this gold
myne, and hauing measured their pathes neere the same place
this last yeere, could not iudge it to bee fifteene miles from vs.
I doe well remember howe comming that way with Putijma the
yeere before, he pointed to this same mountaine, making signes
to haue me goe with him thither.   I vnderstood his signes and
marked the place, but mistooke his meaning, imagining that he
would haue shewed mee the ouerfall of the Riuer Curwara from
the mountaines.   My Indian shewed me in what sort without
digging they gather the gold in the sand of a small riuer, named
Macawini, that springeth and falleth from the rockes where this
myne is.   And farther tolde me, that hee was with Putijma, at
what time Morekito was to be executed by the Spaniardes, and
that then the chiefe of Morekito his friends were in consultation,
to shewe this myne vnto them if so they might redeeme their
Captaines life, but vpon better aduise, supposing them in this
case to bee implacable, and that this might prooue a meanes to
loose not onely their king, but their Countrey also : they haue to
this day concealed it from them, being of all others the richest

and most plentifull.   The aged sort to keepe this from common
knowledge, haue deuised a fable of a dangerous Dragon that
haunteth this place and deuoureth all that come neere it.   But
our Indian, if when we returne, we doe bring store of strong
wine (which they loue beyond measure) with it will vndertake so
to charme this Dragon, that he shall doe vs no harme.

I, that for this ende came from home, and in this iourney had
taken much more paines to lesse purpose, would very gladly
from this mountaine haue taken so good a proofe to witnes my
being in the Countrey : but withall considering that not one
Indian of our knowne friends came unto vs : that Don Iuan the
cousin of Gualtero, who liueth here a reuolt from the Spaniard,
was now in election to bee chiefe commander of all the Indian
forces in these partes, cannot in pollicie, for Gualtero his sake,
whose inheritance hee sought to vsurpe, bee a fast friend vnto
vs : that the Spaniardes abiding in Winicapora (for there were
tenne) might well before wee could doe any thing, and returne,
cause some others of Berreo his men to ioyne with them, in the
way to intercept vs : and forethinking withall, that there being no
meanes but our selues, to make knowne our discouerie, if wee
returned not ; in our misfortune the hope of following this voyage
would bee buried : but besides all this, and the respect of such
spyals, as the Spaniardes kept to obserue our dooings, foreknowing that if the enemie should by our lingring, stop our passage,
which in one or two places of aduantage, fewe of them might
easilie doe : it would bee a question howe with our shippe to get
out of the Riuer, except first wee could remooue them :
I thought it best (all other possibilities set apart) to seeke
in time to bee free from the hazard of the aforesaid euill
passages.

Whilest wee were searching at the shoare for the Indians, my
Barge tooke a Canoa, with three men in her: the one a seruant
to Berreo, (as before is mentioned) the other two marchants of
Cassaui.   They had a letter sent from the Gouernour to bee con-
ueied to Trinidad, which I receiued.   There was also a great
hatchet, and twentie kniues, wherewith this Indian seruant should
buy a Canoa, and hire Indians to cary her vp the Riuer towards
Nueuo Reyno.   This Canoa forsooth with foure other

The small
forces of
Ximenes.

were to be sent to bring downe Berreo his sonne with
all his forces, which nowe haue bene, I thinke, full
three yeers in preparing.   If fiue such boats be

sufficient to conuoy him, his men and all their prouision : it may seeme, hee commeth with no great strength.

This seruant as hee was a man of especiall trust, and neere Berreo: so appeared hee to haue some insight in his proceedings. He shewed mee that the Indians, who with these kniues should be hired, were to passe vp so high, as where some of the Cassanari doe dwell in small villages. That Berreo This transplanting of Indians is worthy of consideration. his purpose was, when they came thither to leaue them there, and make them officers ouer the other Indians: and in their places some of the Cassanari should returne, who likewise should be made Iustices and Constables ouer them of Guiana : that from Trinidad he meant to remoue most of the olde inhabitants, that would be tractable ; and interpose them amongst the Cassanarians of Guiana, and the Guianians of the Cassanari. That the Arwaccas should wholly possesse Trinidad, and the riuer side of Raleana. That they already were prouided of threescore Negros, to worke the mynes in these places. And that by this meanes Berreo hoped to keepe these seuerall nations in mutuall enmitie each against other, all to serue his turne, and neuer to become strong, or likely to ioyne themselues against him. He farther shewed me, that Topiawary, soone after our departure from the riuer, fledde into the mountaines, carying Hugh Godwyn with him, and leauing a Substitute in his Countrey, as aforesaide : and that the next newes they heard of him was, that hee was dead, and the English boy eaten by a Tyger. That the Spaniardes beleeue neither the one nor the other. That about the ende of Iune, when the Riuer shall be impassable, the tenne shippes shall depart from Trinidad. And that Berreo euer since his comming to Guiana, hath spent his time altogether in purueying of victuals, whereof there is such scarsitie, by reason that the Indians forsaking their houses, haue not this halfe yeere planted any of their grounds, so that the Spaniards are inforced to seeke their bread farre off, and content themselues to liue with litle.

In sayling vp the Riuer, wee passed by Toparimacko his Port, which in one place is very shoalde, the chanell lying close aboord the shore. Wee returned therefore another way by the maine riuer on the South side : this branch wee found large, deepe, and without danger. When wee were come neere Carapana his Port, hee sent fiue or six seuerall Canoas, promising

x

this day and the next, that hee would come and speake with vs. Thus wee lingred sixe or seuen dayes, but hee came not. In the ende hee sent one of his aged followers, to certifie vs, that hee was sicke, olde, and weake : that the wayes neere his dwelling are not easie : and that therefore he desired vs to holde him excused for not comming. This olde man dilated vnto vs, that Carapana in hope of our returne, hath euer since your Lordshippes being in that Countrey, kept the mountaines, where the Spaniardes can hardly any way inforce him ; that they haue taken from him and his people many of their wiues, because they refused to furnish them weekely with a certaine proportion of bread and victuals: that Don Iuan otherwise called Eparacano hath the commandement of all his subiects, excepting onely a choise guarde of men sufficient to keepe the place hee nowe dwelleth in. That it repenteth him of his ambition, euer to haue sought by the Spaniardes meanes, to haue enlarged his Countreys and people. For true it is, that from the beginning hee was a Lorde of no other then ordinary power amongst them, vntill hee had entered into friendshippe with Berreo : for then the Indians on all sides left some their habitations, and manie their commanders to become his subiectes, that they might haue the priuiledge to trade with the Spaniardes for hatchets and kniues, which are iewels of great price amongst them : that hee nowe sawe no other choise, but that the Indians must, if they will doe well, without farther dissembling of their necessitie, either entertaine vs their friendes, or else giue place to the Spaniardes their enemies. For the plentie of golde that is in this countrey, beeing nowe knowen and discouered, there is no possibilitie for them to keepe it : on the one side they coulde feele no greater miserie, nor feare more extremitie, then they were sure to finde, if the Spaniardes preuayled, who perforce doe take all things from them, vsing them as their slaues, to runne, to rowe, to bee their guides, to cary their burthens, and that which is worst of all, to bee content, for safetie of their liues, to leaue their women, if a Spaniard chance but to set his eye on any of them to fancie her : on the otherside they could hope for, nor desire no better state and vsage, then her Maiesties gracious gouernment, and Princely vertues doe promise, and assure vnto them. For sayde hee, the other yeere, when wee fledde into the mountaines, and measured your doings by the Spaniards in like case, we made no other account, but that your

Commander being able, as hee was, would doubtlesse haue per-
secuted vs to the vttermost, as the onely maintainers and
supporters of your enemies, and would at the least, if hee could
not reach vs, take our Townes, and make vs ransome our wiues
and children : wee found it farre otherwise, and that none of
your well gouerned companie durst offer any of vs wrong or
violence, no not by stealth, when unknowne they might haue
done it. We then beleeuing it to bee true, that your grand
Captaine reported of his Princesse, tooke this for a good proofe
of her royall commandement and wisedome, that had framed
her subiectes to such obedience, and of your happinesse, that
inioyed the benefite thereof: that Carapana weighing
the good and friendly course of our proceedings,
doeth humbly craue of her Maiestie for himselfe and
his people, that with the rest of the Indians, which
wholly depende on her Princely regarde towardes
them, hee also may inioy her fauourable protection :
that hee doeth this, not as a man left vnto himselfe and forsaken
by the Spaniardes, but as one that knoweth their iniustice, hateth
their cruelties, and taketh it for his best choise, vtterly to dis-
claime their friendshippe. It may bee pertinent (as surely it is
a thing worth the noting) to consider howe this president of your
moderation and good order, which to vs seemeth a matter but of
small and ordinarie respect, hath both alienated their heartes
altogether from the Spaniard, and stirred vp in them true loue
and admiration thereof. For as gouernement is the onely bond
of common societie : so to men lawlesse, that each one to another
are, Omnes hoc iure molesti, quo fortes : To men, I say, that liue
in dayly tumultes, feares, doubtes, suspitions, barbarous cruelties,
neuer sleeping secure, but alwayes either drunke, or practising
one anothers death : to such men as these bee, who wanting dis-
cipline, iustice and good order to confirme them in a quiet and
peaceable course of liuing, knowing not where to finde it : the
sence and sweetnesse thereof is as the dewe of Hermen : it
is as the Harmonie of a well tuned Instrument : to bee briefe,
it carieth in it selfe not onely a due and worthy commendation ;
but is auaylable without stroke striking to gaine a kingdome.
For the Indians in all partes within and neere Guiana, doe offer
their seruice, and promise to prouide victuall, and what else their
countrey yeeldeth, desiring onely that some force of men may
remaine with them, to deliuer them from oppression and

[marginal note: Carapana a great Lord bordering vpon Guiana craueth her Maiesties protection.]

tyrannie. And nowe by generall consent (though hatchets and kniues bee the onely things of request and vsefull vnto them) they haue agreed by no meanes to trade with the Spaniard for any thing.

Farther this old man shewed mee, whence most of their golde commeth, which is formed in so many fashions: whence their Spleene-stones, and others of al sorts are to be had in plentie: where golde is to bee gathered in the sandes of their riuers: from what partes the Spaniards, both by trade, and otherwise, haue returned much gold. This he vttered with Carapana his consent (I doubt not) 'hoping thereby to induce vs to returne againe. For contrarie to their lawe of secrecie, which in this case they doe all generally obserue, sharply punishing the breakers thereof, as enemies vnto their natiue Countrey: I found this man no whit scrupulous, but very free and liberall of speech in all things.

And because we might knowe, that wee should not want handes or helpe, in this or any other our enterprises, if perhaps wee should finde cause to passe vp to the head of this Riuer: hee declared that the Spaniardes haue no Indians to trust vnto but some of the Arwaccas, which since they were not many, could bee but of small force; That the Charibes of Guanipa, the Ciawannas amongst the Tiuitiuas, the Shebaios, Iaos, Amai-pagotos, Cassipagotos, Parpagotos, Samipagotos, Serowos, Etai-guinams, Cassamari, with the rest of the nations farre and neere, were all ready, on what side soeuer the Spaniards shall stirre, to fight against them: that the Ptriagotos, through whose countrey they must first passe, are alone sufficient to encounter them, such is the strength of their countrey, and the valure of the men. The Indians holde opinion, that they are notable sorcerers, and inuulnerable. In the mountaines where they dwell, white stones are found of such hardnesse, that by no arte or meanes they can bee pierced; they imagine that these Pariagotos become inuul-nerable, by eating these stones. The fable omitted, happily they may prooue good Diamonds.

Then he shewed howe the Iwarewakeri haue nourished grasse in all places, where passage is, these three yeeres, and that it is at this present so high, as some of the trees; which they meane to burne, so soone as the Spaniard shall bee within danger thereof. Lastly, hee shewed mee that Wariarimagoto the Emperours chiefe Captaine for those partes, hath gathered together many thousandes of the Epuremei, to keepe the the borders of the Empire ; and that hee lay now on the South side of the mountaines, some one dayes iourney or little more from the Spaniard. To be short, hee certified mee, that they all were resolued not to seeke vpon them (for indeede they feare their shot) but to defend their owne, and to expect our comming. *Wariarima-goto one of the Emperour of Guiana his chiefe Cap-taines vp in armes against the Spani-ardes.* In the meane time they take opportuni-ties, when they finde any of them straggling or deuided from their strength, by litle and litle to lessen their number.

The place where wee were at ancor was but one dayes iourney from Carapana : I therefore made motion to this Captaine to stay with two or three of his company aboord the shippe, and to cause his men to bring mee with my Interpreter to Carapana his dwelling : hee answered mee that it were not good so to doe, least perhaps some Spie might informe the Spaniardes thereof, whereby danger would growe to Carapana. For they haue many times vsed many meanes to reconcile him vnto them : but hee from time to time hath dalyed with them, neither professing him-selfe their enemie, nor in ought shewing them any friendshippe. Nowe (sayde hee) if the Spaniardes shall by any meanes come to knowledge, that you haue conferred together, they will take this occasion to persecute him with all extremitie, as their open enemie, whom they now neglect, or at the least feare not, as being an harmelesse old man. And for this cause only hath Carapana forborne to come vnto you.

By this I perceiued, that to stay longer for him (though gladly I could haue bene content to spend one seuenights more to speake with him) would be purposelesse. Wherefore hauing assured so many of the Indians as at any time came vnto vs, of our speedie returne, promising them plentie of kniues, beades, and hatchets, if they would reserue their Cassaui, and prouide store of their pieces of golde for vs : I desired this Captaine to bee a meanes that our friends of Trinidad might vnderstand of our being in the Riuer and that we meant to relieue them so soone, as conueniently might bee. Hee promised in Carapana his behalfe, that this should not bee forgotten. One of the Captaines of the Cyawannas, who doe now dwell in the Riuer Arawawo, neere Trinidad, undertooke also without fayle to ascertaine them thereof. I was the more carefull herein, because so many ships being heere, I doubted least they would take order

that no Indian should speake with vs.   For so indeede it
fell out.

This Captaine of the Cyawannas came likewise to ioyne with
vs, and had prouided fifteene Canoas for that purpose.   Their
dwelling was lately in Macureo, where the Spaniardes one night
stealing on them, killed twentie of their men, and burnt their
houses, because they refused to trade with them for certaine
images of golde made with many heades which they had gotten
out of Guiana.   I sent a present of Yron to Carapana, and then
set sayle.

In turning downe the riuer wee spent eight dayes.   In many
places where the channell lyeth wee found twentie fathome
depth : where it is sholdest, wee had two fathome and a halfe, and
that but in one or two places.   Of the worthinesse of this Riuer,
because I cannot say ynough, I will speake nothing.   Wee haue
presumed to call it by the name of Raleana, because your selfe
was the first of our nation that euer entred the same, and I
thinke it nothing inferior to Amazones, which is best knowen by
the name of Orellana, the first discouerer thereof.   By turning
onely, without helpe of oares to passe so long away
The chanel in so short a time, against the winde, may sufficiently
of Raleana, prooue, that the chanell is very large, good, and likely
or Orenoque to second our hopes in all that wee can desire.
very large Without the mouth of this Riuer, our Pinnesse, the
and good. Discouerer, whome wee lost neere the coast of
They meete England, came vnto vs. Shee fell with this land
with their somewhat to the Southwarde of Cape Cecyl, and had spent
Pinnesse. three weekes and odde dayes in ranging alongst the coast, when
shee mette with vs.   William Downe the master informed mee
that they entred, and searched these foure riuers.   In Wiapoco
they sayled so farre, vntill the rocks stopped their passage.   In
Caiane they went vp one dayes iourney.   In Cunanama they
found many inhabitantes.   Curitini was the last Riuer they had
beene in.   Whence, hauing no other meanes to finde Raleana,
they were inforced to borrow a Pilot against his will : whom
afterwardes I would haue returned with reward to his contentment ; but he would not.

Our English that to steale the first blessing of an vntraded
place, will perhaps secretly hasten thither, may bee beholding to
A good caueat. mee for this caueat, if they take notice thereof.
They may be assured, that this people, as they no

way sought our harme, but vsed our men with all kindnesse : so are they impatient of such a wrong, as to haue any of their people perforce taken from them, and will doubtlesse seek reuenge. The example of the like practise vpon the coast of Guinie, in the yeere 1566, and againe at Dominica, where Alderman Wats his shippe hardly escaped being taken, may serue for our warning in like case to looke for no good, before they bee satisfied for this iniury.

When wee had taken aboorde vs such victuals as were in the Pinnesse : wee set fire in her, (for her Rudder could serue her to no longer vse) and stopping the floodes, plyed to windwarde with the ebbe neere the shoare, vntill wee were sixteene leagues to the Eastwarde of the Riuers mouth, and then standing off to Sea, wee fell in twentie foure houres sayling with Punta de Galera the Northeastermost part of Trinidad. But The Isle of Tabaco island in sight, wee first went thither. This Tabago. Island is plentifull of all things, and a very good soyle. It is not nowe inhabited, because the Charibes of Dominica are euill neighbours vnto it. They of Trinidad haue a meaning and purpose to flie thither, when no longer they can keepe Trinidad. Their onely doubt is, that when they are seated there, the Spaniard will seeke to possesse it also. The Gouernour of Margarita went lately in a Pinnesse to viewe this Island. Gilbert my Pilot who sometime liued there, noteth it for the best and fruitfullest ground that hee knoweth.

Thence wee returned to Punta de Galera and ancored in tenne fathome vnder the North side of the Island some fiue or sixe miles from the sayde point. The flood-tyde striketh alongst the coast to the Eastward very strongly. Wee discharged a peece of ordinance, and afterwards went to the shore in our boat : but no Indian came vnto vs. I would haue sent Iohn of Trinidad to procure some of them to speake with vs : but he was altogether, vnwilling, alleaging that their dwellings were farre within the mountaines, and that he knew no part of that side of the Island. From this place we set sayle for Santa Lucia, but fell with Granata, which wee found not inhabited. Saint Vincent we hardly recouered, by turning vnder the lee of the island. The Tabaco of this place is good : but the Indians being Canibals, promising vs store, and delaying vs from Most danger-ous Canibals. day to day, sought onely opportunitie to betray, take, and eate vs, as lately they had deuoured the whole companie of a French shippe. This their treacherie being by one of their slaues reuealed, from thenceforth they did all forbeare to come vnto vs. To sit downe on their lowe stooles, when they by offering such ease, will seeme to shew curtesie, abodeth death to strangers, that shall trust them. At Matalino or Martinino we found not any inhabitants. Lastly, wee came to Dominica, where we could get no good Tabaco. But hauing intelligence of a Spanish shippe, that was taking in of fresh water, at the Northwest side of the Island, wee wayed ancor to seeke him. Hee discrying vs, stole away by night. The Indians of this place haue determined to remooue, and ioyne with them of Guanipa, against the Spaniardes, who lately dis-peopled one of their Islands, and at our being there one of their Canoas returned from Guanipa, and certified vs, that the tenne Spanish shippes at Trinidad doe ride, some of them at Conquerabia, the rest at the small Ilands neere the disemboging place. Herehence we steered North and by East, taking the directest course to shorten our way homewards.

Thus haue I emptied your purse, spending my time and trauell in following your lordships directions for the full discouerie of this coast, and the riuers thereof. Concerning the not making of a voyage for your priuate profite, I pretend nothing. Sorie I am, that where I sought no excuse, by the Spaniardes being there I found my defect remedilesse. And for mine owne part, I doe protest, that if the consideration of the publique good that may ensue, had not ouerpoysed all other hopes and desires : I would rather haue aduentured by such small and weake meanes as I had, to doe well with danger, then to returne onely with safetie. Nowe although in a cause not doubtfull, my allegation is no way needefull : yet because the weightinesse thereof, and the expecta-tion of others, seemeth of due and right to claime something to bee sayde by mee, whome your especiall trust and fauour hath credited and graced with this employment : Pardon it (I beseech your honour) if, where my lampe had oyle, it borrow light also ; and my speach, which is altogether vnsauorie, season it selfe with some of the leauen of your owne discourse touching this dis-couerie. The particular relation of some certaine things I haue reserued, as properly belonging to yourselfe, who onely, as knowing most, can make best vse thereof. So much in generall is here touched, as (I hope) may serue to refresh the memorie of this worthie enterprise in those whome it may concerne, and testifie your care and expence in following the same : that in a second age, when in time trueth shall haue credite, and men wondering at the riches, and strength of this place (which nature it selfe hath maruelously fortified, as her chiefe treasure-house) shall mourne and sigh to holde idle cicles, whilest others reape and gather in this haruest, it bee not sayde, that Sir Walter Ralegh was of all men liuing in his dayes, most industrious in seeking, most fortunate in attaining to the fulnesse of an inestimable publique good : if, knowing that for enuie and priuate respectes, his labours were lessened, his informations mistrusted, his proffers not regarded, and the due honour of his deserts imparted to others ; If (I say) seeing, knowing and bearing all this, hee with patience had persisted in so good a way in doing his Princesse, and countrey seruice ; and had but perfected his first discouerie by sending a shippe or two for that purpose : for then surely all lets and doubts being remooued, and so large a kingdome, so exceeding rich, so plentiful of all things, as this by his discourse appeared to bee, being offered : no deuises and vaine surmises could haue taken place, no illusions could haue preuailed : it had bene blindnesse and deafenesse in those, that being neere her Maiestie doe spend their dayes in seruing the common weale, not to see, and knowe in so weightie a matter : it had bene malicious obstinacie, impotencie of minde, and more then treason to the common wealth, the matter standing onely vpon acceptance, to seeke either to foreslowe so fit an occasion, or forsake so generall a blessing.   This (if) is nowe cut off through a singular and incomparable temper, in ouercomming euill with good.

This your seconde discouerie hath not onely founde a free and open entrance into Raleana, which the Naturals call Orenoque : but moreouer yeeldeth choyse of fourtie seuerall great riuers (the lesser I do not reckon) being for the most part with small vessels nauigable for our marchants and others, that do now finde little profit in setting forth for reprisall, to exercise trade in.   To such as shall be willing to aduenture in search of them, I could propose some hope of gold mines, and certaine assurance of peeces of made golde, of Spleene-stones, Kidney-stones, and others of better estimate.   But because our beleefe seemeth to bee mated in these greater matters, and a certaintie of smaller profits is the readiest inducement to quicken our weake hopes ; I not going so farre as mine owne eyes might

Y

warrant mee, doe onely promise in the aforesayd riuers Brasil-
wood, honey, cotton, Balsamum, and drugs to helpe to defray
charges : and further, because without a beginning there can
bee no continuance of these benefites vnto our countrey to any
that shall be the first vndertakers hereof, I am gladly content to
giue such light and knowledge, as by conference with the Indians
I haue attained vnto.

My selfe, and the remaine of my fewe yeeres, I haue
bequeathed wholly to Raleana, and all my thoughts liue onely
in that action.   The prosecuting whereof -is in it selfe iust,
profitable, and necessarie.   Iust, because it is intended for the
defence of harmlesse people, who fearing thralldome and
oppression, desire to protect themselues and their countrey
vnder her Maiesties tuition : Profitable, as may bee gathered not
onely by many Spanish letters intercepted, but also by the
proofes mentioned in the discourse of the first discouerie, and
since that, by the Indians owne voluntarie relations ; and lastly,
by the prouision that the Spaniards doe make to acquite vs
thereof.   Necessarie it is, as being the onely helpe to put a
bitte in the mouth of the vnbrideled Spaniard ; the onely way
to enter into his treasurie of Nueuo Reyno, and Peru ; the
onely meanes to animate the wronged Indians, with our assistance to seeke reuenge for the extreme murthers and cruelties,
which they haue endured, and to ruinate his naked cities in all
those parts of the Inland; whose foundations haue beene layd in
the blood of their parents and ancesters.

The forces that the Spaniard hath already sent to Trinidad, to
fortifie there, and keepe the passage of this riuer, are an euident
argument that the king feareth and doubteth the sequele of this
discouerie.   For can it bee a small matter ?   Or hath hee so
waste imployment for his men and shipping, that vpon no
ground, hee would send eight and twentie shippes, to keepe vs
onely from Tabacco: For what els that good is can Trinidad
yeelde vs : No doubtlesse, if the returne of Berreo his Campe-
master with tenne of these shippes bee compared with precedent
aduertisements concerning him : it will appeare more then
probable, that the Guiana-golde waged these men and shipping :
and that they are nowe more carefull to obtaine this place, then
to keepe others, which they haue already gotten, which note,
except in matters of extraordinarie account, is not incident to
their policie and proceedings.   Againe, it cannot bee thought

that either it was senselesse madnesse in the gouernours of
Margarita, and the Caracas, to bring their states and liues in
question, by seeking, contrarie to their kings order, to enter
Guiana, and kill Berreo with his followers : or else the abundance of pearle in Margarita, and the golde mines in the Caracas,
seeming matters of small account : Guiana onely was in their
iudgement, rich, plentifull, and able of it selfe to redeeme their
trespasse and offence, howe great soeuer it should bee.

The sundry attemptes and ouerthrowes of the Spaniardes
being men of power, and honourable place, in labouring threescore and three yeeres and vpwardes, to inlarge the kingdome
of Spaine with this mightie and great empire, doe plainely shewe,
that they long time sought a path, where in one moneth a high
way was found : that the losse of their liues witnesseth their
desires, and the worthinesse of the thing, where to vs the easi-
nesse of obteining discrediteth the greatnes of the attempt : and
that if now at the last they doe preuaile, they must holde by
tyrannie that which they get by the sword ; where then our
returne nothing by the Indians is more wished for, nothing
expected more earnestly.

Those obiections, which haue beene made by many seeming
wise, and the impediments likely to arise, as they haue supposed,
are best answered by the vnreproued witnesse of those mens
actions. Some haue termed these discoueries fables, and fan-
tasies, as if there had beene no such land or territorie : others
allowing both of the place, and that such a kingdome or countrey
is discouered, make conclusion, that if it had beene so rich as
wee haue supposed, that no doubt the king of Spaine would by
this time haue possessed it. But if they consider that the
Spanish nation hath already conquered the two empires of
Mexico and Peru, with so many other kingdoms and prouinces :
wee may very well answere, that his power is not infinite, and
that hee hath done well for the time. And yet it is manifest,
that this very empire hath beene by all those seuerall Spaniardes
(the catalogue of whose names is by it selfe hereunto annexed)
at sundry times vndertaken, and neuer perfourmed. Howbeit,
the world hath reason to admire their constancie, and their great
labours, and wee may well blush at our owne idle, despairefull,
and loytering dispositions, that can finde abilitie in another
barren, and sterued nation, to possesse so much of the worlde,
and can doe nothing but frame arguments against our selues, as

vnfit and powerlesse to possesse one prouince already discouered, and of which our nation hath assurance of the people's loue, and that all the Chieftains and principals haue vowed their obedience to her Maiestie ; the nauigation being withall so short, danger-lesse, and free from infectious sickenesse. If doubt of perils might moderate the mindes of our men once mooued with steadfast hope, that golde shall bee the reward of their trauels : it may easily bee perceiued, that all those lets and hinderances that can any way bce alleaged, or wrested so much, as but to touch vs, doe deepely and neerely concerne the Spanish king, and in a maner violently withold him from that, which hee not~ withstanding carrieth with successe, whilest wee out of season do affect the bare stile, to be named men stayed and circumspect in our proceedings. It is reported, that Calanus the Indian threw downe before Alexander the great, a drie seare peece of leather, and then put his foot on one of the endes of it : the leather being trode downe at that side, rose on all parts else. By this the wise man did shewe vnto him a figure and similitude of his kingdome, which being exceeding large, must of necessitie in all other parts, excepting the place of the kings residence, be alwayes full of stirs, tumults and insurrections.   The end after-wards confirmed, that this empire consisting of sundry nations, could not keepe it selfe from dissolution.   No potentate liuing hath, or can haue so faithfull and incorrupt counsellers, as bee the examples and histories of forepassed times and ages. Wee may therefore bee bolde to thinke that the Gouernours of the Spanish affaires should minde it, that their kings lustfull desire, and ambi-tious thoughts to establish ouer all Europe one lawe, one Lord, one religion, are built and erected on a dangerous vngrounded resolu-tion : Considering that many of the neighbour kingdomes being of equall force in men, or greater then hee can make, are settled in a long continued estate, are entire within themselues, and hate to heare the voyce of a stranger.   It is not vnlikely that they in this case should lay before their king the fatall destinies of many worthies, that haue beene constrained for wante of sufficient numbers of their naturall subiects, after many yeeres spent in the warres, to retire to their owne countreys, and haue beene glad peaceably to holde their owne Signiories at home, resigning all that vnto others, which they haue gotten abroad by hard aduenture, and much effusion of blood.   The King of Spaine cannot but discerne, that his spacious empires and kingdomes being so many, and so farre diuided one from another, are like the members of a monstrous bodie, tyed together with cables only. For take away the traffique of vnnecessarie commodities transported out of Spaine : those huge countreys of the Indies hauing no common linke of affinitie, lawe, language, or religion, and being of themselues able to maintaine themselues without forreine commerce, are not so simple, as not to knowe their owne strength, and to finde, that they doe rather possesse Spaniardes, then that they are possessed by them. Hee cannot bee ignorant that Spaine it selfe is on all sides enuironed with many puissant enemies, mightie and great princes, who knowing it to bee rich without men, confident without reason, proud and aduenturous without meanes sufficient ; may happily confederate to chastise him, as an insolent intruder, and disturber of all quietnesse ; and going no further then Spaine it selfe may euen there shake the foundation of his long contriued deuises, and in one acte redeeme the time, controll his aspiring humor, and breake the bandes in sunder, that import seruitude, and subuersion to all the dominions of Christendome. Againe his counsell may well informe him, that to dispeople and disable himselfe at home, in hope to obtaine Guiana, being a countrey strong of it selfe, and defended with infinite multitudes of Indian enemies, being rich, and by the inhabitants offered vnto the English : his contempt towardes vs would seeme so intollerable and despightfull, as might bee sufficient to prouoke vs, though otherwise wee had no such inclination ; if hee vnprouided of able helpes to effect it, should rest him-selfe on a carelesse presumption, that wee cannot, wee dare not, wee will not stirre in a matter that promiseth vs so great benefite, and may so highly offend him. Hee may bee perswaded, that to leaue no other succour or safetie to his naked-nesse, but the olde stale practise of spreading rumours, and giuing out false intelligences of preparations to inuade England, thereby to keepe vs at home ; or els of hyring and suborning some Machauellian vnder hande by secret conueyance, to stop the course of our proceedings ; or lastly, of procuring some wilde outlaw to disquiet our tranquilitie ; is but a poore, weake, and vncertaine stay to vpholde his estate by. And yet setting such like driftes aside : what can bee imagined likely to hinder vs from preuailing in Guiana, rather then him, whose disaduantage is to bee encombred with the selfe same, and manifolde more

impediments, then can any way bee supposed, with good cause
to impeach, or diuorce vs from so profitable an attempt? All this
notwithstanding, if the Spanish king not being able to dissemble
his desire, or beare the losse of this one kingdome; putting himselfe out of his strength at home, and exposing his people to the
hazard of all casualities abroad, bee resolued, whatsoeuer shall
happen, not to relinquish Guiana, but to keepe this one yron
more in the fire, on no other assurance, but a peremptorie disdaine
of preuention : If hee appeare so eagerly bent for Guiana, as if it
were enacted for a lawe amongst themselues, Viis et modis to
thrust for it,- and not to heare, conceiue, or beleeue any thing,
that may disswade or deterre from the conquest thereof: it then
appertaineth vnto vs, not to inforce those obiections against ourselues, which hee with lesse reason reiecteth as friuolous : since
by howe much the more earnest hee is in following this purpose,
by so much the lesse cause haue wee to bee diuerted from it.
To such as shall bee willing further to wade in this argument;
for breuities sake, I doe propose onely this bare assertion : that
England and Guiana conioyned, are stronger, and more easily
defended, then if England alone should repose her selfe on her
owne force, and powerfulnesse. The reasons that might bee inferred
to proue this neede no rationall discourse : they are all
intimated in the onely example of Spaine it selfe; which
without the Indies is but a purse without money, or a painted sheath
without a dagger. In summe : it seemeth vnto me, that whereas
the difficultie of performing this enterprise hath bene produced
for a discouragement : it were a dull conceite of strange weakenes
in our selues, to distrust our own power so much, or at least, our
owne hearts and courages; as valewing the Spanish nation to
be omnipotent; or yeelding that the poore Portugal hath that
mastering spirit and conquering industrie, aboue vs : as to bee
able to seate himselfe amongst the many mightie princes of the
East Indies, to frontire China, to holde in subiection The
Phillippians, Zeilan, Calecut, Goa, Ormus, Mozambique, and the
rest; the nauigation being so tedious and full of perill : to suffer
our selues to bee put backe for worthlesse cyphers, out of place,
without account. All which Regions being nowe also by the
late conquest of Portugall, entituled to the Spanish king : to
whom the Colonies of those parts doe yet generally refuse to
sweare fealtie and allegiance : and the care depending on him,
not onely in gouerning them in the East, so farre off; but also of

ordering and strengthening of those disunited, scattered, and ill
guarded empires and prouinces in the West : It might very
well bee alleaged to the sayde Spanish king, that it were more
wisedome for him to assure and fortifie some part of those
already gotten, then to begin the conquest of Guiana, so farre
separate from the rest of his Indies : in which hee hath had so
many misfortunes, and against whom the naturall people are so
impetuously bent, and opposed : were it not, that it exceedeth
all the rest in abundance of gold, and other riches.   The case
then so standing, is it not meere wretchednesse in vs, to spend
our time, breake our sleepe, and waste our braines, in contriuing
a cauilling false title to defraude a neighbour of halfe an acre of
lande : whereas here whole shires of fruitfull rich grounds, lying
now waste for want of people, do prostitute themselues vnto vs,
like a faire and beautifull woman, in the pride and floure of
desired yeeres.

If wee doe but consider, howe vnhappily Berreo his affairs, with
his assistants haue of late yeeres, in our owne knowledge
succeeded : who can say, if the hand of the Almighty be not
against them, and that hee hath a worke in this place, in stead of
Papistrie, to make the sincere light of his Gospell to shine on
this people ? The effecting whereof shall bee a royall crowne of
euerlasting remembrance to all other blessings, that from the
beginning the Lorde hath plentifully powred on our dread
Soueraigne, in an eminent and supreme degree of all perfection.
If the Castilians, pretending a religious care of planting Christianitie in those partes, haue in their doings preached nought els
but auarice, rapine, blood, death, and destruction to those naked,
and sheeplike creatures of God ; erecting statues and trophees
of victorie vnto themselues, in the slaughters of millions of
innocents : doeth not the crie of the poore succourlesse ascend
vnto the heauens ? Hath God forgotten to bee gracious to the
workmanship of his owne hands ? Or shall not his iudgements in
a day of visitation by the ministerie of his chosen Her Maiestie.
seruant, come on these bloodthirstie butchers, like
raine into a fleece of wooll ? Aliquando manifesta ; aliquando
occulta ; semper iusta sunt Dei iudicia.

To leaue this digression, It is fit onely for a prince to begin,
and ende this worke : the maintenance and ordering thereof
requireth soueraigne power, authoritie, and commaundement.
The riuer of Raleana giueth open and free passage, any prouision

that the Spaniards can make to the countrary notwithstanding, (for once yeerely the landes neere the riuer be all drowned) to conuey men, horse, munition, and victuall for any power of men that shall be sent thither.

I doe speake it on my soules health, as the best testimonie, that I can in any cause yeelde to auerre a trueth, that hauing nowe the second time beene in this countrey, and with the helpes of time and leisure well aduised my selfe vpon all circumstances to bee thought on : I can discerne no sufficient impediment to the contrary, but that with a competent number of men, her Maiestie may to her and her successours enioy this rich and great empire : and hauing once planted there, may for euer, (by the fauour of God) holde and keepe it, Contra Iudæos et Gentes. Subiects, I doubt not, may through her Maiesties gracious sufferance, ioyning their strength together, inuade, spoyle, and ouerunne it, returning with golde and great riches. But what good of perpetuitie can follow thereof? . Or who can hope that they will take any other course then such, as tendeth to a priuate and present benefite : considering that an Empire once obteined, is of congruitie, howe, and wheresoeuer the charge shall growe, to bee annexed vnto the crowne? The riches of this place are not fit for any priuate estate : no question they will rather prooue sufficient to crosse and counteruaile the Spaniard his proceedings in all partes of Christendome, where his money maketh way to his ambition.

If the necessitie of following this enterprise doth nothing vrge vs, because in some case better a mischiefe, then an inconuenience : let the conuenience thereof somewhat mooue vs, in respect both of so many Gentlemen, souldiers, and younger brothers, who, if for want of employment they doe not die like cloyed cattell in ranke easefulnesse ; are enforced for maintenance sake, sometimes to take shamefull and vnlawfull courses : and in respect of so many handycraftsmen hauing able bodies, that doe liue in cleannesse of teeth and pouertie. To sacrifice the children of Belial vnto the common weale, is not to defile the lande with blood, because the lawe of God doeth not prohibite it, and the execution of iustice requireth it to bee so : but yet if the waterboughes, that sucke and feede on the iuice, and nourishment that the fruitefull branches should liue by, are to bee cut downe from the tree, and not regarded : luckie and prosperous bee that right hande, that shall plant and possesse a soyle, where they may fructifie, increase and growe to good : thrise honourable and blessed bee the memorie of so charitable a deede, from one generation to another.

To conclude, your lordship hath payd for the discouerie and search, both in your owne person and since by mee. You haue framed it, and moulded it readie for her Maiestie, to set on her seale. If either enuie or ignorance, or other deuise frustrate the rest, the good which shall growe to our enemies, and the losse which will come to her Maiestie and this kingdome, will after a fewe yeeres shewe it selfe. Wee haue more people, more shippes, and better meanes, and yet doe nothing. The Spanish king hath had so sweete a taste of the riches thereof, as notwithstanding that hee is lorde of so many empires and kingdomes already, notwithstanding his enterprises of France and Flanders, notwithstanding that hee attended this yeere a home inuasion : yet hee sent twentie eight saile to Trinidad, whereof tenne were for that place and Guiana, and had some other shippes ready at Cadiz, if the same had not beene by my Lordes her Maiesties Generals and your lordship set on fire.

In one worde ; The time serueth, the like occasion seldome happeneth in many ages, the former repeated considerations doe all ioyntly together importune vs, nowe, or neuer to make our selues rich, our posteritie happy, our Prince euery way stronger then our enemies, and to establish our countrey in a state flourishing and peaceable. O let not then such an indignitie rest on vs, as to depraue so notable an enterprise with false rumours, and vaine suppositions, to sleepe in so serious a matter, and renouncing the honour, strength, wealth, and soueraigntie of so famous a conquest, to leaue all vnto the Spaniard.

A Table of the names of the Riuers, Nations, Townes, and Casiques or Captaines that in this second voyage were discouered.

Riuers.	Nations.	Townes.	Captains.
1 Arowari great.	Arwaos, Paraweas, Charibes.		
2 Iwaripoco very great.	Mapurwanas, Iaos.		
3 Maipari great.	Arricari.		
4 Caipurogh great,	Arricurri.		
5 Arcooa great.	Marowanas, Charibes.		
6 Wiapoco great.	Coonoracki, Wacacoia, Wariseaco.		
7 Wanari.	Charibes.		
8 Capurwacka great.	Charibes.		
9 Cawo great.	Iaos.	Icomana.	Wareo.

1 These are enemies to the Iaos, their money is of white and greene stones. Theyspeake the Tiuitiuas language : so likewise doe the nation of the Arricari, who haue greater store of those moneyes then any others.

2 Here it was as it seemeth, that Vincent Pinçon the Spaniard had his Emeralds. In one of these two riuers certain Frenchmen that suffred shipwrack some 2. or 3. yeres since, doe liue.

3. 4. 5. These with the other two seeme to bee branches of the great riuer of Amazones. When wee first fell with land, wee were, by ye Indians report, but 1. dayes iourney from the greatest riuer, that is on that coast.

6 The first mountaines yt appeare within lande, doe lie on the East side of this riuer. From the mouth thereof, the inhabitants doe passe with their canoas in 20. dayes to the salt lake, where Manaostandeth. The water hath many Cata-

Riuers.	Nations.	Townes.	Captains.
10 Wia great.	Maworia, Charib. Wiaco, Ch.	Parammona, great.	Mashwipo.
11 Caiane g. Gowateri a great iland.	Wiaco. Ch. Shebaios.	Canawi. g. Orinikero.	Parawetteo.
12 Macuria.	Piraos. Ch.		
13 Cawroora.	Arrawacos Charib.		
14 Manmanuri.	Ipaios. Ch.		
15 Cureey.	Shebaios.		
16 Curassiwini.	Shebaios.	Musswara. great.	Ocapanio.
17 Cunanama.	Iaos. Arwaccas.	Waritappi. great.	Carinamari. Curipotoore.
18 Vracco. Moruga.	Arwaccas. Arwaccas.		Marwabo. Eramacoa.
19 Mawari.	Winicinas. Arwaccas.	Iwanama.	Aranacoa.
20 Mawarpai.	Arwaccas.	Awaricana.	Mahaho-nero.

racts like Caroli, but that they are of greater distance one from another: where it falles into the sea, hils do inclose it on both sides.

10 The freshet shoots out into the sea, with great force: the sea doth here sometimes campe high, and breake, as it were full of rocks : but in proofe it is nothing els but the pride and force of the tydes. In this bay, and round about, so far as the mountaines do extend there is great store of Brasill wood, some of it bearing farre darker colour then other some. Here are also many sortes of other good woods.

14 These speake the language of the Indians of Dominica. They are but few, but very cruel to their enemies. For they bind, and eat them aliue peecemeale. This torment is not comparable to the deadly paine that commeth of hurts, or woundes, made by those arrowes that are inuenomed wt the iuice of ye herbe Wapototo. These Indians because they eate them whome they kill, vse no poyson. The sea coast is nowhere populous, for they haue much wasted themselues, in mutuall warres.

Riuers.	Nations.	Townes.	Captains.	
				But now in all parts so farre as Orenoque, they liue in league and peace.
21 Amonna very great. Gapellepo. g.	Charibes.	Iaremappo. very great.		21. Neere the head of this riuer, Capeleppo falleth out of the plaines, and runneth into the Sea with Curitini. Some of the Guianians liue in this riuer.
22 Marawini. g.	Paracuttos.			
23 Owcowi.				
24 Wiawiami.				
25 Aramatappo.				
26 Wiapo.				
27 Macuruma.				
28 Carapi.				
29 Vraca.				
30 Chaimawimini great.	Carepini. Charib.		Caponaiarie.	
31 Ecrowto.	Vpotommas.			
32 Pawro.	Arwaccas.	Maripoma.		
33 Shurinama. g	Carepini. Chari.			
34 Shurama g.	Carepini.	Cupari.		
35 Northumbria or Cupanama very g.	Char. Arwaccas.			
36 Wioma.				
37 Cushwini.	Neekeari.	Tawrooromene.	Neperwari.	
38 Inana. g.	Carepini.	Owaripoori.		
39 Curitini. g.	Arwaccas. Parawianni.	Mawronama.		39. This riuer, as also most of the rest, is not nauigable aboue sixe dayes iourney by reason of rockes. It is tenne dayes iourney to the head, where the Guianians do dwel : hony, yarne or cotton, silke, Balsamum, and Brasil beds are here to bee had in plentie, and so all the coast alongst Eastward. Some images of golde, spleenestones, and others may bee gotten on this coast, but they doe somewhat * extraordinarily esteeme of
40 Winitwari g.		Maiapoore. Cariwacka.		
41 Berbice. g.	Arwaccas.	Aneta. Manacobeece. Eppera. Parawiannos. Lupulee.	Warawaroco.	
42 Wapari.	Shebaios. Arwaccas.	Madewini.	Benmurwagh.	
43 Maicawini.	Panapi. Arwaccas.	Itewee.	Caporaco. great Cap.	
44 Mahawaica.	Arwaccas.	Maburessa g.		
45 Lemerare g.	Wacawaios.	Maburessa g.		
46 * Deuoritia or Dessekebe very g.	Arwaccas. Iaos. Shebaios. Arwaccas.			

---

* Marginal note.--So called after the name of the right honourable the Earle of Essex.

Rivers.	Nations.	Townes.	Captains.
Matorooni.	Charibes.		
Coowini.	Maripai.		
Chipanama.	Wocowaios.		
Arawanna.	Parawianni.		
Itorebece.	Iwarewakeri.	Caiaremappo.	
47 Pawrooma.		Waroopana.	
g.	Iaos.	Maripa.	Macapowa.
Aripacoro.		Chipariparo.	
Ecawini.	Panipi.	Towtwi.	Shuracoima.
Manurawini.		Sarinbugh.	
		Wariwagh.	
48 Moruga. g.	Iaos.	Cooparoore.	Manare-
Piara.	Arwaccas.	g.	cowa.
Chaimera-		Awiapari.	Iarwarema.
goro.		Topoo.	
49 Waini. g.	Charibes.	Tocoopoima. g.	Parana.
50 Barima. g.	Charibes.	Pekwa g.	Anawra.
Caitooma.	Arwaccas.	Arwakima.	Aparwa.
Arooca.			Arracurri.
51 Amacur. g.			
52 Aratoori. g.			
Cawrooma. g.			
Raleana, or			
Orenoque.			
Maipar	⎧ Ilands in		
Ita caponea	⎨ the mouth		
Owarecapa-	of Rale-		
ter.	⎩ ana.		
Waruca-			
nasso.			

The 29. day of Iune we arriued in Portland road, hauing spent fiue moneths in going, staying, and returning.

them, because euery where they are current money. They get their Moone3, and other pieces of gold by exchange, taking for each one of their greater Canoas, one piece or image of golde. with three heades, and after that rate for their lesser Canoas, they receiue pieces of golde of lesse value. One hatchet is the ordinarie price for a Canoa. They haue euery where diuers sorts of drugs, gummes, and rootes, which I doubt not by farther trial, will be found medicinable.

NAMES OF POY-
SONED HEARES.
Ourari.
Carassi.
Apareepo.
Parapara.

HEARBES GOOD
AGAINST POYSON.
Turara.
Cutarapama.
Wapo.
Macatto.

Here follow the names of those worthie Spaniards that haue sought to discouer and conquer Guiana: Extracted out of the writings of Iuan de Castellanos clerigo, who compiled the booke intituled, Primera parte de las Elegias de varones illustres de Indias.

THe enterprise of Guiana was vndertaken by Diego de Ordas of the kingdome of Leon, in the yeere 1531. Hee was one of the captaines of Cortes in the conquest of Mexico.

The riuer of Amana by which Sir Walter Ralegh first entred called by Diego de Ordas Viapari: and by Barth. de Casas Iuia Pari.

This Ordas made his entrance by the riuer of Amana, by which wee entred, and spent fiftie dayes before hee came to the riuer of Orenoque, which we past in fifteene. Hee named the riuer by which hee entred, Viapari ; which name it still retaineth in the Spanish descriptions. It lyeth South from Trinidad some fiue leagues. He transported out of Spaine a thousand souldiers. He dyed afterwards at sea in returning for Spaine.

2. Iuan Cortesso arriued at the riuer of Amazones or Orellana with three hundred men : Hee marched vp into the countrey. But neither hee nor any of his companie did returne againe.

3 Gaspar de Sylua, with his two brothers, departed from Teneriff, accompanied with two hundred men to assist Diego de Ordas. They sought El Dorado by the riuer of Amazones : but staying there a short time, they fell downe to Trinidad, where they all three were buried.

4 Iuan Gonsales set saile from Trinidad to discouer Guiana. He reposed himselfe more on the faith of his guides, then on his small number of men. Hee by triall founde the confines of Guiana, so farre as hee entred, to bee populous, plentifull of victuall, and rich in golde. Vpon such proofes as he brought with him, to make good his report, many others aduentured to follow his steps.

5, 6. Philip de Vren, and after him Pedro de Limpias, who both successively commanded the Almaines, were leaders in this action. Limpias was slaine by an Indian Casique named Porima.

7 Ieronimo de Ortal vndertooke it by the way of Maracapana. After great trauell and his substance all spent, he dyed on the sudden at S. Domingo.

8. 9. Ximenes, brother of Don Ximenes de Quesida the Adelantado, and Pedro de Orsua were both at sundry times in the same conquest.

10 Father Iala, a Frier, taking with him onely one companion, and some Indian guides passed into the prouinces of Guiana. Hee returned with good intelligence, and brought with him Eagles, idols, and other iewels of golde, An. 1560. Hee assayed the second time to pass in like manner, but was slaine by the Indians.

11 Hernandez de Serpa also vndertooke it. The Indians of Cumanawgoto killed him, and defeated his armie.

12 Afterwardes, Diego de Vargas, and his sonne Don Iuan followed this enterprise, and at their first setting out, were slaine by the Indians.

13 Caceres vndertooke this discouery from Nueuo Reyno de Granada. Hee came no neerer to it then Matachines, which borders vpon the sayd kingdome of Granada. Hee rested there and peopled that place.

14 It was also attempted by Alonço de Herera, at two seuerall times. Hee endured great miserie, but neuer entred one league into the countrey. He sought it by Viapari or Amana, and was at last slaine by a nation of Indians called Xaguas.

15 It was also vndertaken by Antonio Sedenno, with whom Herrera and Augustine Delgado ioyned in the conquest of Trinidad, against Bawcunar a famous king of that place. He passed by Maracapana in the yeere 1536 to discouer El Dorado with 500 chosen men. In this iourney hee got much gold, and tooke many Indian prisoners, whom he manacled in yrons ; and many of them dyed as they were led in the way. The Tigers being fleshed on those dead carkeisses, assaulted the Spaniards, who with much trouble hardly defended themselues from them. Sedenno was buried within the precinct of the empire neere the head of the riuer Tinados. Most of his people perished likewise.

16 Augustine Delgado searched the countrey to the Southward of Cumanawgoto with 53. footemen, and three horsemen. The warres that were then betweene the Indians of the vale, and those of the mountaines, serued well for his purpose. By which occasion he found meanes to passe so farre, vntill he came to an Indian Casique, named Garamental, who entertained him with all kindnesse, and gaue him for a present some rich iewels of golde, sixe seemely pages, tenne young slaues, and three nymphes very beautifull, which bare the names of three prouinces from whence they were sent to Garamental chiefe commander of all that countrey. Their names were Guanba, Gotoguane, and Maiarare. These prouinces are of an excellent temperature, very healthfull, and haue an admirable influence in producing faire women. The Spaniards afterwardes to requite the manifold curtesies that they receiued in that countrey, tooke and carried away, besides all the golde that they could get, all the Indians

that they could lay holde on : they conueyed them in yrons to
Cubagua, and sould them for slaues.   Delgado afterwards was
shot in the eye by an Indian : of which hurt he died.

17 Diego de Losada succeeded in his brothers place.   Hee
had many more men ; who in the ende wasted themselues in
mutinies : those that liued returned to Cubagua.

18 Reynoso vndertooke this iourney : but hauing endured exceeding troubles, in the discomfort of his minde, he gaue it ouer,
and was buried in Hispaniola.

19 Pedro de Orsua, in the yeere 1560. sought it with 400.
Spaniards by the riuer of Orellana.   Hee imbarqued his men in
the countrey of the Motijones.   As they passed downe the riuer,
they found Synamon trees.   His men murthered him, and afterward the sayde rebels beheaded lady Anes his wife, who forsooke
not her lord in all his trauels vnto death.

20 Frier Francis Montesino was in the prouince of Maracapana
with 100. souldiers bound for Guiana, when Lopez Aguirri
the tyrant made insurrection in all those parts of the Indies.
What became of this intended iourney is not expressed.

In this discouerie of Guiana, you may reade both of Orellana,
who discouered the riuer of Amazones An. 1542. and of Berreo,
with others that haue trode this maze, and lost themselues in
seeking to finde this countrey.

An aduertisement to the Reader.

IN the Breuiarie, the names onely are comprised of such, as
being led with the generall fame of Guiana, haue endeuoured to
discouer and possesse it.   The whole histories are long and cannot suddenly be translated or englished at large, as we in these
Elegies finde them.   It may perhaps seeme strange and incredible, that so many caualleros should all faile in this one
attempt, since in many parts of the Indies, far smaller numbers
in shorter time haue performed as great matters, and subdued
mighty kingdomes : I haue therefore thought it good here to
alleage those reasons, which by circumstance may bee gathered
to haue beene chiefe impediments to the Spaniard in this intended
search and conquest.

The first may bee the remotenesse or distance of their places
of Rendeuous, from El Dorado : which appeare to be foure,

Nueuo reyno, the mouth of Amazones or Orellana, Cubagua or the coast of the Caracas, and Trinidad.

1 From Moiobamba, where Orellana hath his head-spring, to his mouth, the Spaniards account it 2000. leagues. Raleana riseth neere the said mountaines in Moiobamba, and tributeth his waters to the sea, not farre from the other : Guiana is enuironed with these 2 freshwaterseas, where their distance is greatest from their risings, and is besides guarded with impassable mountaines which inclose and defend it on all parts, excepting Topiawaries countrey. It is no maruel then, if the vigor, heart, and life of those Spaniards, who sought it from Nueuo Reyno, were allayed and spent, before they came neere to it, in those long, desolate and vncomfortable wayes.

2 From Cubagua to seeke it by sea in vessels of any burthen, is a worke of far greater labour, then to saile directly from Spaine. And to passe ouer land is a matter of great diffi-cultie, by reason that the Indian nations inhabiting betweene the coast of The Caracas and Guiana, being wearied and harried with the daily incursions of the Spaniards, haue now turned their abused patience into furie, refusing to suffer any forces of men to be led through their countreys. For the Spaniards trauelling in those parts, when they found not gold answer-able to their expectation, ouerlaid them with cruelties, tyrannie, and thraldome : forbearing neither men, women, friends, nor foes. Which maner of dealing, though in some part it satisfied their desire of present profit ; yet hath it otherwise done them much harmè, in hardening and driuing those nations to desperate resolutions.

3 From the mouth of Orellana to seeke entrance with any number of men, and to bore a hole through the mountaines is all one. Neither finde wee, that any seeking it that way, haue at any time boasted of their gaines or pleasurable iourneys.

4 From Trinidad, as the course is shortest, so doeth it promise best likelyhood of successe. Howbeit, impossible it is with any vessell of ordinarie burthen by that way to recouer the riuer of Raleana.

The second, The Spaniards haue bene so farre from helping and furthering one another, or admitting partners or coadiutors in the Guiana-cause, that amongst so many attemptes, from the beginning to the last, I cannot find any one, when they were otherwise likeliest to preuaile, free from discords, mutinies, and cruell murthers amongst themselues.

A 2

Thirdly, The Spaniards in this place haue mist that aduantage, which elsewhere hath steeded themselues in all their conquestes: namely, the dissentions and mutuall warres of the Indians. Which of what force it is, may be gathered by the example of Arauco in Chili. For the Indians of that one prouince conteining in circuit not aboue 20 leagues, haue maintained warres aboue these 30. yeeres against all the Spaniards, and in despight of them haue kept their owne countrey, oftentimes discomfiting their enemies in many set battels, burning and destroying some of their strongest townes. The chiefe reason whereof I take to bee, because no Indian nation was enemie vnto them. And howsoeuer the Spaniards vaunt of their redoubted exploits in the Indies : yet doe their owne writings in effect testifie, that without the ayde of the Indians diuided among themselues, Mexico, Peru, and the rest, had neuer beene Spanish.

Lastly, I can impute it to no cause so rightly, as immediatly to the diuine prouidence : for by him princes raigne. And in my beleefe (except we will look to be warned by miracle from heauen) wee need no further assurances, then we already haue to perswade our selues, that it hath pleased God of his infinite goodnesse, in his will and purpose to appoint and reserue this empire for vs.

The thirde voyage set forth by Sir Walter Ralegh to Guiana, with a pinnesse called The Watte, in the yeere 1596. Written by M. Thomas Masham a gentleman of the companie.

VPon Thursday the 14. of October 1596, we set saile from Limehouse vpon the riuer of Thames, and through much contrarietie of winds and other accidents, we made it the 27. of December, before we could get out of Waimouth. The 25. of Ianuarie in the morning we came to the North side of the Island of Grand Canaria, where we hoped to haue gotten a boate to serue vs vpon the coast of Guiana, but the winde was so great that we could not lanch our shalope : so we past along by the roade and the towne, and at length saw a boate lying on shoare, which being too bigge for vs, wee ripped vp, and wooded our selues with her. That day wee descryed a saile, which at length wee found to be a flieboate of Dartmouth, of 200. tunnes, bound to the Island of Mayo for salte. Wee fell in consort with her, and that night stoode for the Southermost part of the Island there to water, where wee stayed all the next day, and watered at the Southsouthwest part thereof. That night wee weyed and stoode away together Southsoutheast, and South and by East, purposing by their perswasion to goe for the riuer Doro. The 28. of Ianuarie wee made the furthermost part of Barbarie ; and this morning we met with ·M. Beniamin Wood with his fleete of 3 sailes bound for the straights of Magellan and China, to wit, The Beare, The Whelpe, and The Beniamin : who told vs that there was no good to be done in the riuer Doro. Whereupon we stood along with them for Cape Blanco, vnto which we came vpon Sunday night next following. And vpon Munday morning the first of Februarie, we saw two ships in a sandie bay : so we stirred in with them, which were Frenchmen bound for the West Indies, and put all into the bay, where wee refreshed our selues with fish, in which there was infinite store, and stayed there vntill Thursday the 5. at which time wee stood vp with the Cape againe, where rode the Frenchman and his pinnesse, who put foorth right afore vs, and another Frenchman and his carauel well manned : So all we 5. English came to an anker by them, where after kinde greeting with many shots out of euery ship both English and French, all our captaines were inuited to a feast aboord the French admirall : where after great cheere and kinde entertainment, it was concluded on all handes to take the Isle of Fogo, if God would giue vs leaue.

(margin note: M. Beniamin Wood bound for The South Sea.*)*

The same day we all weyed and stoode along for the Isle of Sal, vnto which we came the 8. of Februarie, and ankered altogether at a bay in the West part thereof : in which Island wee had good store of goates and fresh fish. There is no man dwelling vpon the Island that we could see. Wee could finde no fresh water vpon it, but one standing puddle of bad water : it hath foure great mountaines, vpon the 4. corners of it. Here the Frenchmen (as it seemeth being ouercome with drinke, hauing bene aboord our Generall at a feast) being on shoare, one of the gentlemen of their companie was slaine, and their chiefe captaine sorely wounded : by reason whereof, and of the setting together of a pinnesse which they were about, the French admiral and the carauel stayed behind. So wee in the Watte, and the other 6. ships weyed the 10. of Februarie, and stood away for the isle of Maio. This night the other two French shippes that came from

Sal with vs (as it seemeth of purpose, because their ccnsorts were not with them) lost vs. The next morning wee sawe Maio. So wee and the flieboate of Dartmouth compassed the Northermost part of the Island, and master Beniamin Wood in the China-fleete, the Southermost, and came all to an anker together
36 sailes of at the Southwest part thereof : where rode sixe sayles **Flemmings at** of Flemmings lading salte; who had brought their **Maio for salt.** horses and cartes, and wheele-barrowes, and plankes for their barrowes to runne vpon. Here is abundance of salte in this Island made by Gods hande without mans labour. These tolde vs that there were thirtie sayles more, which fell to leeward of Fogo, who, as I heard since, beat it vp with much adoe, and came thither also for salte. This trade may bee very beneficiall to England, considering the dearnesse of salte. Of goates on this Island there is such store, as is incredible, but to those that haue seene them : and it is a wonder howe they liue one by the other, the ground being stonie and barren. It is thought that there are dwelling in it some twentie Mountainiers, which got one of the Flemmings men stragling, and God knoweth what they did with him : for they sawe him no more. This Island is somewhat lowe and round, hauing no great mountaines vpon it.

Here ended our determination concerning the inuading of Fogo. And here wee left the flieboat of Dartmouth lading salte, and the China-fleete to refresh themselues with goates, who as I haue heard since had at the village (from whence the Mountainiers were fledde into the furthest partes of the Island and rocks) great store of dryed goates which they carried along with them : which were like to bee a great helpe vnto them in their long voyage. So vpon Saturday the 12 of Februarie at night wee set sayle and stood for the coast of Wiana, which wee were bound for.

Vpon Sunday the twentieth of Februarie wee came into the maine current that setteth from the Cape of Buena Esperança, along the coast of Brasil, and so toward the West Indies, for the most part setting away Northwest.

The Tuesday night following, whereas before our course was Westsouthwest, wee stoode away West and by South : by reason whereof, and of the current that set vs to the Northward, wee were the next day by noone twentie minutes further to the Northward then the day before. So that then we lay away Southwest, because wee were loath to fall to the Northward of our place intended : which if wee should bee put to leeward of, there was small hope left to recouer it.

By Thursday wee were within one degree $\frac{1}{2}$ of the Equinoctiall line : therefore this day wee halled away West and by South, and West among. This night wee sounded, but had no ground at 90 fathoms.

The next day in the morning the colour of the water began to change, and to bee more white, so wee made another sound and had ground at thirtie fathoms, but saw no lande, and in the afternoone wee halled away Westnorthwest, Northwest, and Northnorthwest. In the night wee sounded diuers times, and had twelue, ten, and nine fathoms water.

All Saturday we had a thick red water, and had seuen and eight fathoms both day and night, and vpon Sunday morning by day being the seuen and twentieth of Februarie, wee made the lande which appeared lowe, and trended neerest as wee fell with it, South and by East, North and by West about two degrees $\frac{1}{2}$ toward the North. Right on head of vs was a Cape or head land so that had wee beene shot a little further into the bay, the winde being more Northerly, wee should hardly haue doubled it off. For with much adoe making many boords, and stooping euery tyde, it was the Tuesday following before we cleered our selues of the bay, and recouered the Cape. Nowe the land trended Northwest and by North, and Southeast and by South. And still wee were faine to anker euery tyde sometimes in foure fathoms, and sometimes in three, as farre as wee could Cape Cecil see land. So about night we sawe Cape Cecill : and in 3 degrees after some two houres came to an anker. Betweene and a halfe. these two Capes the lande lyeth lowe and euen.

Vpon Wednesday morning, hauing the winde large at Eastnortheast, wee layd it away vpon a board into the bay of Wiapoucou and came to an anker in the riuers mouth in two fathoms : ouer the barre there is little water, as 6 and 7 foote and lesse in many places. And this riuer of Wiapoucou standeth almost in 4 degrees to the Northward of the line.

The next morning wee weyed, and standing in with our pinnesse by night, wee got some eight leagues vp the riuer. This day sometimes wee had but 5 foote water and drew 7 foot, but being soft oaze we went cleere : and a little before wee came to anker wee were on ground vpon a rocke, but with some trouble and labour wee got off and had no hurt.

Vpon Friday the 4 of March towards night wee came to the falles. The next day M. Leonard Berrie our captaine, the Master, my selfe and some 5 more, went through the woods, and spent all the day in searching the head of the falles, but could not finde it: for though wee passed by many, yet were there more still one aboue the other. So that finding no Indians in this riuer to buy victuals of, neither any kind of thing that might intice vs to come to so short allowance, as wee must haue done, if wee had spent any long time here, finding it ouer hard to passe the falles, wee fell downe the riuer againe, and by Friday the 11 of March wee cleered our selues of the riuer and bay. This riuer from the mouth to the falles is some 16. leagues, in many places a mile ouer, but for the most part halfe a mile. There are many Islands in it: as are also in most of the riuers vpon the coast. This night wee ankered against Cawo in two fathoms; whereinto wee thought to haue put with our pinnesse: but found the water so shoald, and the sea so growen, that neither with our shippe nor shallope wee durst goe in.

The 7 Ilands.   On Saturday by noone wee came to anker vnder one of tne 7. Islands: vpon which going on shoare wee found neither man nor beast, but great store of yellow plumbes which are good to eate.

Vpon Sunday after dinner our Master William Dowle and 6 more went off with our boat to a towne called Aramatto; where they found many inhabitants, and brought victuals and some Tobacco with them, and one Indian named Caprima, who lying aboord all night, the next day being Munday the 14 of March went with our Captaine into Wias, and there traded with the Caribes for such things as they had. And afterward they of Aramatto came off with their canoas to vs, and wee went on shoare to them: and from thence our Captaine sent a canoa with seuen men, which had euery one of them a knife to goe backe to the riuer of Cawo, and to tell Ritimo captaine of that place, that because wee coulde not come to him, wee would stay at Chiana for him, whither wee intreated him to come to vs. So vpon Thursday the 17 wee stoode in for Chiana, and came to an anker without in the bay in 3 fathoms that night: and had the Caribes comming continually to vs with their canoas, which brought vs great store of victuals and some Tabacco, shewing themselues

Marginal notes:
Aramatto a great towne.

The Caribes of Wias tractable people.

Chiana a riuer and bay.

very kinde and louing, and came all from their townes, and dwelt on shoare by vs vntill Ritimo came : at whose comming they returned all vp to their townes againe, which was vpon the Sunday following. All this day we feasted him and his traine, and the next day we traffiqued with them for such things as they brought, which was principally tabacco.

After that they had made knowen their mindes of the desire that they had to haue the English come and kill the Spaniards, and to dwell in Orenoque and in the countrey, they departed with their 3 canoas the next day. And wee with the helpe of the Caribes of Chiana, hauing by their meanes from the shoare watered, because the riuers mouth was salte, departed out of the bay the Thursday following, and passing by Macerea, Couroura, and Manamanora, by reason of shoalds, rockes, and great windes, beeing a lee shoare ; and for want of a good shalope, wee came to an anker the next day being good Friday in five fathoms neere The Triangle Islands called The Careres. And vpon Saturday standing to the Westward, wee stopped against the towne of Maware, which is a little to the Westward of the towne Comanamo : from whence and from the other townes in that bay, which are some 6 or 7, wee had canoas come off to vs as before with such things as they had themselues in vse, with parrots, monkeys, and cotton-wooll, and flaxe. From whence wee departed vpon Munday following the 28 of March 1597.

And passing by the riuers of Euracco and Amano, which openeth but a small riuer, and is shoald off, Marawinne a a riuer. wee came to Marawinne the next day : And finding a chanell of three, foure, and fiue fathoms, wee stood into the riuer: and the same day came to an anker some 2 leagues in against the mouth of Cooshepwinne, which riuer goeth into Amana. Into which, (vnderstanding that there were Arwaccawes dwelling) this night we sent our boat and came to a towne called Marrac one league in : And finding the people something pleasant, hauing drunke much that day, being as it seemed a festiuall day with them, yet were they very fearefull and ready to run away at the first sight of vs, hauing seldome seene any Christian before. But assoone as Henry our Indian interpreter had tolde them what wee were, and our intent, they came to vs and vsed vs kindely, and brought vs victuals and other things. And the next day their captaine Mawewiron came out into Marawinne, with diuers canoas, and traded with vs, and wee went in againe to them on shore, who made very much of vs, and carried vs from house to house, and made vs eate and drinke in euery house which wee came in.   And the next day following being the last of March, hauing the captaine of Marrack with vs, wee weyed and stoode into the riuer, and about two of the clocke in the afternoone came to an anker some eight leagues within the riuer, a little short of a towne called Quiparia, the people whereof are Caribes : who, when they sawe vs come toward their towne with our boate, began all to runne into the woods, vntill the captaine of Marrac which was with vs in the boate, leaped ouer-boord and swamme on shoare vnto them, and told them that wee were Englishmen, and came in friendship to trade with them.

Vpon whose report they came before night sixe or seuen canoas aboord vs, yet very fearfull, because there was neuer either shippe or Christian seene in that riuer before.   The first of Aprill, wee weighed againe, and stood in to the next towne called Macirria : where comming to anker, there came a canoa from Amana to vs, with great store of victuals, which canoa wee bought : and because wee mette with some sholds, we were loath to goe any farther with our Pinnesse : so there wee mored her, and the next day at three of the clocke in the afternoone, eleuen of vs (Master Monax hauing the gouernment of the action, by the Captaines appointment) with Mawerirou, Henry, and William of Cawo, in the canoa which we bought, went into the riuer farther to search it so farre as wee .could, and that night gatte some fiue leagues from our shippe. And betweene two villages, Awodwaier and Ma-peributto, we tooke vp our lodging in the woods.   The third of Aprill, betimes in the morning, we tooke our course still vnto the riuer, and in the afternoone came to one house where wee found many Indians, where wee hired another canoa and foure Indians, into the which I went, and one more of our men, and this night gat twelue leagues farther, and as before, lodged among the wilde beastes.

On Munday the fourth of Aprill, wee came to the falles of this riuer about two in the afternoone : and hauing shotte vp some of the rockes, wee went on shore vpon an island, and there con-ferred of our farther proceeding.   And inquiring of the Indians that wee hired for our Pilots of the last house, whether the falles were passable or not : their first answere was, that they had nothing to eate : but wee being loath to loose so much labour, and the sight of that vpper rich countrey, A rich . countrey. which wee desired, told them that they should haue victuals of vs (though God knoweth wee had none for our selues) who seeing vs so importunate, sayde farther, that the rockes would kill the canaos : which they sayde because indeed they had no victuals : which by some was taken for sufficient to proceede no farther, and so wee left off, and onely stayed some two houres vpon the island, and with the swiftnesse of the current, fell that night downe 10 leagues againe. Though I for mine owne part offered in that small canoa that I was in, being so leake, that my selfe did nothing but laue out the water, to lead them the way, and if they sawe any danger to mee, they might chuse whether they would come into it or not themselues.

For seeing the countrey aboue was rich as wee were informed, that their bowes were handled with golde, (being men of an extraordinarie stature for talnes) wee should haue taken the more paines, and haue fared the harder, vntill wee had gotten vp in the countrey which wee sawe with our eyes : for though wee had not victuals in any sort to cary vs vp, yet the woods doe yeld fruites and the palmito trees afforde meate, whereby wee might haue made shift to liue, vntill wee had come to the inhabitants, by whome we might both bee refreshed with victuals, and also haue reaped that, which might haue done vs good as long as wee had liued.

But to returne to the rest of our voyage : the day after wee went from the falles wee came to our shippe, which was the fifth of Aprill 1597. On Wednesday wee fell with our Pin-nesse to Quiparia againe : where we brought her on Pitch to trim shippes. ground right before the town, and trimmed her with the pitch of the countrey : and vntill wee had done, kept a corps du guard, night and day on shore, which was vpon Saturday follow-ing the ninth of Aprill. All the while we were there we had an house of the Caribes, and were kindely vsed of them, and had victuals, and euery thing we needed of them.

And so taking our leaue on Tuesday being the twelfth of Aprill, wee came to the mouth of Cusse-winne, where the The riuer of Cusse-winne. Arwaccas of Marrac and of the riuer had prouided and brought to vs such infinite store of potatoes, and Guiney-wheate, that the stewarde sayd wee had no stowage for them ; and so they were turned backe, and wee by that meanes came to shorter allowance home ward bound, then (if there had bene any good care) wee needed to haue done.

On Fryday the fifteenth of Aprill, wee put foorth of Marawinne, which is some foure leagues ouer, and within one league and an halfe for the most part broad ; full of islands, and diuers small riuers running into it : and it is betweene forty and fifty leagues, from the mouth to the falles, and lyeth for the most part South Southwest vp, altering some 3 poynts, being almost streight. And standing along to the Westward, this night we tryed with our mayne coarse and bonnet.   On Saturday night we came to an anker, in three fathomes against Sewramo.   On Sunday morning we thought to haue gone into Cuppanamo : but sending off our boat and finding vncertaine sounding, sometime 3 fathomes and presently 9 foote, we stood along to Coritine and came into it vpon the Munday being the 18 of Aprill : and the next night wee came to anker against Warrawalle in 10 fathoms.   On Wednesday the Indians of the towne hauing hunted a Doe, shee tooke soyle and came neer our ship, and putting off with our boat we tooke her, being like vnto our deere in England, not altogether so fat, but very good flesh and great bodied.   In this riuer we met a Barke called the Iohn of London captaine Leigh being in her.   And being both fallen downe within some fiue leagues of the mouth of the riuer, vpon intelligence that one Marracon, (whom wee brought along with vs) gaue vs, namely that the riuer Desekebe, in which he dwelt (and wherein there were some three hundred Spaniards, which for the most part now are destroyed and dead) doeth lead so farre into the countrey, that it commeth within a dayes iourney of the lake called Perima, whereupon Manoa is supposed to stand ; and that this riuer of Coritine doeth meete with Desekebe vp in the land : by meanes whereof wee make account to goe vp into the countrey, and to haue discouered a passage vnto that rich citie.   So hauing concluded both shippes, we stood vp into the riuer againe, and comming to Warawalle the 24 of Aprill there our shippes roade vntill we went vp to Mawranamo to speake with Marracon, to know the trueth of these things : whom when we had found, he verified al that before he had spoken : Master Monax being the man that of Leonard of Cawe tooke all the intelligence : who being brought vp with Antonie Berreo could speake some Spanish and Marracons language also.   And besides wee our selues by signes, and drawing the two riuers on the ground, and the meeting of them aloft, did perceiue as much.   Now comming

(Marginal notes:)
Coritine riuer.

The great lake Perima.

downe with our boates the sixe and twentieth of April we went vp with our ships to Mawranamo, where we morred them, and taking some twentie out of both, vpon Thursday the eight and twentieth in They bring their shippes vp to the Mawranamo.
the afternoone with two shallops and two Canoas, in one of which Henry the Indian was and some twentie Indians more, wee went vp the river; and by night getting some three leagues farther wee lodged in the woods, and the next morning wee with our boate and the two Canoas went into a small riuer called Tapuere, to a towne called Macharibi, thinking to haue had Casaui and other victuals, which they were altogether vnprouided of, by reason that they make no more ready then serueth themselues from hand to mouth, liuing in this towne for the most part by fish. By meanes of going into this riuer, though wee rowed very hard it was noone before we ouertooke the bigger shallop wherein both the Captaines were. This night we came to a towne called Vaperon, where wee stayed all Saturday and the night following, for Casaui: whereof they baked good store for vs being but a fewe left in the towne. For not a moneth before wee came thither, the Waccawaes that dwell aboue the falles came downe to the towne, and slewe some tenne of them, and many of the rest fled away, so that wee found most of the houses emptie. Vpon Sunday morning being May day, wee went from this place, and by night gotte some twelue leagues beyond and being past all townes wee lodged as before in the woods, and the next day came to the falles of the riuer: vp some of which falles we shotte with our boates, and going vpon a rocke there came some nine canoas up the riuer to vs, and would haue gone vp with vs to kill the Waccawayans, because they had killed some of them, as before is said. Whereupon the Captaines and Master Monax tooke aduise: and because nowe they had learned, as they sayde, that fiue dayes iourney farther there was a fall not passable, and that by this meanes they should make the Wacchawayans their enemies, which would turne to our great hurt, when Sir Walter Ralegh should come thither, hauing occasion to vse this riuer, where wee were informed was good store of golde, they resolued to returne, though I yeelded diuers reasons to the contrary. So vpon Tuesday night, we came backe to Vaperon, where we lodged.

And vpon Wednesday the fourth of May, wee came to our shippes: where it was reported that the Spaniardes were gonne

out of Desekebe, which was not so : but as it seemed in policie
by them giuen out to make our men that wee left in our shippes
more careless, that they might the easier haue surprised them in
our absence. The next night we had newes brought vs to
Mawranamo, where we yet roade, that there were tenne canoas
of Spaniardes in the mouth of Coritine ; and fearing lest they
had intended to come to vs in the night, we fitted all our gunnes
and muskets, and kept good watch to preuent them of their
purpose ; who, as it was afterwards tolde vs, went along the coast
to buy bread and other victuals for them in Orenoque, Marowgo,
and Desekebe. Vpon Fryday the sixth of May we weighed and
made downe the riuer, and vpon Sunday the eight we gat cleare
of it.

This riuer is much like vnto Marawynne in bredth, and about
fiftie leagues from the mouth to the first falles full of Islandes as
the other : in which three riuers, Mano, Tapuere, and Tabuebbi,
otherwise Tapuellibi : with sixe Townes, Warrawalle, Mawranamo,
Maapuere, Maccharibi, Yohoron, and Vapéron. And so clering
our selues of this coast, wee tooke our course to the Islands of
the West Indies.

Now I thinke it not amisse to speak something of this countrey.
And first touching the climate ; though it stand within the
Tropick, and something neere to the Equinoctiall, so that the
Sunne is twise a yeere ouer their heads and neuer far from them,
yet is it temperate ynough in those partes. For besides that
wee lost not a man vpon the coast, one that was sicke before
hee came there, was nothing sicker for being there, but came
home safe, thanks be to God. And for mine owne part, I was
neuer better in body in all my life, and in like sort fared it with
the rest of the company ; for indeed it is not so extreame hote as
many imagine. The people in all the lower parts of the countrey
goe naked, both men and women, being of seuerall languages,
very tractable, and ingenious, and very louing and kinde to
Englishmen generally ; as by experience we found, and vpon our
owne knowledge doe report. In the vpper countreys they goe
Great store apparelled, being, as it seemeth, of a more ciuill dis-
of golde in position, hauing great store of golde, as we are
Wiana. certeinely informed by the lower Indians, of whom
we had some golde, which they brought and bought in the high
countrey of Wiana, being able to buy no more, because they
wanted the things which now wee haue left among them. They

keepe no order of marriage : but haue as many wiues as they can buy, or win by force of their enemies, which principally is the cause of all their warres. For bread there is infinite store of casaui, which is as good bread as a man need to eate, and better then we can cary any thither. We spent not a bit of our owne all the while we were vpon the coast. It is made of a root so called ; which they take and scrape, and crush all the iuyce out, being poison ; and when it is drie it is as fine floure as our white meale maketh : which drie as it is, without any moisture, they strew vpon a round stone, hauing a still fire vnder it, and so it congealeth to a cake ; and when it commeth new off, it eateth like to our new white bread. Besides there is great store of Guiny-Wheat (whereof they make passing good Passing good drinke) which after it is once sowed, if you cut off drinke made the eare, on the same stalke groweth another. of maiz.

For victuals, wee either did not, or at least needed not to haue spent any of our owne : for there is great store of as good fish in the riuers, as any is in the world. Great store of fowle, of diuers sorts. Tortoise-flesh plentifull, and Tortoise egges innumerable. Deere, swine, conies, hares, cockes and hennes, with potatoes more then wee could spend. Besides, all kinde of fruits, at all times of the yeere : and the rarest fruits of the world, the pine, the plantan, with infinite other variable and pleasant, growing to their handes, The commo- without planting or dressing. For commodities, dities of though wee had but small time to search, because Wiana. wee spent so much time in searching the riuers : yet wee haue brought examples of some, which the countrey yeeldeth in great plenty : as a kinde of long hempe like vnto steele hempe, fine cotton wooll, which the trees yeeld great store of; and where- with the women make a fine threed, which will make excellent good fustians or stockings. Great store of pitch, diuers sorts of sweet gummes, and West Indian pepper, balsamum, parrots and monkies. Besides diuers other commodities, which in good time may be found out to the benefit of our countrey, and profit of the aduenturers, who as yet hauing ventured much, haue gained litle.

Now leauing the riuer of Coritine, passing by Saint Vincent, Santa Lucia, and Matalina, we came to Dominica vpon the Friday following, being the thirteenth of May, hauing lost the barke that came out with vs the Wednesday before. Vpon

They lost cap-
taine Leigh
in yᵉ Iohn of
London.
Sunday morning, the fifteenth of May, we came to Guadalupe, where wee watered at the souther part of the Island, and hauing done by night, we set saile, and stood away to the Nòrthward, but were becalmed all night, and vntill tenne of the clocke on Munday night: at which time hauing a faire gale at East, and after at Southeast, wee passed along in the sight of Monserate, Antigua, and Barbuda. Vpon the ninth of Iune, being Thursday, we made the Islands of Flores and Coruo: and the eight and twentieth of Iune we made the Lisart, and that night came all safe to Plymmouth, blessed be God.

Betweene the Isle of Barbuda in the West Indies and England we had three mighty stormes, many calmes, and some contrary windes. And vpon the foureteenth of Iune 1597, there being diuers whales playing about our pinnesse, one of them crossed our stemme, and going vnder, rubbed her backe against our keele : but by none of all these we susteined any losse. Thanks be to him that gouerneth all things.

Written by Master
Thomas Masham.

CERTAINE BRIEFE TESTIMONIES

CONCERNING THE MIGHTIE RIUER OF AMAZONES OR ORELLANA, AND OF THE MOST WONDERFULL DOWNEFALL OR CATARACT OF WATERS AT THE HEAD THEREOF, NAMED BY THE SPANIARDS EL PONGO : TOGETHER WITH SOME MENTION OF THE RICH AND STATELY EMPIRE OF DORADO, CALLED BY SIR WALTER RALEIGH AND THE NATURAL INHABITANTS GUIANA, AND OF THE GOLDEN COUNTREY OF PAYTITY NEERE ADIOINING, WITH OTHER MEMORABLE MATTERS : TAKEN OUT OF IOSEPHUS DE ACOSTA* HIS NATURALL AND MORALL HISTORIE OF THE WEST INDIES.

The first Testimonie out of Iosephus de Acosta, lib. 2. cap. 6.

BVt when we intreat of Riuers, that which some men call the riuer of Amazones, others Marannon, others the riuer of Orellana,

*Born *circa* 1540. Died in 1600. He was Provincial of the Jesuits of Peru. His principal works are : *History of the Indies* (here quoted), Seville 1590, 4to. ;—and *De Christo revelato*, Rome 1590. 4to.

doeth iustly put to silence all the rest, whereunto our Spaniards haue gone and sayled. And I stand in doubt, whether I may cal it a riuer or a sea. This riuer runneth from the mountaines of Piru, from which it gathereth infinite store of waters, of raine, and riuers, which runneth along, gathering it selfe together, and passing through the great fieldes and plaines of Paytiti, of Dorado, and of the Amazones, and falleth at length into the Ocean sea, and entreth into it almost ouer against the Isles of Margarita and Trinidad. But it groweth so broad, especially towardes the mouth, that it maketh in the middest many and great Isles : and that which seemeth incredible, sayling in the middle chanel of the riuer, men can see nothing but the skie and the riuer, although men say that there are hilles neere the bankes thereof, which can not be kenned, through the greatnesse of the Riuer. Wee vnderstood by very good meanes the wonderfull bredth and largenesse of this Riuer, which iustly may bee called the Emperour of Riuers, to wit by a brother of our companie, which being a boy was there, and sayled it wholy through, being personally present in all the successes of that strange enterance, which Pedro de Orsua made, and in the mutinies and perilous conspiracies of that wicked Diego de Aguirre, out of all which troubles and dangers the Lord deliuered him, to make him one of our societie.

The second Testimonie out of Iosephus de Acosta, lib. 3. cap. 20.

AMong all the riuers not onely of the West Indies but also of the whole world, the chief is the Riuer of Marannon or of the Amazones, whereof I haue spoken in the second booke. The Spaniards haue diuers times sayled along this riuer, with determin-ation to discouer countries, which according to report, are of great riches, especially that which they call Dorado, and Paytiti. The Adelantado or admirall Iuan de Salians made a very notable entrance, although to small profite. It hath a salt or fall of water which they call El Pongo, which is one of the most dangerous places in the world : for being restrained betweene two exceeding hie diuided mountaines, it maketh a fall of terrible depth, where the water with the great descent maketh such whirlepooles that it seemeth impossible but that it should sink it self there into the ground. For all this the boldnes of men hath attempted to passe the said El Pongo for the greedines to come to that so famous renowmed Dorado. They suffered themselues to bee caryed from aloft, being throwne downe headlong with the furie of the riuer, and sitting fast in their Canoas or boats in which they sayled, although they were ouer-turned in the fal, and they and their Canoas suncke downe to the bottome, yet they rose vp againe aboue the water, and at length with their hands and force gat out of the whirlepooles. The whole army in a maner escaped, sauing a very fewe which were drowned : and which I most maruel at, they handled the matter so well, that they lost not their victuals and powder which they caryed with them. In their returne (for after great trauels and dangers they returned that way againe) they clymed vp ouer one of those aforesaide exceeding high mountaines, creeping vp vpon their hands and feete.

Captaine Pedro de Orsua made another enterance by the selfe same riuer, and after hee was slaine by a mutinie of his people, other captaines followed the discouerie, by the arme that falleth into the North Sea. One of our companie told me (who while he was a secular man was in al that expedition) that they entred vp the Riuer almost an hundred leagues with the tydes, and that when the fresh water and the salt meeteth, which is either almost vnder or very neere the Equinoctial line, the riuer is 70 leagues broad, a thing incredible, and which exceedeth the bredth of the Mediterran sea. Howbeit other in their descriptions make it not past 25 or 30 leagues broad at the mouth.

The Third Testimonie out of Iosephus de Acosta, lib. 3. cap. 25.

IN that part of America, whereof the coasts be thoroughly known, the greater part of the Inland is not knowen, which is that which falleth betweene Piru and Brasil, and there are diuers opinions of some, which say, that it is all sunken land full of lakes and bogges, and of others, which affirme that there are great and florishing kingdomes there, and there they place the Countrey of Paytity, and Dorado, and great Emperours, and say, that there are wonderfull things there. I heard of one of our companie my selfe, a man of credite, that hee had seene great townes, and high wayes as broad and as much beaten, as the wayes betweene Salamanca and Validolid : and this was when the great entrance or discouerie was made by the great riuer of the Amazones or Marannon by Pedro de Orsua, and afterwardes by others that succeeded him : and they supposing that Dorado which they sought, was farther vp in the countrey, did not inhabite there, and afterward returned without discouering Dorado (which they neuer found) and without that great prouince which they left.

~~~~~~~~~~~~~~~~~~~

A short description of the riuer of Marannon or Amazones, and the Countries thereabout, as also of the sea of Freshwater, taken out of an ancient discourse of all the Portes, Creekes, and Hauens of the West Indies, Written by Martin Fernandez de Enciça, and dedicated to Charles the Emperour, Anno 1518.

MArannon lyeth in seuen degrees and a halfe Northward of the Equinoctial, it is a great riuer, and hath more then fifteene leagues in bredth eight leagues within the land. It hath many islands, and in this riuer within the land fortie leagues there is neere to the sayde riuer a mountaine, whereupon growe trees of Incense, the trees be of a good height, and the boughs thereof be like to Plumtrees, and the Incense doeth hang at them, as the yce doeth at the tiles of a house in the winter season when it doeth freeze. In this riuer were taken foure Indians in a smal boat, called in the Indian language a Canoa, that came downe by the riuer, and there were taken from them two stones of Emeralds, the one of them being as great as a mans hand. They sayd that so many dayes iourney going vpward by the riuer, they found a rocke of that stone. Likewise there were taken from them two loaues made of floure, which were like to cakes of Sope, and it seemed that they were kneaded with the licour of Balsamum. All this coast from the Cape of S. Austine vnto Marannon is a cleare coast and deep, but neere to the riuer are certaine sholds towardes the East part. And by the West part the riuer is deepe,

and it hath a good entrie.   From this riuer Marannon, vnto the
riuer which is called The sea of fresh water, are 25 leagues : this
riuer hath 40 leagues of bredth at the mouth, and carieth such
abundance of water that it entreth more then 20 leagues into the
Sea, and mingleth not it selfe with the salt water : this bredth
goeth 25 leagues within the land, and after it is diuided into
partes, the one going toward the Southeast, and the other
towards the Southwest. . That which goeth towards the Southeast
is very deepe and of much water, and hath a channel half a
league of bredth, that a Carack may goe vp through it : and the
tydes be so swift, that the ships haue need of good cables.   The
riuer of this port is very good, and there haue bene some that
haue entred 50 leagues within it, and haue seene no mountaines.
The Indians of this countrey haue their lips made full of small
holes in 4 parts, and through those holes be put small rings, and
likewise at their eares : and if any man ask of them where they
had their gold, they answer, that going vp by the riuer so many
dayes iourney, they found certaine mountaines that had much of
it, and from those mountaines they brought it when they would
haue it, but they made no great account of it, for they
neither buy nor sell, and amongst them is nothing but change.
In this countrey they eate bread of rootes, and Maiz, and they
eate certaine rootes which they call Aies and Batatas, but the
Batatas bee better then the other rootes, and being rawe they
haue a smell of Chestnuts : they are to be eaten rosted.   These
Indians doe make wine of the fruit of Date-trees, which fruit is
yellow in colour, and is as great as a little Doues egge, and being
in season is good to be eaten, and of it proceedeth good wine, and
is preserued for a long time.   These kinde of people do make
their houses with vpper roomes, and they sleepe in them, as also
al their habitation is in the vpper roomes, and that which is
belowe, they leaue open : and also they vse certaine mantels of
cotten wooll, and these they tie at the endes with ropes, and the
one ende of the rope they make fast to one part of the house, and
the other ende to the other part of the house : and in these they
lye, which bee their beddes, and these kinde of beds bee vsed in
all India, and there is not in any part of India any chambers that
the people do vse to lodge in aloft from the ground, nor they
make any hie roomes, but only in this part of India : and in al
other places they make their houses without any loftes or chambers,
and they couer their houses with the leaues of date-trees, and of

grasse. And from this fresh water sea vnto Paria, the coast lyeth West Northwest, and is so ful of sholds that the ships cannot come neer to the land. There are from this riuer to Paria 250 leagues. In this fresh water sea, the tydes do ebbe and flow as much as they do in Britayne, and it standeth in 6 degrees and a halfe. Paria standeth on the other side of the Equinoctial towards the North, in seuen degrees : In Paria the sea floweth but little, and from Paria towards the West, the sea doth not flow. From the entry of the gulfe of Paria vnto the Cape that lyeth towards the West, are 35 leagues, and from the coast turneth towardes the Northeast other 35 leagues, and from thence the coast turneth toward the West. Before this gulfe standeth the Island of Trinidad, and towards the West doeth appeare the gulfe of Paria like to halfe a round circle, after the fashion of a Diameter, and at the end of this circle is the entery in of Paria, and at this entery there is betweene the land and the Island 8 leagues, and on the other side there is but litle space betweene the Iland and the land, but it is deepe, and hath a good entry : this Iland of Trinidad hath in length 25 leagues, and as many in bredth, and standeth in eight degrees, and is inhabited of many people, and as yet not vnder subiection. Here the Indians do vse to shoote with bowes, and arrowes which are of a fathome in length, made of reeds, which grow in that Countrey, and at the ende of them is artificially ioyned a piece of wood very strong, vnto the which piece of wood at the end of it, they put a bone of a fish, in place of an arrow head : these kinde of bones bee harder then Diamonds, and euery one of them be three or foure fingers long, and they are taken out of a fish that hath three of these bones, one vpon the backe, another vnder euery wing : but that which groweth vpon the backe is the strongest and the greatest. In this Island the people saith that there groweth golde : and in this Island and in Paria growe reedes so great, that they make staues of them and cary of them into Spaine. Likewise there bee Popiniayes very great and gentle, and some of them haue their foreheads yellow, and this sort do quickly learne to speak, and speak much. There be likewise in the gulf of Paria pearles, although not many, but very good and great.

THE PRINCIPAL VOYAGES OF
THE ENGLISH NATION TO THE ISLES OF TRINIDAD, MARGARITA, ETC.

The voyage of Sir Thomas Pert, and Sebastian Cabot, about the eight yeere of King Henry the eight, which was the yere 1516. to Brasil, Santo Domingo, and S. Iuan de Puerto rico.

THat learned and painefull writer Richard Eden in a certaine Epistle of his to the duke of Northumberland, before a worke which he translated out of Munster in the yeere 1553, called A treatise of new India, maketh mention of a voyage of discouerie vndertaken out of England by sir Thomas Pert and Sebastian Cabota, about the 8. yere of King Henry the eight of famous memorie, imputing the ouerthrow thereof vnto the cowardise and want of stomack of the said Sir Thomas Pert, in maner following. If manly courage, saith he, (like vnto that which hath bene seene and proued in your Grace, as well in forreine realmes, as also in this countrey) had not bene wanting in other in these our dayes, at such time as our soueraigne lord of famous memorie king Henry the 8. about the same yeere of his raigne, furnished and sent out certaine shippes vnder the gouernance of Sebastian Cabot yet liuing and one Sir Thomas Pert, whose faint heart was the cause that the voyage took none effect; if, I say, such manly courage, whereof wee haue spoken, had not at that time beene wanting, it might happily haue come to passe, that that rich treasurie called Perularia, (which is nowe in Spaine in the citie of Siuill, and so named, for that in it is kept the infinite riches brought thither from the newfoundland of Peru) might long since haue beene in the tower of London, to the kings great honour and wealth of this realme. Hereunto that also is to bee referred which the worshipfull M. Robert Thorne wrote to the sayde king Henry the 8. in the yeere 1527 by doctor Leigh his ambassadour sent into Spaine to the Emperour Charles the fift whose wordes bee these. Now rest to be discouered the North parts, the which it seemeth vnto me, is onely your highnes charge and dutie, because the situation of this your realme is thereunto neerest and aptest of all other: and also, for that already you haue taken it in hand. And in mine opinion it will not seeme well to leaue so great and profitable an enterprise, seeing it may

[margin note:] This sir Thomas Pert was Vice-admirall of England, and dwelt in Poplar at Blackwall.

so easily and with so little cost, labour and danger be followed
and obteined. Though hitherto your grace haue   Note.
made thereof a proofe, and found not the commoditie
thereby as you trusted, at this time it shalbe none impediment :
for there may be now prouided remedies for things then lacked,
and the inconueniences and lets remooued, that then were cause
your graces desire tooke no full effect : which is, the courses to
be changed, and to follow the aforesayd new courses. And concerning the mariners, ships, and prouision, an order may be
deuised and taken meete and conuenient, much better then
hitherto : by reason whereof, and by Gods grace, no doubt your
purpose shall take effect. And whereas in the aforesayd wordes
M. Robert Thorne sayth, that he would haue the old courses to
bee changed, and the newe courses (to the North) to bee
followed : It may plainely be gathered, that the former voyage,
whereof twise or thrise he maketh mention, wherein it is like
that sir Thomas Pert and Sebastian Cabot were set foorth by the
king, was made towarde Brasill and the South parts. Moreouer
it seemeth that Gonsaluo de Ouiedo,* a famous Spanish writer
alludeth vnto the sayde voyage in the beginning of the 13.
chapter of the 19. booke of his generall and natural historie of
the West Indies, agreeing very well with the time about which
Richard Eden writeth that the foresaid voyage was begun. The
authors wordes are these, as I finde them translated into Italian
by that excellent and famous man Baptista Ramusius. Nel 1517.
Vn Corsaro Inglese, sotto colore di venire à dis-   An English
coprire, se ne venne con vna gran naue alla volta del great shippe
Brasil nella costiera di Terra ferma, e indi attrauerso   at Brasill
à questa isola Spagnuola, e giunse presso la bocca del   1517.
porto di questa città di S. Domenico, e mandò in terra il suo
battello pieno di gente, e chiese licentia di potere qui entrare,
dicendo che venia con mercantie a negotiare. Ma in quello
instante il castellano, Francesco di Tapia fece tirare alla naue vn
tiro d'artiglieria da questo castello, perche ella se ne veniua dìritta
al porto. Quando gli Inglesi viddero questo si ritirarono fuori,
e quelli del battello tosto si raccolsero in naue. E nel vero il
Castellan fece errore : perche se ben fosse naue entrata nel porto,
non sarebbono le genti potuto smontare à terra senza volontà e

* Born at Madrid in 1478. He happened to be in *Barcelona* on the return
of Columbus in 1493, and was intimate with the explorer. His History was
published at Salamanca in 1535, folio.

D 2

San Iuan della città e del castello. La naue adunque veggendo
de puerto come vi era riceuuta, tirò la volta dell' isola di San
Rico. Giouanni, ed entrata nel porto di San Germano
parlarono gli Inglesi con quelli della terra, e dimandarono vettouaglie e fornimenti per la naue, e si lamentarono di quelli di
questa città, dicendo che essi non veniuano per fare dispiacere,
ma per contrattare, e negotiare con suoi danari e mercantie.
Hora quiui hebbero alcune vettouaglie, ed in compensa essi
diedero e pagarono in certi stagni lauorati ed altre cose. E poi
si partirono alla volta d'Europa, doue si crede, che non gun-
gessero, perche non se ne seppe piu nuoua mai. This extract
importeth thus much in English, to wit : That in the yeere 1517.
an English Rouer vnder the colour of trauelling to discouer, came
with a great shippe vnto the parts of Brasill on the coast of the
firme land, and from thence he crossed ouer vnto this Iland of
Hispanolia, and arriued neere vnto the mouth of the hauen of
this citie of S. Domingo, and sent his shipboate full of men on
shoare, and demaunded leaue to enter into this hauen, saying
that hee came with marchandise to traffique. But at that very
instant the gouernour of the castle Francis de Tapia caused
a tire of ordinance to be shot from the castle at the ship, for she
bare in directly with the hauen. When the Englishmen sawe
this, they withdrew themselues out, and those that were
in the shipboate, got themselues with all speede on shipboord.
And in trueth the warden of the castle committed an ouersight :
for if the shippe had entred into the hauen, the men thereof could
not haue come on lande without leaue both of the citie and of
the castle. Therefore the people of the ship seeing how they
were receiued, sayled toward the Iland of S. Iohn, and entring
into the port of S. Germaine, the English men parled with those
of the towne, requiring victuals and things needefull to furnish
their ship, and complained of the inhabitants of the city of S.
Domingo, saying that they came not to doe any harme, but to
trade and traffique for their money and merchandise. In this
place they had certaine victuals, and for recompence they gaue
and paid them with certain vessell of wrought tinne and other
things. And afterward they departed toward Europe, where it is
thought they arriued not : for wee neuer heard any more newes
of them. Thus farre proceedeth Gonsaluo de Ouiedo, who
though it please him to call the captain of this great English ship
a rouer, yet it appeareth by the Englishmens owne words, that

they came to discouer, and by their traffique for pewter vessel'
and other wares at the towne of S. Germaine in the Iland o.
S. Iohn de puerto rico, it cannot bee denied but that they were
furnished with wares for honest traffique and exchange. But
whosoeuer is conuersant in reading the Portugall and Spanish
writers of the East and West Indies, shall commonly finde that
they account all other nations for pirats, rouers, and theeues,
which visite any heathen coast that they haue once sayled by or
looked on. Howbeit their passionate and ambitious reckoning
ought not to bee preiudiciall to other mens chargeable and painefull enterprises and honourable trauels in discouerie.

A briefe note concerning a voyage of one Thomas Tison an
  English man, made before the yeere 1526. to the West
  Indies, and of his abode there in maner of a secret factor
  for some English marchants, which vnder hand had trade
  thither in those dayes : taken out of an olde ligier-booke
  of M. Nicolas Thorne the elder, a worshipfull marchant of
  Bristol.

IT appeareth out of a certaine note or letter of remembrance,
in the custodie of mee Richard Hakluyt, written 1526. by
master Nicolas Thorne the elder, a principall marchant of Bristol,
vnto his friend and factour Thomas Midnall, and his seruant
William Ballard at that time remaining at S. Lucar in Andaluzia:
that before the sayd yeere one Thomas Tison an Englishman had
found the way to the West Indies, and was there resident : vnto
whom the aforesayd M. Nicolas Thorne sent armour and other
commodities specified in the letter aforesayd. This Thomas
Tison (so farre as I can coniecture) may seeme to haue bene some
secret factour for M. Thorne and other English marchants in those
remote partes ; whereby it is probable that some of our marchants
had a kinde of trade to the West Indies euen in those ancient
times and before also : neither doe I see any reason why the
Spaniards should debarre vs from it at this present.

The first voyage of the right worshipfull and valiant knight sir
  Iohn Hawkins, sometimes treasurer of her Maiesties nauie
  Roial, made to the West Indies 1562.

MAster Iohn Haukins hauing made diuers voyages to the Iles

of the Canaries, and there by his good and vpright dealing being growen in loue and fauour with the people, informed himselfe amongst them by diligent inquisition, of the state of the West India, whereof hee had receiued some knowledge by the instructions of his father, but increased the same by the aduertisments and reports of that people. And being amongst other particulars assured, that Negros were very good marchandise in Hispaniola, and that store of Negros might easily bee had vpon the coast of Guinea, resolued with himselfe to make triall thereof, and communicated that deuise with his worshipfull friendes of London : namely with Sir Lionell Ducket, sir Thomas Lodge, M. Gunson his father in law, sir William Winter, M. Bromfield, and others. All which persons liked so well of his intention, that they became liberall contributers and aduenturers in the action. For which purpose there were three good ships immediatly prouided : The one called the Salomon of the burthen of 120. tunne, wherein M. Haukins himselfe went as Generall : The second the Swallow of 100. tunnes, wherein went for Captaine M. Thomas Hampton : and the third the Ionas a barke of 40. tunnes, wherein the Master supplied the Captaines roome : in which small fleete M. Hawkins tooke with him not aboue 100. men, for feare of sicknesse and other inconueniences, whereunto men in long voyages are commonly subiect.

With this companie he put off and departed from the coast of England in the moneth of October 1562. and in his course
Sierra Leona touched first at Teneriffe, where hee receiued friendly
called intertainement. From thence he passed to Sierra
Tagarin. Leona, vpon the coast of Guinea, which place by the people of the countrey is called Tagarin, where he stayed some good time, and got into his possession, partly by the sworde, and partly by other meanes, to the number of 300. Negros at the least, besides other merchandises which that countrey yeeldeth. With this praye hee sayled ouer the Ocean sea vnto the Iland of Hispaniola, and arriued first at the port of Isabella : and there hee had reasonable vtterance of his English commodities, as also of some part of his Negros, trusting the Spaniards no further, then that by his owne strength he was able still to master them. From the port of Isabella he went to Puerto de Plata, where he made like sales, standing alwaies vpon his guard : from thence also hee sayled to Monte Christi another port on the North side of Hispaniola, and the last place of his touching, where he had

peaceable traffique, and made vent of the whole number of his Negros : for which he receiued in those 3. places by way of exchange such quantitie of merchandise, that hee did not onely lade his owne 3. shippes with hides, ginger, sugars, and some quantitie of pearles, but he fraighted also two other hulkes with hides and other like commodities, which hee sent into Spaine. And thus leauing the Iland, he returned and disemboqued, passing out by the Ilands of the Caycos, without further entring into the bay of Mexico, in this his first voyage to the West India. And so with prosperous successe and much gaine to himselfe and the aforesayde aduenturers, he came home, and arriued in the moneth of September 1563.

The voyage made by M. Iohn Hawkins Esquire, and afterward knight, Captaine of the Iesus of Lubek, one of her Maiesties shippes, and Generall of the Salomon, and other two barkes going in his companie, to the coast of Guinea, and the Indies of Noua Hispania, begun in An. Dom. 1564.

MAster Iohn Hawkins with the Iesus of Lubek, a shippe of 700. and the Salomon a shippe of 140. the Tiger a barke of 50. and the Swallow of 30. tunnes, being all well furnished with men to the number of one hundreth threescore and tenne, as also with ordinance and victuall requisite for such a voyage, departed out of Plymmouth the 18. day of October, in the yeere of our Lord 1564. with a prosperous winde : at which departing, in cutting the foresail, a marueilous misfortune happened to one of the officers in the shippe, who by the pullie of the sheat was slaine out of hand, being a sorowfull beginning to them all. And after their setting out ten leagues to the sea, he met the same day with the Minion a ship of the Queenes Maiestie, whereof was Captaine Dauid Carlet, and also her consort the Iohn Baptist of London, being bounde to Guinea also, The Minion, who hailed one the other after the custome of the the Iohn Baptist, and sea with certaine pieces of ordinance for ioy of their the Merlin, meeting : which done, the Minion departed from bound for him to seeke her other consort the Merlin of Lon- Guinea. don, which was a sterne out of sight, leauing in M. Hawkins companie the Iohn Baptist her other consort.

Thus sayling forwards on their way with a prosperous winde

vntill the 21. of the same moneth, at that time a great storme arose, the winde being at Northeast about nine a clocke in the night, and continued so 23. houres together, in which storme M. Hawkins lost the companie of the Iohn Baptist aforesayd, and of his pinnesse called the Swallow, his other 3. shippes being sore beaten with a storme. The 23. day the Swallow to his no small reioycing, came to him againe in the night, 10. leagues to the Northward of Cape Finister, he hauing put roomer, not being able to double the Cape, in that there rose a contrary winde at Southwest. The 25. the wind continuing contrary, hee put into a place in Galicia, called Ferroll, where hee remained fiue dayes, and appointed all the Masters of his shippes an order for the keeping of good companie in this manner : The small shippes to bee always a head and aweather of the Iesus, and to speake twise a day with the Icsus at least : if in the day the Ensigne bee ouer the poope of the Iesus, or in the night two lights, then shall all the shippes speake with her : If there bee three lights aboord the Iesus, then docth she cast about : If the weather bee extreme, that the small shippes cannot keepe companie with the Iesus, then all to keepe companie with the Salomon, and foorthwith to repaire to the Iland of Teneriffe, to the Northward of the road of Sirroes ; If any happen to any misfortune then to shew two lights, and to shoote off a piece of ordinance. If any lose companie, and come in sight againe, to make three yawes, and strike the Myson three times : Serue God daily, loue one another, preserue your victuals, beware of fire, and keepe good companie.

Good orders for a fleete in a long voyage.

The 26. day the Minion came in also where hee was, for the reioycing whereof hee gaue them certaine pieces of ordinance, after the courtesie of the sea for their welcome : but the Minions men had no mirth, because of their consort the Merline, whome at their departure from Master Hawkins vpon the coast of England they went to seeke, and hauing met with her, kept companie two dayes together, and at last by misfortune of fire (through the negligence of one of their gunners) the powder in the gunners roome was set on fire, which with the first blast strooke out her poope, and therewithall lost three men, besides many sore burned (which escaped by the brigandine being at her sterne) and immediatly, to the great losse of the owners, and most horrible sight to the beholders, she sunke before their eyes.

A dreadfull mischance by fire.

The 20. day of the moneth M. Hawkins with his consorts and companie of the Minion, hauing nowe both the brigandines at her sterne, wayed anker, and set saile on their voyage, hauing a prosperous winde thereunto.

The fourth of Nouember they had sight of the Iland of Madera, and the sixt day of Teneriffe, which they thought to haue beene the Canarie, in that they supposed themselues to haue beene to the Eastward of Teneriffe, and were not : but the Minion being three or foure leagues a head of vs, kept on her course to Teneriffe, hauing better sight thereof then the other had, and by that meanes they parted companie. For M. Hawkins and his companie went more to the West, vpon which course hauing sayled a while, hee espied another Iland, which hee thought to bee Teneriffe, and being not able by meanes of the fogge vpon the hils, to discerne the same, nor yet to fetch it by night, went roomer vntill the morning, being the seuenth of Nouember, which as yet hee could not discerne, but sayled along the coast the space of two houres, to perceiue some certaine marke of Teneriffe, and found nò likelyhood thereof at all, accompting that to bee, as it was in deede, the Ile of Palmes : and so sayling forwards, espied another Iland called Gomera, and also Teneriffe, with the

The Ile of Palmes. Gomera and Teneriffe.

which hee made, and sayling all night, came in the morning the next day to the port of Adecia, where he found his pinnesse which had departed from him the sixt of the moneth, being in the weather of him, and espying the pike of Teneriffe all a high, bare thither. At his arriuall somewhat before hee came to anker, hee hoysed out his shippes pinnesse rowing a shoare, intending to haue sent one with a letter to Peter de Ponte, one of the gouernours of the Iland, who dwelt a league from the shoare : but as hee pretended to haue landed, suddenly there appeared vpon the two points of the roade, men leuelling of bases and harguebuzes to them, with diuers others to the number of foure-score, with halberds, pikes, swordes and targets, which happened so contrary to his expectation, that it did greatly amaze him, and the more, because hee was nowe in their danger, not knowing well howe to auoyde it without some mischiefe. Wherefore hee determined to call to them for the better appeasing of the matter, declaring his name, and professing himselfe to bee an especiall friend to Peter de Ponte, and that he had sundry things for him which he greatly desired. And in the meane time, while hee was

thus talking with them, whereby he made them to holde their
hands, hee willed the marriners to rowe away, so that at last he
gat out of their danger: and then asking for Peter de Ponte, one
of his sonnes being Sennor Nicolas de Ponte, came forth, whom
hee perceiuing, desired to put his men aside, and he himselfe
would leape a shoare, and commune with him, which they did:
so that after communication had betweene them of sundry things,
and of the feare they both had, master Hawkins desired to haue
certaine necessaries prouided for him.   In the meane space, while
these things were prouiding, hee trimmed the maine mast of the
Iesus which in the storme aforesayd was sprung: here he
soiourned 7. dayes, refreshing himselfe and his men.   In the
Santa Cruz. which time Peter de Ponte dwelling at S. Cruz, a
citie 20. leagues off, came to him, and gaue him as
gentle intertainment as if he had bene his owne brother.   To
A briefe   speake somewhat of these Ilands, being called in olde
description time Insulæ fortunatæ, by the meanes of the flourish-
of the com-
modities of ing thereof, the fruitfulnesse of them doeth surely
the Canarie exceede farre all other that I haue heard of : for they
Ilands.   make wine better then any in Spaine, they haue grapes
of such bignesse, that they may bee compared to damsons, and
in taste inferiour to none: for sugar, suckets, raisins of the
Sunne, and many other fruits, abundance : for rosine and raw
silke, there is great store, they want neither corne, pullets, cattell,
nor yet wilde foule : they haue many Camels also, which being
young, are eaten of the people for victuals, and being olde, they
are vsed for caryage of necessaries : whose propertie is as hee is
taught to kneele at the taking of his loade, and vnlading againe :
his nature is to ingender backward contrary to other beastes : of
vnderstanding very good, but of shape very deformed, with a
little bellie, long misshapen legges, and feete very broad of flesh,
without a hoofe, all whole, sauing the great toe, a backe bearing
vp like a molehill, a large and thin necke, with a little head, with
a bunch of hard flesh, which nature hath giuen him in his breast
to leane vpon.   This beast liueth hardly, and is contented with
strawe and stubble, but of force strong, being well able to carrie
Fierro.   500. weight. , In one of these Ilands called Fierro,
there is by the reports of the inhabitants, a certaine
tree that raineth continually, by the dropping whereof the
inhabitants and cattell are satisfied with water, for other water
haue they none in all the Iland.   And it raineth in such abund-

ance, that it were incredible vnto a man to beleeue such a vertue to bee in a tree, but it is knowen to be a diuine matter, and a thing ordeined by God, at whose power therein wee ought not to maruell, seeing he did by his prouidence as we read in the Scriptures, when the children of Israel were going into the land of promise, feede them with Manna from heauen, for the space of 40. yeeres. Of the trees aforesaid wee saw in Guinie many, being of great height, dropping con- tiually, but not so abundantly as the other because the leaues are narrower, and are like the leaues of a peare tree. About these Ilands are certaine flitting Ilands, which haue beene oftentimes seene, and when men approched neere them, they vanished : as the like hath bene of these Ilands nowe knowen by the report of the inhabitants, which were not found of long time one after the other : and therefore it should seeme hee is not yet borne to whom God hath appoynted the finding of them. In this Iland of Teneriffe there is a hill called The Pike, because it is piked, which is in height by their reports twentie leagues, hauing both winter and summer abundance of snowe in the top of it : This pike may bee seene in a cleere day fiftie leagues off, but it sheweth as though it were a blacke cloude a great heigth in the element. I haue heard of none to be compared with this in heigth, but in the Indias I haue seene many, and in my iudgement not inferiour to the Pike, and so the Spaniards write.

Trees dropping water in Guinie.

The pike of Teneriffe.

The 15. of Nouember at night we departed from Teneriffe, and the 20. of the same wee had sight of ten Carauals, that were fishing at sea, with whome we would haue spoken, but they fearing vs, fled into a place of Barbarie, called Cape de las Barbas.

Cape de las Barbas.

The twentieth, the ships pinnesse with two men in her, sayling by the ship, was ouerthrowne by the ouersight of them that went in her, the winde being so great, that before they were espied, and the ship had cast about for them, she was driuen halfe a league to leeward of the pinnesse, and had lost sight of her, so that there was small hope of recouerie, had not Gods helpe and the Captaines deligence bene, who hauing wel marked which way the pinnesse was by the Sunne, appointed 24 of the lustiest rowers in the great boate, to rowe to the wind-wardes, and so recouered, contrary to all mens expectations, both the pinnesse and the men sitting vpon the keele of her.

E 2

Cape Blanco. The 25 we came to Cape Blanco, which is vpon the coast of Africa, and a place where the Portugals do ride, that fish there in the moneth of Nouember especially, and is a very good place of fishing, for Pargoes, Mullet, and Dogge fish. In this place the Portugals haue no holde for their defence, but haue rescue of the Barbarians, whom they entertaine. as their souldiers, for the time of their being there, and for their fishing vpon that coast of Africa, doe pay a certaine tribute to the king of the Moores. The people of that part of Africa are tawnie, hauing long haire without any apparell, sauing before their priuie members. Their weapons in warres are bowes and arrowes.

The 26 we departed from S. Auis Baye, within Cape Blanco, where we refreshed our selues with fish, and other Cape Verde necessaries : and the 29 wee came to Cape Verde, in 14 degrees. which lieth in 14 degrees, and a halfe. These people are all blacke, and are called Negros, without any apparell, sauing before their priuities : of stature goodly men, and well liking by reason of their food, which passeth all other Guyneans for kine, goats, pullin, rise, fruits, and fish. Here wee tooke fishes with heades like conies, and teeth nothing varying, of a iolly thickenesse, but not past a foote long, and is not to be eaten without flaying or cutting off his head. To speake somewhat of the sundry sortes of these Guyneans : the people of Cape Verde are called Leophares, and counted the goodliest men of all other, sauing the Congoes, which do inhabite on this side the cape de Buena Esperança. These Leophares haue warres against the Ieloffes, which are borderers by them : their weapons are bowes and arrowes, targets, and short daggers, darts also, but varying from other Negros : for whereas the other vse a long dart to fight with in their hands, they cary fiue or sixe small ones a peece, The trafficke which they cast with. These men also are more ciuill of the French then any other, because of their dayly trafficke with men at Cape the Frenchmen, and are of nature very gentle and Verde. louing : for while we were there, we tooke in a Frenchman, who was one of the 19 that going to Brasile, in a Barke of Diepe, of 60 tunnes, and being a sea boord of Cape Verde, 200 leagues, the plankes of their Barke with a sea brake out vpon them so suddenly, that much a doe they had to saue themselues in their boats : but by Gods prouidence, the wind being Westerly, which is rarely seene there, they got to the shore, to the Isle Braua, and in great penurie gotte to Cape Verde, where they remained sixe weekes, and had meate and drinke of the same people. The said Frenchman hauing forsaken his fellowes, which were three leagues off from the shore, and wandring with the Negros too and fro, fortuned to come to the waters side : and communing with certaine of his countreymen, which were in our ship, by their perswasions came away with vs : but his entertainment amongst them was such, that he desired it not: but through the importunate request of his Countreymen, consented at the last. Here we stayed but one night, and part of the day : for the 7 of December wee came away, in that pretending to haue taken Negros there perforce, the Mynions men gaue them there to vnderstand of our comming, and our pretence, wherefore they did auoyde the snares we had layd for them.

The 8 of December wee ankered by a small Island called Alcatrarsa, wherein at our going a shore, we found nothing but sea-birds, as we call them Ganets, but by the Portugals, called Alcatrarses, who for that cause gaue the said Island the same name. Herein halfe of our boates were laden 'with yong and olde fowle, who not being vsed to the sight of men, flew so about vs, that we stroke them down with poles. In this place the two shippes riding, the two Barkes, with their boates, went into an Island of the Sapies, called La Formio, to see if they could take any of them, and there landed to the number of 80 in armour, and espying certaine made to them, but they fled in such order into the woods, that it booted them not to ;follow : so going on their way forward till they came to a riuer which they could not passe ouer, they espied on the otherside two men, who with their bowes and arrowes shot terribly at them. Whereupon wee discharged certaine harque-buzers to them againe, but the ignorant people wayed it not, because they knewe not the danger thereof : but vsed a marueilous crying in their fight with leaping and turning their tayles, that it was most strange to see, and gaue vs great pleasure to beholde them. At the last, one being hurt with a harquebuz vpon the thigh, looked vpon his wound and wist not howe it came, because hee could not see the pellet. Here Master Hawkins perceiuing no good to be done amongst them, because we could not finde their townes, and also not knowing how to goe into Rio grande, for want of a Pilote, which was the very occasion of our comming thither: and finding so many sholes, feared with our great ships to goe in, and therefore departed on our pretended way to the Idols.

The 10 of December, we had a Northeast winde, with raine and storme, which weather continuing two dayes together, was the occasion that the Salomon, and Tygre loste our companie : for whereas the Iesus, and pinnesse ankered at one of the Islands called Sambula, the twelfth day, the Salomon and Tygre came not thither till the 14. In this Iland wee stayed certaine daies, going euery day on shore to take the Inhabitants, with burning and spoiling their townes, who before were Sapies, and were conquered by the Samboses, Inhabitants beyond Sierra Leona. These Samboses had inhabited there three yeres before our comming thither, and in so short space haue so planted the ground, that they had great plentie of Mil, Rise, Rootes, Pompions, Pullin, goates, of small frye dried, euery house full of the Countrey fruite planted by Gods prouidence, as Palmito trees, fruites like dates, and sundry other in no place in all that Countrey so aboundantly, whereby they liued more deliciously then other. These inhabitants haue diuerse of the Sapies, which they tooke in the warres as their slaues, whome onely they kept to till the ground, in that they neither haue the knowledge thereof, nor yet will worke themselues, of whome wee tooke many in that place, but of the Samboses none at all, for they fled into the maine. All the Samboses haue white teeth as we haue, farre vnlike to the Sapies which doe inhabite about Rio grande, for their teeth are all filed, which they doe for a brauerie, to set out themselues, and doe iagge their flesh, both legges, armes, and bodies, as workemanlike, as a Ierkin maker with vs pinketh a ierkin. These Sapies be more ciuill then the Samboses : for whereas the Samboses liue most by the spoile of their enemies, both in taking their victuals, and eating them also. The Sapies doe not eate mans flesh, vnlesse in the warre they be driuen by necessitie thereunto, which they haue not vsed, but by the example of the Samboses, but liue onely with fruites, and cattell, whereof they haue great store. This plentie is the occasion that the Sapies desire not warre, except they be thervnto prouoked by the inuasions of the Samboses, whereas the Samboses for want of foode are inforced thereunto, and therefore are not woont onely to take them that they kill, but also keepe those that they take,

The Samboses man-eaters.

vntill such time as they want meate, and then they The Sapies burie their dead with golde.
kill them.   There is also another occasion that
prouoketh the Samboses to warre against the Sapies,
which is for couetousnes of their riches.   For whereas
the Sapies haue an order to burie their dead in certaine places
appointed for that purpose, with their golde about them, the
Samboses digge vp the ground, to haue the same treasure : for
the Samboses haue not the like store of golde, that the Sapies
haue.   In this Island of Sambula we found about 50
boates called Almadyes, or Canoas, which are made The Canoas of Affrica.
of one peece of wood, digged out like a trough but of
a good proportion, being about 8 yards long, and one in
breadth, hauing a beakhead and a sterne very proportionably
made, and on the out side artificially carued, and painted red and
blewe : they are able to cary twenty or thirty men, but they are
about the coast able to cary threescore and vpward.   In these
canoas they rowe standing vpright, with an oare somewhat longer
then a man, the ende whereof is made about the breadth and
length of a mans hand, of the largest sort.   They row very
swift, and in some of them foure rowers and one to steere
make as much way, as a paire of oares in the Thames of
London.

Their townes are pretily diuided with a maine The forme of their townes.
streete at the entring in, that goeth thorough their
Towne, and another ouerthwart street, which maketh
their townes crosse wayes : their houses are built in a ranke very
orderly in the face of the street, and they are made round, like a
douecote, with stakes set full of Palmito leaues, in stead of a
wall : they are not much more then a fathome large, and two of
height, and thatched with Palmito leaues very close, other some
with reede, and ouer the roofe thereof, for the better garnishing
of the same, there is a round bundle of reede, pretily contriued
like a louer : in the inner part they make a loft of stickes, whereupon they lay all their prouisions of victuals : a place they reserue
at their enterance for the kitchin, and the place they lie in is
deuided with certaine mattes artificially made with the rine of
Palmito trees : their bedsteades are of small staues layd along,
and raysed a foote from the ground, vpon which is
layde a matte, and another vpon them when they list : for
other couering they haue none.   In the middle of the town there
is a house larger and higher then the other, but in forme alike,

The consulta- adioyning vnto the which there is a place made of
tion house or foure good stancions of woode, and a round roofe
towne-howse. ouer it, the grounde also raised round with claye a
foote high, vpon the which floore were strawed many fine mats :
this is the Consultation-house, the like whereof is in all Townes,
as the Portugals affirme : in which place, when they sitte in
Counsell the King or Captaine sitteth in the midst, and the
Elders vpon the floore by him : (for they giue reuerence to their
Elders) and the common sorte sitte round about them.   There
they sitte to examine matters of theft, which if a man be taken
with, to steale but a Portugal cloth from another, hee is sold to
the Portugals for a slaue.   They consult also, and take order
what time they shall goe to warres : and as it is certainely reported
by the Portugals, they take order in gathering of the fruites in the
season of the yeere, and also of Palmito wine, which
Palmito is a is gathered by a hole cut in the top of a tree, and a
wilde date. gourde set for the receiuing thereof, which falleth in
by droppes, and yeeldeth fresh wine againe within a moneth, and
this diuided part and portion-like to euery man, by the iudgement
of the Captaine and Elders, euery man holdeth himselfe contented :
and this surely I iudge to be a very good order : for otherwise,
whereas scarsitie of Palmito is, euery man would haue the same,
which might breed great strife : but of such things, as euery man
doeth plant for himselfe, the sower thereof reapeth it to his owne
vse, so that nothing is common, but that which is vnset by mans
hands.   In their houses there is more common passage of
Lizardes like Euats, and other greater, of blacke and blew colour,
of neere a foote long, besides their tailes, then there is with vs of
Mise in great houses.   The Sapies and Samboses also vse in
their warres bowes, and arrowes made of reedes, with heads of
yron poysoned with the iuyce of a Cucumber, whereof
A venemous I had many in my handes.   In their battels they haue
Cucumber. target-men, with broad wicker targets, and darts with
heades at both endes of yron, the one in forme of a two edged
sworde, a foote and an halfe long, and at the other ende, the yron,
long of the same length made to counterpease it, that in
casting   it   might   flie   leuel,   rather   then   for   any   other
purpose as I can iudge.   And   when they espie the
enemie, the Captaine to cheere his men, cryeth Hungry, and
they answere Heyre, and with that euery man placeth himselfe
in order, for about euery target man three bowemen will

couer themselues, and shoote as they see aduantage : and
when they giue the onset, they make such terrible cryes, that
they may bee heard two miles off. For their beliefe, I can
heare of none that they haue, but in such as they themselues
imagine to see in their dreames, and so worshippe
the pictures, whereof wee sawe some like vnto deuils. Idoles like deuils.
In this Island aforesayde wee soiourned vnto the one
and twentieth of December, where hauing taken certaine Negros,
and asmuch of their fruites, rise, and mill, as we could well cary
away (whereof there was such store, that wee might haue laden one of
our Barkes therewith) wee departed, and at our departure diuers
of our men being desirous to goe on shore, to fetch Pompions,
which hauing prooued, they found to bee very good, certaine of
the Tygres men went also, amongst the which there was a Car-
penter, a young man, who with his fellowes hauing fet many, and
caryed them downe to their boates, as they were ready to depart,
desired his fellow to tary while he might goe vp to fetch a few
which he had layed by for him selfe, who being more The extreme
licorous then circumspect, went vp without weapon, negligence of
and as he went vp alone, possibly being marked of one of the
the Negros that were vpon the trees, espying him companie.
what hee did, perceauing him to be alone, and without weapon,
dogged him, and finding him occupyed in binding his Pompions
together, came behinde him, ouerthrowing him and straight cutte
his throate, as hee afterwardes was found by his fellowes, who
came to the place for him, and there found him naked.

The two and twentieth the Captaine went into the Riuer,
called Callowsa, with the two Barkes, and the Iohns Pinnesse,
and the Salomons boate, leauing at anker in the Riuers mouth
the two shippes, the Riuer being twenty leagues in, where the
Portugals roade : hee came thither the fiue and twentieth, and
dispatched his businesse, and so returned with two Carauels,
loaden with Negros.

The 27. the Captaine was aduertised by the Portugals of a
towne of the Negros called Bymba, being in the way as they
returned, where was not onely great quantitie of golde, but
also that there were not aboue fortie men, and an hundred
women and children in the Towne, so that if hee would giue the
aduenture vpon the same, hee might gette an hundreth slaues ;
with the which tydings hee being gladde, because the Portugals
shoulde not thinke him to bee of so base a courage, but that hee

durst giue them that, and greater attempts : and being thereunto
also the more prouoked with the prosperous successe hee had in
other Islands adiacent, where he had put them all to flight, and
taken in one boate twentie together, determined to stay before
the Towne three or foure houres, to see what hee could doe :
and thereupon prepared his men in armour and weapon together,
to the number of fortie men well appointed, hauing

Portugals not to be trusted. to their guides certaine Portugals, in a boat, who
Want of cir- brought some of them to their death : wee landing
cumspection in our men. boat after boat, and diuers of our men scattering
themselues, contrary to the Captaines will, by one or
two in a company, for the hope that they had to finde golde in
their houses, ransacking the same, in the meane time the Negros
came vpon them, and hurte many being thus scattered, whereas
if fiue or sixe had bene together, they had bene able, as their
companions did, to giue the ouerthrow to 40 of them, and being
driuen downe to take their boates, were followed so hardly by a
route of Negros, who by that tooke courage to pursue them to their
boates, that not onely some of them, but others standing on
shore, not looking for any such matter by meanes that the Negros
did flee at the first, and our companie remained in the towne,
were suddenly so set vpon that some with great hurt recouered
their boates : othersome not able to recouer the same, tooke the
water, and perished by meanes of the ooze.   While this was
doing, the Captaine who with a dosen men, went through the
towne, returned, finding 200 Negros at the waters side, shooting
at them in the boates, and cutting them in pieces which were
drowned in the water, at whose comming, they ranne all
away : so he entred his boates, and before he could put off from
the shore, they returned againe, and shot very fiercely and hurt
diuers of them.   Thus wee returned backe somewhat discom-
forted, although the Captaine in a singular wise maner caried
himselfe, with countenance very cheerefull outwardly, as though
hee did litle weigh the death of his men, nor yet the great
hurt of the rest, although his heart inwardly was broken in
pieces for it ; done to this ende, that the Portugals being with
him, should not presume to resist against him, nor take
occasion to put him to further displeasure or hinderance for the
death of our men : hauing gotton by our going ten Negros, and
lost seuen of our best men, whereof M. Field Captaine of the
Salomon, was one, and we had 27 of our men hurt.   In the

same houre while this was doing, there happened at the same
instant, a marueilous miracle to them in the shippes, who road
ten leagues to sea-ward, by many sharkes or Tiburons, who came
about the ships: among which, one was taken by the Iesus, and
foure by the Salomon, and one very sore hurt escaped: and so
it fell out of our men, whereof one of the Iesus men, and foure
of the Salomons were killed, and the fift hauing twentie wounds
was rescued, and scaped with much adoe.

The 28 they came to their ships, the Iesus, and the Salomon,
and the 30 departed from thence to Taggarin.

The first of Ianuary the two barkes, and both the boates
forsooke the ships, and went into a riuer called the Casserroes,
and the 6 hauing dispatched their businesse, the two barkes
returned, and came to Taggarin, where the two ships were at
anker. Not two dayes after the comming of the two ships
thither, they put their water caske a shore and filled it with water,
to season the same, thinking to haue filled it with fresh water
afterward: and while their men were some on shore, and some
at their boates, the Negros set vpon them in the boates, and
hurt diuers of them, and came to the caskes, and
cut of the hoopes of twelue buts, which lost vs 4 or 5 A new assult
by the Negros.
dayes time, besides great want we had of the same:
soiourning at Taggarin, the Swallow went vp the riuer about her
trafficke, where they saw great townes of the Negros,
and Canoas, that had threescore men in a piece: Very great
Canoas.
there they vnderstood by the Portugals, of a great
battell betweene them of Sierra Leona side, and them of Taggarin:
they of Sierra Leona, had prepared three hundred Canoas to
inuade the other. The time was appointed not past six dayes
after our departure from thence, which we would haue seene
to the intent we might haue taken some of them, The contagion
of the
had it not bene for the death and sicknesse of our countrey of
men, which came by the contagiousnes of the place, Sierra Leona.
which made vs to make hast away.

The 18 of Ianuarie at night, wee departed from Taggarin, being
bound for the West Indies, before which departure certaine of
the Salomons men went on shore to fill water in the night, and
as they came on shore with their boat being ready to leape on
land, one of them espied a Negro in a white coate, standing vpon
a rocke, being ready to haue receiued them when they came on
shore, hauing in sight of his fellowes also eight or nine, some in

F 2

one place leaping out, and some in another, but they hid themselues streight againe: whereupon our men doubting they had
bene a great companie, and sought to haue taken them at more
aduantage, as God would, departed to their ships, not thinking
there had bene such a mischiefe pretended toward them, as then
was in deede.   Which the next day we vnderstood of a Portugal
that came downe to vs, who had trafficked with the Negros, by
whom hee vnderstood, that the king of Sierra Leona had made
all the power hee could, to take some of vs, partly for the desire
he had to see what kinde of people we were, that had spoiled his
people at the Idols, whereof he had newes before our comming,
and as I iudge also, vpon other occasions prouoked by the
Tangomangos, but sure we were that the armie was come downe,
by meanes that in the euening wee saw such a monstrous fire,
made by the watring place, that before was not seene, which fire
is the only marke for the Tangomangos to know where their
armie is alwayes.   If these men had come downe in the euening,
they had done vs great displeasure, for that wee were on shore
filling water : but God, who worketh all things for the best, would
not haue it so, and by him we escaped without danger, his name
be praysed for it.

The 29 of this same moneth we departed with all our shippes
from Sierra Leona, towardes the West Indies, and for the space
of eighteene dayes, we were becalmed, hauing nowe and then
contrary windes, and some Ternados amongst the same calme,
which happened to vs very ill, beeing but reasonably watered,
for so great a companie of Negros, and our selues, which pinched
vs all, and that which was worst, put vs in such feare that many
neuer thought to haue reached to the Indies, without great death
of Negros, and of themselues : but the Almightie God, who neuer
suffereth his elect to perish, sent vs the sixteenth of Februarie,
the ordinary Brise, which is the Northwest winde, which neuer
left vs, till wee came to an Island of the Canybals,
Dominica   called Dominica, where wee arriued the ninth of March,
  Island.
vpon a Saturday : and because it was the most desolate place in all the Island, we could see no Canybals, but some of
their houses where they dwelled, and as it should seeme forsooke
the place for want of fresh water, for wee could finde none there but
raine water, and such as fell from the hilles, and remained as a
puddle in the dale, whereof wee filled for our Negros.   The Canybals of that Island, and also others adiacent are the most desperate

warriers that are in the Indies, by the Spaniardes re- Canyballs
port, who are neuer able to conquer them, and they exceeding
are molested by them not a little, when they are cruell and to
driuen to water there in any of those Islands : of very be auoyded.
late, not two moneths past, in the said Island, a Carauel being
driuen to water, was in the night sette vpon by the inhabitants,
who cutte their cable in the halser, whereby they were driuen a
shore, and so taken by them and eaten.   The greene Dragon of
Newhauen, whereof was Captaine one Bontemps, in March also,
came to one of those Islands, called Granada, and being driuen
to water, could not doe the same for the Canybals, who fought
with him very desperatly two dayes.   For our part also, if we had
not lighted vpon the desertest place in all that Island, wee could
not haue missed, but should haue bene greatly troubled by them,
by all the Spaniards reports, who make them deuils in respect
of me.
   The tenth day at night, we departed from thence,
and the fifteenth had sight of nine Islands, called the The Testigos
Testigos : and the sixteenth of an Island, called Island.
Margarita, where wee were entertayned by the   Margarita
Alcalde, and had both Beeues and sheepe giuen vs,   Island.
for the refreshing of our men : but the Gouernour of the Island,
would neither come to speak with our Captaine, neither yet giue
him any licence to trafficke : and to displease vs the more,
whereas wee had hired a Pilote to haue gone with vs, they would
not onely not suffer him to goe with vs, but also sent word by a
Carauel out of hand, to the Santo Domingo, to the Vice-roy, who
doeth represent the kings person, of our arriuall of those partes,
which had like to haue turned vs to great displeasure, by the
meanes that the same Vice-roy did send word to Cape de la
Vela, and to other places along the coast, commanding them
that by the vertue of his authoritie, and by the obedience that
they owe to their Prince, no man should trafficke with vs, but
should resist vs with all the force they could.   In this Island,
notwithstanding that wee were not within foure leagues of the
Towne, yet were they so afraid, that not onely the Gouernour
himselfe, but also all the inhabitants forsooke their Towne,
assembling all the Indians to them and fled into the mountaines,
as wee were partly certified, and also sawe the experience our
selues, by some of the Indians comming to see vs who by three
Spaniards a horsebacke passing hard by vs, went vnto the

Indians, having euery one of them their bowes, and arrowes, procuring them away, who before were conuersant with vs.

Here perceiuing no trafficke to be had with them, nor yet water for the refreshing of our men, we were driuen to depart the twentieth day, and the 2 and twentieth we came to a place in the maine called Cumana, whither the Captaine going in his Pinnisse, spake with certaine Spaniards, of whom he demanded trafficke, but they made him answere, they were but souldiers newely come thither, and were not able to by one Negro : whereupon hee asked for a watring place, and they pointed him a place two leagues off, called Santa Fè, where we found marueilous goodly watering, and commodious for the taking in thereof : for that the fresh water came into the Sea, and so our shippes had aboord the shore twentie fathome water.   Neere about this place, inhabited certaine Indians, who the next day after we came thither, came down to vs, presenting mill and cakes of breade, which they had made of a kinde of corn called Maiz; in bignesse of a pease, the eare whereof is much like to a teasell, but a spanne in length, hauing thereon a number of granes.   Also they brought down to vs Hennes, Potatoes and Pines, which we bought for beades, pewter whistles, glasses, kniues, and other trifles.

These Potatoes be the most delicate rootes that may be eaten, and doe farre exceed our passeneps or carets.   Their pines be of the bignes of two fists, the outside whereof is of the making of a pine-apple, but it is soft like the rinde of a Cucomber, and the inside eateth like an apple, but it is more delicious than any sweet apple sugred.   These Indians being of colour tawnie like an Oliue, hauing euery one of them both men and women, haire all blacke, and no other colour, the women wearing the same hanging downe to their shoulders, and the men rounded, and without beards, neither men nor women suffering any haire to growe in any part of their body, but dayly pull it off as it groweth.   They goe all naked, the men couering no part of their body but their yard, vpon the which they weare a gourd or piece of cane, made fast with a thrid about their loynes, leauing the other parts of their members vncouered, whereof they take no shame.   The women also are vncouered, sauing with a cloth which they weare a handbreadth, wherewith they couer their priuities both before and behind.   These people be very small feeders, for trauelling they

The description of the Indians of Terra firma.

cary but two small bottels of gourdes, wherein they put in one the iuice of Sorrell whereof they haue great store, and in the other flowre of their Maiz, which being moist, they eate, taking sometime of the other. These men cary euery man his bowe and arrowes, whereof some arrowes are poisoned for warres, which they keepe in a Cane together, which Cane is of the bignesse of a mans arme, other some, with broad heades of iron wherewith they stricke fish in the water: the experience whereof we saw not once nor twise, but dayly for the time we taried there, for they are so good archers that the Spaniards for feare thereof arme themselues and their horses with quilted canuas of two ynches thicke, and leaue no place of their body open to their enemies, sauing their eyes which they may not hide, and yet oftentimes are they hit in that so small a scant- The making ling: their poyson is of such a force, that a man of their being stricken therewith dyeth within foure and poyson. twentie howers, as the Spaniards do affirme, and in my iudgement it is like there can be no stronger poyson as they make it, vsing thereunto apples which are very faire and red of colour, but are a strong poyson, with the which together with venemous Bats, Vipers, Adders and other serpents, they make a medley, and therewith anoint the same.

The Indian women delight not when they are yong in bearing of children, because it maketh them haue hanging The maners breastes which they account to bee great deforming of the yong of them, and vpon that occasion while they bee women. yong, they destroy their seede, saying, that it is fittest for olde women. Moreouer, when they are deliuered of a childe, they goe straight to washe themselues, without making any further ceremonie for it, not lying in bed as our women doe. The beds which they haue are made of Gossopine cotton, and wrought artificially of diuers colours, which they cary about with them when they trauell, and making the same fast to two trees, lie therein they and their women. The people be surely gentle and tractable, and such as desire to liue peaceably, or els had it bene vnpossible for the Spaniards to haue conquered them as they did, and the more to liue now peaceably, they being so many in number, and the Spaniards so few.

From hence we departed the eight and twentie, and the next day we passed betweene the maine land and the The Isle of Island of Tortuga, a very lowe Island, in the yeere Tortuga.

of our Lorde God one thousande fiue hundred sixty fiue
aforesaide, and sayled along the coast vntill the first of
Aprill, at which time the Captaine sayled along in the Iesus
pinnesse to discerne the coast, and saw many Caribes on shore,
and some also in their Canoas, which made tokens vnto him of
friendship, and shewed him golde, meaning thereby that they
would trafficke for wares.   Whereupon he stayed to see the
maners of them, and so for two or three trifles they gaue such
things as they had about them, and departed : but the Caribes
were very importunate to haue them come on shore, which if it
had not bene for want of wares to trafficke with them, he would
not haue denyed them, because the Indians which we saw before
were very gentle people, and such as do no man hurt.   But as
God would haue it, hee wanted that thing, which if hee had
had, would haue bene his confusion : for these were no such
kinde of people as wee tooke them to bee, but more deuilish a
thousand partes and are eaters and deuourers of any man they
can catch, as it was afterwards declared vnto vs at Burboroata,
by a Carauel comming out of Spaine with certaine souldiers, and
a Captaine generall sent by the king for those Eastward parts of
the Indians, who sayling along in his pinnesse, as our Captaine
did to descry the coast, was by the Caribes called a shoare with
sundry tokens made to him of friendshippe, and golde shewed as
though they desired trafficke, with the which the Spaniard beeing
mooued, suspecting no deceite at all, went ashore amongst them :
who was no sooner a shore, but with foure or fiue more was
taken, the rest of his company being inuaded by them saued
themselues by flight, but they that were taken, paied their ransome with their liues, and were presently eaten.   And
this is their practise to toll with their golde the
ignorant to their snares : they are bloodsuckers both
of Spaniards, Indians, and all that light in their laps, not sparing
their owne countreymen if they can conueniently come by them.
Their pollicie in fight with the Spaniards is maruellous : for they
chuse for their refuge the mountaines and woodes where the
Spaniards with their horses cannot follow them, and if they
fortune to be met in the plaine where one horseman may ouer-
runne 100. of them, they haue a deuise of late practised by them
to pitch stakes of wood in the ground, and also small iron pikes
to mischiefe their horses, wherein they shew themselues politique
warriers.   They haue more abundance of golde then all the

The crueltie
of the
Caribes.

Spaniards haue, and liue vpon the mountaines where the Mines are in such number, that the Spaniards haue much adoe to get any of them from them, and yet sometimes by assembling a great number of them, which happeneth once in two yeeres, they get a piece from them, which afterwards they keepe sure ynough.

Thus hauing escaped the danger of them, wee kept our course along the coast, and came the third of April to a Towne called Burboroata, where his ships came to Burboroata. an ancker, and hee himselfe went a shore to speake with the Spaniards, to whom hee declared himselfe to be an Englishman, and came thither to trade with them by the way of marchandize, and therefore required licence for the same. Vnto whom they made answere, that they were forbidden by the king to trafique with any forren nation, vpon penaltie to forfeit their goods, therefore they desired him not to molest them any further, but to depart as he came, for other comfort he might not looke for at their handes, because they were subiects, and might not goe beyond the law. But hee replied that his necessitie was such, as hee might not so do: for being in one of the Queens Armadas of England, and hauing many souldiers in them, hee had neede both of some refreshing for them, and of victuals, and of money also, without the which hee coulde not depart, and with much other talke perswaded them not to feare any dishonest part of his behalfe towards them, for neither would hee commit any such thing to the dishonour of his prince, nor yet for his honest reputation and estimation, vnlesse hee were too rigorously dealt withall, which he hoped not to finde at their handes, in that it should as well redound to their profite as his owne, and also hee thought they might doe it without danger, because their princes were in amitie one with another, and for our parts wee had free trafique in Spaine and Flanders, which are in his dominions, and therefore he knew no reason why he should not haue the like in all his dominions. To the which the Spaniards made answere, that it lay not in them to giue any licence, for that they had a gouernour to whom the gouernment of those parts was committed, but if they would stay tenne dayes, they would send to their gouernour who was threescore leagues off, and would returne answere within the space appointed, of his minde.

In the meane time they were contented hee should bring his ships into harbour, and there they would deliuer him any victuals he would require. Whereupon the fourth day we went in, where being one day and receiuing all things according to promise, the Captaine aduised himselfe, that to remaine there tenne dayes idle, spending victuals and mens wages, and perhaps in the ende receiue no good answere from the gouernour, it were meere follie, and therefore determined to make request to haue licence for the sale of certaine leane and sicke Negros which hee had in his shippe like to die vpon his hands if he kept them ten dayes, hauing little or no refreshing for them, whereas other men hauing them, they would bee recouered well ynough. And this request hee was forced to make, because he had not otherwise wherewith to pay for victuals and for necessaries which he should take: which request being put in writing and presented, the officers and towne-dwellers assembled together, and finding his request so reasonable, granted him licence for thirtie Negros, which afterwards they caused the officers to view, to the intent they should graunt to nothing but that were very reasonable, for feare of answering thereunto afterwards. This being past, our Captaine according to their licence, thought to haue made sale, but the day past and none came to buy, who before made shewe that they had great neede of them, and therefore wist not what to surmise of them, whether they went about to prolong the time of the Gouernour his answere because they would keepe themselues blamelesse, or for any other pollicie hee knew not, and for that purpose sent them worde, marueiling what the matter was that none came to buy them. They answered, because they had granted licence onely to the poore to buy those Negros of small price, and their money was not so ready as other mens of more wealth. More then that, as soone as euer they sawe the shippes, they conueyed away their money by their wiues that went into the mountaines for feare, and were not yet returned, and yet asked two dayes to seeke their wiues and fetch their money. Notwithstanding, the next day diuers of them came to cheapen, but could not agree of price, because they thought the price too high. Whereupon the Captaine perceiuing they went about to bring downe the price, and meant to buy, and would not confesse if hee had licence, that he might sell at any reasonable rate, as they were worth in other places, did send for the principals of the Towne, and made a shewe hee would depart, declaring himselfe to be very sory that he had so much troubled them, and also that he had sent for the gouernour to come downe, seeing nowe his pretence was to depart, whereat they marueiled much, and asked him what cause mooued him there-unto, seeing by their working he was in possibilitie to haue his licence.

To the which he replied, that it was not onely a licence that he sought, but profit, which he perceiued was not there to bee had, and therefore would seeke further, and withall shewed him his writings what he payed for his Negros, declaring also the great charge he was at in his shipping and mens wages, and therefore to counteruaile his charges, hee must sell his Negros for a greater price then they offered. So they doubting his departure, put him in comfort to sell better there then in any other place. And if it fell out that he had no licence, that he should not loose his labour in tarying, for they would buy without licence. Whereupon, the Captaine being put in comfort, promised them to stay, so that hee might make sale of his leane Negros, which they granted vnto. And the next day did sell some of them, who hauing bought and payed for them, thinking to haue had a discharge of the Customer, for the custome of the Negros, being the kings duetie, they gaue it away to the poore for Gods sake, and did refuse to giue the discharge in writing, and the poore not trusting their wordes, for feare, least hereafter it might bee demaunded of them, did refraine from buying any more, so that nothing else was done vntill the Gouernours comming downe, which was the fourteenth day, and then the Captaine made petition, declaring that hee was come thither in a shippe of the Queenes Maiesties of England, being bound to Guinie, and thither driuen by winde and weather, so that being come thither, hee had neede of sundry necessaries for the repara-tion of the said Nauie, and also great need of money for the paiment of his Souldiours, vnto whom hee had promised paiment, and therefore although he would, yet would not they depart without it, and for that purpose he requested licence for the sale of certaine of his Negros, declaring that although they were for-bidden to trafique with strangers, yet for that there was a great amitie between their princes, and that the thing perteined to our Queens highnesse, he thought hee might doe their prince great seruice, and that it would bee well taken at his hands, to doe it in this cause. The which allegations with diuers others put in request, were presented vnto the Gouernour, who sitting in counsell for that matter, granted vnto his request for licence.

But yet there fell out another thing which was the abating of the kings Custome, being vpon euery slaue 30. duckets, which would not be granted vnto.

Whereupon the Captaine perceiuing that they would neither come neere his price hee looked for by a great deale, nor yet would abate the Kings Custome of that they offered, so that either he must be a great looser by his wares, or els compell the officers to abate the same kings Custome which was too vnreasonable, for to a higher price hee coulde not bring the buyers: Therefore the sixteenth of April hee prepared one hundred men well armed with bowes, arrowes, harquebuzes and pikes, with the which hee marched to the townewards, and being perceiued by the Gouernour, he straight with all expedition sent messengers to knowe his request, desiring him to march no further forward vntill he had answere againe, which incontinent he should haue. So our Captaine declaring how vnreasonable a thing the Kings Custome was, requested to haue the same abated, and to pay seuen and a halfe per centum, which is the ordinarie Custome for wares through his dominions there, and vnto this if they would not graunt, hee would displease them. And this word being caried to the Gouernour, answere was returned that all things should bee to his content, and thereupon hee determined to depart, but the souldiers and Mariners finding so little credite in their promises, demanded gages for the performance of the premisses, or els they would not depart. And thus they being constrained to send gages, wee departed, beginning our traffique, and ending the same without disturbance.

An hundreth Englishmen in armour.

Thus hauing made traffique in the harborough vntill the 28. our Captaine with his ships intended to goe out of the roade, and purposed to make shew of his departure, because nowe the common sort hauing imployed their money, the rich men were come to towne, who made no shewe that they were come to buy, so that they went about to bring downe the price, and by this pollicie the Captaine knew they would be made the more eger, for feare least we departed, and they should goe without any at all.

The nine and twentie wee being at ancker without the road, a French ship called the Greene Dragon of Newhauen, whereof was Captaine one Bon Temps came in, who saluted vs after the maner of the Sea, with certaine pieces of Ordinance, and we resaluted him with the like againe : with whom hauing communication, he declared that hee had bene at the Mine in Guinie, and was beaten off by the Portugals gallies, and inforced to come thither to make sale of such wares as he had : and further that the like was happened vnto the Minion : besides the Captain Dauie Carlet and a Marchant, with a dozen Mariners betrayed by the Negros at their first arriuall thither, and remayning prisoners with the Portugals ; and besides other misaduentures of the losse of their men, happened through the great lacke of fresh water, with great doubts of bringing home the ships : which was most sorrowfull for vs to vnderstand.

The reports of the mis-haps of the Minion in Guinie.

Thus hauing ended our trafique here the 4. of May, we departed, leauing the Frenchman behinde vs, the night before the which the Caribes, whereof I haue made mention before, being to the number of 200. came in their Canoas to Burboroata, intending by night to haue burned the towne, and taken the Spaniards, who being more vigilant because of our being there, then their custome was, perceiuing them comming, raised the towne, who in a moment being a horsebacke, by meanes their custome is for all doubts to keepe their horses ready sadled, in the night set vpon them, and tooke one, but the rest making shift for themselues, escaped away. But this one, because he was their guide, and was the occasion that diuers times they had made inuasion upon them, had for his traueile a stake thrust through his fundament, and so out at his necke.

The sixt of May aforesaide, wee came to an yland called Curaçao, where wee had thought to haue anckered, but could not find ground, and hauing let fal an ancker with two cables, were faine to weigh it again : and the seuenth sayling along the coast to seeke an harborow, and finding none, wee came to an ancker where we rode open in the Sea. In this place we had trafique for hides, and found great refreshing both of beefe, mutton and lambes, whereof there was such plentie, that sauing the skinnes, we had the flesh giuen vs for nothing, the plentie whereof was so abundant, that the worst in the ship thought scorne not onely of mutton, but also of sodden lambe, which they disdained to eate vnrosted.

Exceeding plentie of cattle in Curazao.

The increase of cattell in this yland is marueilous, which from a doozen of each sort brought thither by the gouernour, in 25.

yeres he had a hundreth thousand at the least, and of other cattel was able to kil without spoile of the increase 1500. yeerely, which hee killeth for the skinnes, and of the flesh saueth onely the tongues, the rest hee leaueth to the foule to deuour. And this I am able to affirme, not only vpon the Gouernours owne report, who was the first that brought the increase thither, which so remaineth vnto this day, but also by that I saw my selfe in one field, where an hundred oxen lay one by another all whole, sauing the skinne and tongue taken away. And it is not so marueilous a thing why they doe thus cast away the flesh in all the ylands of the West Indies, seeing the land is great, and more then they are able to inhabite, the people fewe, hauing delicate fruites and meates ynough besides to feede vpon, which they rather desire, and the increase which passeth mans reason to beleeue, when they come to a great number: for in S. Domingo an yland called by the finders thereof Hispaniola, is so great quantitie of cattell, and such increase therof, that notwith- standing the daily killing of them for their hides, it is not possible to asswage the number of them, but they are deuoured by wilde dogs, whose number is such by suffering them first to range the woods and mountaines, that they eate and destroy 60000. a yeere, and yet small lacke found of them. And no marueile, for the said yland is almost as bigge as all England, and being the first place that was founde of all the Indies, and of long time inhabited before the rest, it ought therefore of reason to be most populous : and to this houre the Viceroy and counsell royall abideth there as in the chiefest place of all the Indies, to prescribe orders to the rest for the kings behalfe, yet haue they but one Citie and 13. villages in all the same yland, whereby the spoile of them in respect of the increase is nothing.

Great num-bers of wilde dogs.

The 15. of the foresaid moneth wee departed from Curaçao, being not a little to the reioycing of our Captaine and vs, that wee had there ended our trafique : but notwithstanding our sweete meate, wee had sower sauce, for by reason of our riding so open at sea, what with blastes whereby our anckers being a ground, three at once came home, and also with contrary windes blowing, whereby for feare of the shore we were faine to hale off to haue anker-hold, sometimes a whole day and a night we turned vp and downe ; and this happened not once, but halfe a dozen times in the space of our being there.

The 16. we passed by an yland called Aruba, and the 17. at night anckered sixe houres at the West ende of Cabo de la vela, and in the morning being the 18. weighed againe, keeping our course, in the which time the Captaine sayling by the shore in the pinnesse, came to the Rancheria, a place where the Spaniards vse to fish for pearles, and there spoke La Rancheria. with a Spaniard, who tolde him how far off he was from Rio de la Hacha, which because he would not ouershoot, he ankered that night againe, and the 19. came thither ; where hauing talke with the kings treasurer of the Indies resident there, he declared his quiet trafique in Burboroata, and shewed a certificate of the same, made by the gouernour thereof, and therefore he desired to haue the like there also : but the treasurer made answere that they were forbidden by the Viceroy and council of S. Domingo, who hauing intelligence of our being on the coast, did sende expresse commission to resist vs, with all the force they could, insomuch that they durst not traffique with vs in no case, alleaging that if they did, they should loose all that they did trafique for, besides their bodies at the magistrates commaundement. Our Captaine replied, that he was in an Armada of the Queenes Maiesties of England, and sent about other her affaires, but driuen besides his pretended voyage, was inforced by contrary windes to come into those parts, where he hoped to finde such friendship as hee should doe in Spaine, to the contrary whereof hee knewe no reason, in that there was amitie betwixt their princes. But seeing they would contrary to all reason go about to withstand his trafique, he would it should not be said by him, that hauing the force he hath, to be driuen from his trafique perforce, but he would rather put it in aduenture to try whither he or they should haue the better, and therefore willed them to determine either to giue him licence to trade, or else to stand to their owne harmes : So vpon this it was determined hee should haue licence to trade, but they would giue him such a price as was the one halfe lesse then he had sold for before, and thus they sent word they would do, and none· otherwise, and if it liked him not, he might do what he would, for they were not determined to deale otherwise with him. Whereupon, the captaine waying their vnconscionable request, M. Hawkins wrote to them a letter, that they dealt too rigorously the Treasurer with him, to go about to cut his throte in the price of of Rio de la his commodities, which were so reasonably rated, as Hacha.

they could not by a great deale haue the like at any other mans handes. But seeing they had sent him this to his supper, hee would in the morning bring them as good a breakfast. And therefore in the morning being the 21. of May, hee shot off a whole Culuering to summon the towne, and preparing one hundred men in armour, went ashore, hauing in his great boate two Faulcons of brasse, and in the other boates double bases in their noses, which being perceiued by the Townesmen, they incontinent in battell aray with their drumme and ensigne displayed, marched from the Towne to the sands, of footemen to the number of an hundred and fiftie, making great bragges with their cries, and weauing vs a shore, whereby they made a semblance to haue fought with vs in deed. But our Captaine perceiuing them so bragge, commanded the two Faulcons to be discharged at them, which put them in no small feare to see, (as they afterward declared) such great pieces in a boate. At euery shot they fell flat to the ground, and as wee approched neere vnto them, they broke their aray, and dispersed themselues so much for feare of the Ordinance, that at last they went all away with their ensigne. The horsemen also being about thirtie, made as braue a shew as might be, coursing vp and downe with their horses, their braue white leather Targets in the one hand, and their iauelings in the other, as though they would haue receiued vs at our landing. But when wee landed, they gaue ground, and consulted what they should doe, for little they thought wee would haue landed so boldly : and therefore as the Captaine was putting his men in aray, and marched forward to haue encountred with them, they sent a messenger on horsebacke with a flagge of truce to the Captaine, who declared that the Treasurer marueiled what he meant to doe to come a shore in that order, in consideration that they had granted to euery reasonable request that he did demaund : but the Captaine not well contented with this messenger, marched forwards. The messenger prayed him to stay his men, and saide, if hee would come apart from his men, the Treasurer would come and speake with him, whereunto hee did agree to commune together, the Captaine onely with his armour without weapon, and the Treasurer on horsebacke with his iaueling, was afraide to come neere him for feare of his armour, which he said was worse than his weapon, and so keeping aloofe communing together, granted in fine to all his requests.

Which being declared by the Captaine to the company, they desired to haue pledges for the performance of all things doubting that otherwise when they had made themselues stronger they would haue bene at defiance with vs : and seeing that now they might haue what they would request, they iudged it to be more wisedome to be in assurance then to be forced to make any more labours about it. So vpon this, gages were sent, and we made our trafique quietly with them. In the mean time while we stayed here, wee watered a good breadth off from the shore, where by the strength of the fresh water running into the Sea, the salt water was made fresh. In this Riuer we saw many Crocodils of sundry bignesses, but some as bigge as a boate, with 4. feete, a long broad mouth, and a long taile, whose skinne is so hard, that a sword wil not pierce it. His nature is to liue out of the water as a frogge doth, but he is a great deuourer, and spareth neither fish, which is his common food, nor beastes, nor men, if he take them, as the proofe thereof was knowen by a Negro, who as hee was filling water in the Riuer was by one of them caried cleane away, and neuer seene after. His nature is euer when hee would haue his prey, to cry and sobbe like a Christian body, to prouoke them to come to him, and then hee snatcheth at them, and thereupon came this prouerbe that is applied vnto women when they weepe, Lachrymæ Crocodili, the meaning whereof is, that as the Crocodile when hee crieth, goeth then about most to deceiue, so doeth a woman most commonly when she weepeth. Of these the Master of the Iesus watched one, and by the banks side stroke him with a pike of a bill in the side, and after three or foure times turning in sight, hee sunke downe, and was not afterward seene. In the time of our being in the Riuers Guinie, wee sawe many of a monstrous big-nesse, amongst the which the captaine being in one of the Barkes comming downe the same, shot a Faulcon at one, which very narrowly hee missed, and with a feare hee plunged into the water, making a streame like the way of a boate.

Now while we were here, whether it were of a feare that the Spaniards doubted wee would haue done them some harme before we departed, or for any treason that they intended towards vs, I am not able to say ; but then came thither a Captaine from some of the other townes, with a dozen souldiers vpon a time when our Captaine and the treasurer cleared al things betweene them, and were in a communication of debt of the gouernors of

Burboroata, which was to be payd by the said treasurer, who
would not answer the same by any meanes.   Whereupon certaine
words of displeasure passed betwixt the Captaine and him, and
parting the one from the other, the treasurer possibly doubting
that our Captaine would perforce haue sought the same, did
immediately command his men to armes, both horsemen and
footemen : but because the Captaine was in the Riuer on the
backe side of the Towne with his other boates, and all his men
vnarmed and without weapons, it was to be iudged he ment him
little good, hauing that aduantage of him, that comming vpon
the sudden, hee might haue mischieued many of his men : but
the Captaine hauing vnderstanding thereof, not trusting to their
gentlenesse, if they might haue the aduantage, departed aboord
his ships, and at night returned againe, and demanded amongst
other talke, what they ment by assembling their men in that
order, and they answered, that their Captaine being come to
towne did muster his men according to his accustomed maner.
But it is to be iudged to bee a cloake, in that comming for that
purpose hee might haue done it sooner, but the trueth is, they
were not of force vntill then, whereby to enterprise any matter
against vs, by meanes of pikes and harquebuzes, whereof they
haue want, and were now furnished by our Captaine, and also 3.
Faulcons, which hauing got in other places, they haue secretly
conueyed thither, which made them the bolder, and also
for that they saw now a conuenient place to do such
The author of a feat, and time also seruing thereunto, by the meanes
this storie. that our men were not onely vnarmed and vnprouided
as at no time before the like, but also were occupied
in hewing of wood, and least thinking of any harme :
these were occasions to prouoke them thereunto.   And I
suppose they went about to bring it to effect, in that
I with another gentleman being in the towne, thinking of
no harme towards vs, and seeing men assembling in armour to
the treasurers house, whereof I marueiled, and reuoking to
minde the former talke betweene the Captaine and him, and
the vnreadinesse of our men, of whom aduantage might haue
bene taken, departed out of the Towne immediately to
giue knowledge thereof, but before we came to our men by a
flight-shot, two horsemen riding a gallop were come neere vs,
being sent, as wee did gesse, to stay vs least wee should cary
newes to our Captaine, but seeing vs so neere our men they

stayed their horses, comming together, and suffring vs to passe, belike because wee were so neere, that if they had gone about the same, they had bene espied by some of our men which then immediatly would haue departed, whereby they should haue bene frustrate of their pretence : and so the two horsemen ridde about the bushes to espie what we did, and seeing vs gone, to the intent they might shadow their comming downe in post, whereof suspition might bee had, fained a simple excuse in asking whether he could sell any wine, but that seemed so simple to the Captaine, that standing in doubt of their courtesie, he returned in the morning with his three boats, appointed with Bases in their noses, and his men with weapons accordingly, where as before he caried none : and thus dissembling all iniuries conceiued of both parts, the Captaine went ashore, leauing pledges in the boates for himselfe, and cleared all things betweene the treasurer and him, sauing for the gouernours debt, which the one by no meanes would answere, and the other, because it was not his due debt, woulde not molest him for it, but was content to remit it vntill another time, and therefore departed, causing the two Barkes which rode neere the shore to weigh and go vnder saile, which was done because that our Captaine demanding a testimoniall of his good behauiour there, could not haue the same vntill hee were vnder saile ready to depart : and therefore at night he went for the same againe, and receiued it at the treasurers hand, of whom very courteously he tooke his leaue and departed, shooting off the bases of his boat for his farewell, and the townesmen also shot off foure Faulcons and 30. harquebuzes, and this was the first time that he knew of the conueyance of their Faulcons.

The 31. of May wee departed, keeping our course to Hispaniola, and the fourth of Iune wee had sight of an yland, which wee made to be Iamaica, maruelling that by the vehement course of the Seas we should be driuen so farre to leeward : for setting our course to the West end of Hispaniola we fel with the middle of Iamaica, notwithstanding that to al mens sight it shewed a headland, but they were all deceiued by the clouds that lay vpon the land two dayes together, in such sort that we thought it to be the head land of the sayd yland. And a Spaniard being in the ship, who was a Marchant, and inhabitant in Iamaica, hauing occasion to goe to Guinie, and being by treason taken of the Negros, and afterwards bought by the Tangomangos, was by our Captaine brought from thence, and had his passage to go into his countrey, who perceiuing the land, made as though he knew euery place thereof, and pointed to certaine places which he named to be such a place, and such a mans ground, and that behinde such a point was the harborow, but in the ende he pointed so from one point to another, that we were a leeboord of all places, and found our selues at the West end of Iamaica before we were aware of it, and being once to lee-ward, there was no getting vp againe, so that by trusting of the Spaniards knowledge, our Captaine sought not to speake with any of the inhabitants, which if he had not made himselfe sure of, he would haue done as his custome was in other places : but this man was a plague not onely to our Captaine, who made him loose by ouershooting the place 2000. pounds by hides, which hee might haue gotten, but also to himselfe, who being three yeeres out of his Couutrey, and in great misery in Guinie, both among the Negros and Tangomangos, and in hope to come to his wife and friends, as he made sure accompt, in that at his going into the pinnesse, when he went to shore he put on his new clothes, and for ioy flung away his old, could not afterwards finde any habitation, neither there or in all Cuba, which we sailed all along, but it fell out euer by one occasion or other, that wee were put be-side the same, so that he was faine to be brought into England, and it happened to him as it did to a duke of Samaria, when the Israelites were besieged, and were in great misery with hunger, and being tolde by the Prophet Elizæus, that a bushell of flower should be sold for a sickle, would not belieue him, but thought it impossible : and for that cause Elizæus prophesied hee should see the same done, but hee should not eate thereof : so this man being absent three yeeres, and not euer thinking to haue seene his own countrey, did see the same, went vpon it, and yet was it not his fortune to come to it, or to any habitation, whereby to remaine with his friends according to his desire.

Thus hauing sailed along the coast two dayes, we departed the seuenth of Iune, being made to beleeue by the Spaniard that it was not Iamaica, but rather Hispaniola, of which opinion the Captaine also was, because that which hee made Iamaica seemed to be but a piece of the land, and thereby tooke it rather to be The deceit- Hispaniola, by the lying of the coast, and also for full force of that being ignorant of the force of the current, he the current. could not beleeue he was so farre driuen to leeward, and therefore setting his course to Iamaica, and after certaine

dayes not finding the same, perceiued then certainly that the
yland which he was at before was Iamaica, and that the cloudes
did deceiue him, whereof he maruelled not a little : and this mis-
taking of the place came to as ill a passe as the ouershooting of
Iamaica : for by this did he also ouerpasse a place in Cuba, called
Santa Cruz, where, as he was informed, was great store of hides
to be had : and thus being disappointed of two of his portes,
where he thought to haue raised great profite by his trafique and
also to haue found great refreshing of victuals and water for his
men, hee was now disappointed greatly, and such want he had of
fresh water, that he was forced to seeke the shore to obteine the
same, which he had sight of after certaine dayes ouerpassed with
stormes and contrary windes, but yet not of the
maine of Cuba, but of certaine ylands in number two   Two hund-
hundred, whereof the most part were desolate of in- red ylands
habitants : by the which ylands the Captaine passing for the most
in his pinnesse, could finde no fresh water vntill hee part not inhabited.
came to an yland bigger then all the rest, called the yle of Pinas,
where wee anckered with our ships the 16. of Iune, and found
water, which although it were neither so toothsome as running
water, by the meanes it is standing, and but the water of raine,
and also being neere the Sea was brackish, yet did wee not refuse
it, but were more glad thereof, as the time then required, then
wee should haue bene another time with fine Conduit water.
Thus being reasonably watered we were desirous to depart,
because the place was not very conuenient for such ships of
charge as they were, because there were many shoales to leeward,
which also lay open to the sea for any wind that should blow :
and therefore the captaine made the more haste away, which was
not vnneedfull : for little sooner were their anckers weyed, and
foresaile set, but there arose such a storme, that they had not
much to spare for doubling out of the shoales : for one of the
barks not being fully ready as the rest, was faine for haste to cut
the cable in the hawse, and loose both ancker and cable to saue
herselfe.

Thus the 17. of Iune, we departed and on the 20. The Cape of
wee fell with the West end of Cuba, called Cape S. Anthony
S. Antony, where for the space of three dayes wee in Cuba.
doubled along, till wee came beyond the shoales, which are
20. leagues beyond S. Anthony. And the ordinary Brise taking
vs, which is the Northeastwinde, put vs the 24. from the shoare,

and therefore we went to the Northwest to fetch wind, and also to the coast of Florida to haue the helpe of the current, which was iudged to haue set to the Eastward : so the 29. wee found our selues in 27. degrees, and in the soundings of Florida, where we kept our selues the space of foure dayes, sailing along the coast as neere as we could, in tenne or twelue fadome water, hauing all the while no sight of land.

The Isles of Tortugas.
Great store of birds.

The fift of Iuly we had sight of certeine Islands of sand, called the Tortugas (which is lowe land) where the captaine went in with his pinnesse, and found such a number of birds, that in halfe an houre he laded her with them ; and if they had beene ten boats more, they might haue done the like.   These Islands beare the name of Tortoises, because of the number of them, which there do breed, whose nature is to liue both in the water and. vpon land also, but breed onely vpon the shore, in making a great pit wherein they lay egges, to the number of three or foure hundred, and couering them with sand, they are hatched by the heat of the Sunne ; and by this meanes commeth the great increase.   Of these we tooke very great ones, which haue both backe and belly all of bone, of the thicknes of an inch : the fish whereof we proued, eating much like veale ; and finding a number of eggs in them, tasted also of them, but they did eat very sweetly.   Heere wee ankered sixe houres, and then a. fair gale of winde springing, we weyed anker, and made saile toward Cuba,

A hill called the Table.

whither we came the sixt day, and weathered as farre as the Table, being a hill so called because of the forme thereof: here we lay off and on all night to keepe that we had gotten to wind-ward, intending to haue watered in the morning, if we could haue done it, or els if the winde had come larger, to haue plied to wind-ward

The port of Hauana.

to Hauana, which is an harborow whereunto all the fleet of the Spanyards come, and doe there tary to haue one the company of another.   This hill we thinking to haue beene the Table, made account (as it was indeed) that Hauana was but eight leagues to wind-ward, but by the per-swasion of a French man, who made the captaine beleeue he knew the table very well, and had beene at Hauana, sayd that it was not the Table, and that the Table was much higher, and neerer to the sea side, and that there was no plaine ground to the Eastward, nor hilles to the Westward, but all was contrary,

and that behinde the hilles to the Westward was Hauana. To
which persuasion credit being giuen by some, and they not of
the woorst, the captaine was perswaded to goe to leeward, and so
sailed along the seuenth and eight dayes, finding no habitation,
nor no other Table ; and then perceiuing his folly to giue eare to
such praters, was not a little sory, both because he did consider
what time he should spend yer he could get so far to wind-ward
againe, which would haue bene, with the weathering which we
had, ten or twelue dayes worke, and what it would haue bene
longer he knew not, and (that which was woorst) he had not
aboue a dayes water, and therfore knew not what shift to make :
but in fine, because the want was such, that his men could not
liue with it, he determined to seeke water, and to goe further to
leeward, to a place (as it is set in the card) called Rio de los
puercos, which he was in doubt of, both whether it were
inhabited, and whether there were water or not, and whether
for the shoalds he might haue accesse with his ships, that he
might conueniently take in the same. And while we were in
these troubles, and kept our way to the place aforesayd, almighty
God our guide (who would not suffer vs to run into any further
danger, which we had bene like to haue incurred, if we had
ranged the coast of Florida along as we did before, which is so
dangerous (by reports) that no ship escapeth which commeth
thither, as the Spanyards haue very wel proued the same) sent
vs the eight day at night a faire Westerly winde, whereupon the
captaine and company consulted, determining not to refuse Gods
gift, but euery man was contented to pinch his owne bellie,
whatsoeuer had happened ; and taking the sayd winde, the ninth
day of Iuly got to the Table, and sailing the same night, vnawares
ouershot Hauana ; at which place wee thought to haue watered :
but the next day, not knowing that wee had ouershot the same,
sailed along the coast, seeking it, and the eleuenth day in the
morning, by certaine knowen marks, we vnderstood that we had
ouershot it 20 leagues : in which coast ranging, we found no
conuenient watering place, whereby there was no remedy but to
disemboque, and to water vpon the coast of Florida : for, to go
further to the Eastward, we could not for the shoalds, which are
very dangerous ; and because the current shooteth to the Northeast, we doubted by the force thereof to be set vpon them, and
therefore durst not approch them :. so making but reasonable
way the day aforesayd, and all the night, the twelfth day in the

morning we fell with the Islands vpon the cape of Florida, which
we could scant double by the meanes that fearing the shoalds to
The state of the Eastwards, and doubting the current comming
the current out of the West, which was not of that force we made
of Florida. account of; for we felt little or none till we fell with
the cape, and then felt such a current, that bearing all sailes
against the same, yet were driuen backe againe a great pace : the
experience whereof we had by the Iesus pinnesse, and the
Salomons boat, which were sent the same day in the afternoone,
whiles the ships were becalmed, to see if they could finde any
water vpon the Islands aforesaid ; who spent a great part of the
day in rowing thither, being further off then they deemed it to
be, and in the meane time a faire gale of winde springing at sea,
the ships departed, making a signe to them to come away, who
although they saw them depart, because they were so neere the
shore, would not lose all the labour they had taken, but determined to keepe their way, and see if there were any water to be
had, making no account but to finde the shippes well enough :
but they spent so much time in filling the water which they had
found, that the night was come before they could make an end.
And hauing lost the sight of the ships, they rowed what they
could, but were wholly ignorant which way they should seeke
them againe ; as indeed there was a more doubt then they knew
of: for when they departed, the shippes were in no current ; and
sailing but a mile further, they found one so strong, that bearing
all sailes, it could not preuaile against the same, but were driuen
backe : whereupon the captaine sent the Salomon, with the other
two barks, to beare neere the shore all night, because the current
was lesse there a great deale, and to beare light, with shooting off
a piece now and then, to the intent the boats might better know
how to come to them.

The Iesus also bare a light in her toppe gallant, and shot off a
piece also now and then, but the night passed, and the morning
was come, being the thirteenth day, and no newes could be
heard of them, but the ships and barkes ceased not to looke still
for them, yet they thought it was all in vaine, by the meanes
they heard not of them all the night past ; and therefore determined to tary no longer, seeking for them till noone,·and if they
heard no newes, then they would depart to the Iesus, who perforce
(by the vehemency of the current) was caried almost out of sight ;
but as God would haue it, now time being come, and they hauing

tacked about in the pinnesses top, had sight of them, and tooke them vp : they in the boats, being to the number of one and twenty, hauing sight of the ships, and seeing them tacking about; whereas before at the first sight of them they did greatly reioyce, were now in a greater perplexitie then euer they were : for by this they thought themselues vtterly forsaken, whereas before they were in some hope to haue found them. Truly God wrought maruellously for them, for they themselues hauing no victuals but water, and being sore oppressed with hunger, were not of opinion to bestow any further time in seeking the shippes then that present noone time : so that if they had not at that instant espied them, they had gone to the shore to haue made prouision for victuals, and with such things as they could haue gotten, either to haue gone for that part of Florida where the French men were planted (which would haue bene very hard for them to haue done, because they wanted victuals to bring them thither, being an hundred and twenty leagues off) or els to haue remained amongst the Floridians ; at whose hands they were put in comfort by a French man, who was with them, that had remained in Florida at the first finding thereof, a whole yeere together, to receiue victuals snfficient, and gentle entertainment, if need were, for a yeere or two, vntill which time God might haue prouided for them. But how contrary this would haue fallen out to their expectations, it is hard to iudge, seeing those people of the cape of Florida are of more sauage and fierce nature, and more valiant than any of the rest ; which the Span-yards well prooued, who being fiue hundred men, who intended there to land, returned few or none of them, but were inforced to forsake the same : and of their cruelty mention is made in the booke of the Decades, of a frier, who taking vpon him to per-suade the people to subiection, was by them taken, and his skin cruelly pulled ouer his eares, and his flesh eaten.

In these Islands they being a shore, found a dead man, dried in a maner whole, with other heads and bodies of men : so that these sorts of men are eaters of the flesh of men, aswel as the Canibals. But to returne to our purpose.

The foureteenth day the shippe and barks came to the Iesus, bringing them newes of the recouery of the men, which was not a little to the reioycing of the captaine, and the whole company : and so then altogether they kept on their way along the coast of Florida, and the fifteenth day came to an anker, and so from

M. Hawkins sixe and twenty degrees to thirty degrees and a halfe,
ranged all where the French men abode, ranging all the coast
the coast of along, seeking for fresh water, ankering euery night,
Florida. because we would ouershoot no place of fresh water,
and in the day time the captaine in the ships pinnesse sailed
along the shore, went into euery creeke, speaking with diuers of
the Floridians, because hee would vnderstand where the French
men inhabited ; and not finding them in eight and twentie
degrees, as it was declared vnto him, maruelled thereat, and
neuer left sailing along the coast till he found them, who inhabited
in a riuer, by them called the riuer of May, and standing in
thirty degrees and better.   In ranging this coast along, the
Florida found captaine found it to be all an Island, and therefore
to be cut into it is all lowe land, and very scant of fresh water, but
Islands. the countrey was maruellously sweet, with both
The commo-
dities of marish and medow ground, and goodly woods among.
Florida. There they found sorell to grow as abundantly as
grasse, and where their houses were, great store of maiz and
mill, and grapes of great bignesse, but of taste much like our
English grapes.   Also Deere great plentie, which came vpon
The houses of the sands before them.   Their houses are not many
Florida. together, for in one house an hundred of them do
lodge ; they being made much like a great barne, and in strength
not inferior to ours, for they haue stanchions and rafters of whole
trees, and are couered with palmito-leaues, hauing no place
diuided, but one small roome for their king and queene.   In
the middest of this house is a hearth, where they make great fires
all night, and they sleepe vpon certeine pieces of wood hewin in
for the bowing of their backs, and another place made high for
their heads, which they put one by another all along the walles
on both sides.   In their houses they remaine onely in the nights,
and in the day they desire the fields, where they dresse their
meat, and make prouision for victuals, which they prouide onely
for a meale from hand to mouth.   There is one thing to be
maruelled at, for the making of their fire, and not onely they but
The maner also the Negros doe the same, which is made onely
of kindling of by two stickes, rubbing them one against another :
fire in and this they may doe in any place they come, where
Florida. they finde sticks sufficient for the purpose.   In their
apparell the men onely vse deere skinnes, wherewith some onely
couer their priuy members, other some vse the same as garments

to couer them before and behind; which skinnes are painted, some yellow and red, some blacke and russet, and euery man according to his owne fancy. They do not omit to paint their bodies also with curious knots, or antike worke, as euery man in his owne fancy deuiseth, which painting, to make it continue the better, they vse with a thorne to pricke their flesh, and dent in the same, whereby the painting may haue better hold. In their warres they vse a sleighter colour of painting their faces, whereby to make themselues shew the more fierce; which after their warres ended, they wash away againe. In their warres they vse bowes and arrowes, whereof their bowes are made of a kind of Yew, but blacker then ours, and for the most part passing the strength of the Negros or Indians, for it is not greatly inferior to ours : their arrowes are also of a great length, but yet of reeds like other Indians, but varying in two points, both in length and also for nocks and feathers, which the other lacke, whereby they shoot very stedy : the heads of the same are vipers teeth, bones of fishes, flint stones, piked points of kniues, which they hauing gotten of the French men, broke the same, and put the points of them in their arrowes heads : some of them haue their heads of siluer, othersome that haue want of these, put in a kinde of hard wood, notched, which pierceth as farre as any of the rest. In their fight, being in the woods, they vse a maruellous pollicie for their owne safegard, which is by clasping a tree in their armes, and yet shooting notwithstanding : this policy they vsed with the French men in their fight, whereby it appeareth that they are people of some policy : and although they are called by the Spanyards Gente triste, that is to say, Bad people, meaning thereby, that they are not men of capacity : yet haue the French men found them so witty in their answeres, that by the captaines owne report, a counseller with vs could not giue a more profound reason.

The women also for their apparell vse painted skinnes, but most of them gownes of mosse, somewhat longer then our mosse, which they sowe together artificially, and make the same surplesse wise, wearing their haire down to their shoulders, like the Indians. In this riuer of May aforesayd, the captaine entring with his pinnesse, found a French ship of fourescore tun, and two pinnesses of fifteene tun a piece, by her, and speaking with the keepers thereof, they tolde him of a fort two leagues vp, which they had built, in

The French fort.

I 2

which their captaine Monsieur Laudonniere was, with certeine souldiers therein. To whom our captaine sending to vnderstand of a watering place, where he might conueniently take it in, and to haue licence for the same, he straight, because there was no conuenient place but vp the riuer fiue leagues, where the water was fresh, did send him a pilot for the more expedition thereof, to bring in one of his barks, which going in with other boats prouided for the same purpose, ankered before the fort, into the which our captaine went ; where hee was by the Generall, with other captaines and souldiers, very gently enterteined, who declared vnto him the time of their being there, which was fourteene moneths, with the extremity they were driuen to for want of victuals, hauing brought very little with them ; in which place they being two hundred men at their first comming, had in short space eaten all the maiz they could buy of the inhabitants about them, and therefore were driuen certeine of them to serue a king of the Floridians against other his enemies, for mill and other

Bread made of acorns.
victuals : which hauing gotten could not serue them, being so many, so long a time : but want came vpon them in such sort, that they were faine to gather acorns, which being stamped small, and often washed, to take away the bitternesse of them, they did vse for bread, eating withall sundry times, roots, whereof they found many good and holesome, and such as serue rather for medecines then for meates alone. But this hardnesse not contenting some of them, who would not take the paines so much as to fish in the riuer before their doores, but would haue all things put in their mouthes, they did rebell against the captaine, taking away first his armour, and afterward imprisoning him : and so to the number of fourescore of them, departed with a barke and a pinnesse, spoiling their store of victuall, and taking away a great part thereof with them, and so went to the Islands of Hispaniola and Iamaica a rouing, where they spoiled and pilled the Spanyards ; and hauing taken two carauels laden with wine and casaui, which is a bread made of roots, and much other victuals and treasure, had not the grace to depart therewith, but were of such haughty stomacks, that they thought their force to be such that no man durst meddle with them, and so kept harborow in Iamaica, going dayly ashore at their pleasure. But God which would not suffer such euill doers vnpunished, did indurate their hearts in such sort, that they lingered the time so long, that a ship and galliasse being made

out of Santa Domingo came thither into the harborow, and tooke
twenty of them, whereof the most part were hanged, and the
rest caried into Spaine, and some (to the number of fiue
and twenty) escaped in the pinnesse, and came to Florida;
where at their landing they were put in prison, and incontinent foure of the chiefest being condemned, at the
request of the souldiers, did passe the harquebuzers, and then
were hanged vpon a gibbet. This lacke of threescore The occasion
men was a great discourage and weakening to the of the falling
rest, for they were the best souldiers that they had : out with the
for they had now made the inhabitants weary of them Floridians.
by their dayly crauing of maiz, hauing no wares left to content
them withall, and therefore were inforced to rob them, and to
take away their victual perforce, which was the occasion that the
Floridians (not well contented therewith) did take certeine of their
company in the woods, and slew them ; whereby there grew great
warres betwixt them and the Frenchmen : and therefore they
being but a few in number durst not venture abroad, but at such
time as they were inforced thereunto for want of food to do the
same : and going twenty harquebuzers in a company, were set
vpon by eighteene kings, hauing seuen or eight hundred men,
which with one of their bowes slew one of their men, and hurt a
dozen, and droue them all downe to their boats ; whose pollicy in
fight was to be maruelled at : for hauing shot at diuers of their
bodies which were armed, and perceiuing that their arrowes did
not preuaile against the same, they shot at their faces and legs,
which were the places that the Frenchmen were hurt in. Thus
the Frenchmen returned, being in ill case by the hurt of their
men, hauing not aboue forty souldiers left vnhurt, whereby they
might ill make any more inuasions vpon the Floridians, and
keepe their fort withall : which they must haue beene driuen vnto,
had not God sent vs thither for their succour ; for they had not
aboue ten dayes victuall left before we came. In which per-
plexity our captaine seeing them, spared them out of The French
his ship twenty barrels of meale, and foure pipes of greatly re-
beanes, with diuers other victuals and necessaries lieued by M.
which he might conueniently spare : and to helpe Hawkins.
them the better homewardes, whither they were bound before
our comming, at their request we spared them one of our barks
of fifty tun. Notwithstanding the great want that the Frenchmen
had, the ground doth yeeld victuals sufficient, if they would

haue taken paines to get the same ; but they being souldiers'
desired to liue by the sweat of other mens browes : for
while they had peace with the Floridians, they had for
sufficient, by weares which they made to catch the
same : but when they grew to warres, the Floridians tooke away
the same againe, and then would not the Frenchmen take the
paines to make any more. The ground yeeldeth naturally grapes
in great store, for in the time that the Frenchmen
Twentie hogs- were there, they made 20 hogsheads of wine. Also
heads of wine it yeeldeth roots passing good, Deere maruellous
made in Flori- store, with diuers other beasts, and fowle, seruiceable
da, like to the to the vse of man. These be things wherewith a man
wine of
Orleans. may liue, hauing corne or maiz wherewith to make
bread : for maiz maketh good sauory bread, and cakes as fine as
flowre. Also it maketh good meale, beaten and sodden with
water, and eateth like pap wherewith we feed children. It
maketh also good beuerage, sodden in water, and nourishable ;
which the Frenchmen did vse to drinke of in the morning, and
Labourers it assuageth their thirst, so that they had no need
necessary to to drinke all the day after. And this maiz was the
inhabit new greatest lacke they had, because they had no labourers
countreys. to sowe the same, and therefore to them that should
inhabit the land it were requisite to haue labourers to till and
sowe the ground : for they hauing victuals of their owne, whereby
they neither rob nor spoile the inhabitants, may liue not onely
quietly with them, who naturally are more desirous of peace then
of warres, but also shall haue abundance of victuals proferred
them for nothing : for it is with them as it is with one of vs,
when we see another man euer taking away from vs, although we
haue enough besides, yet then we thinke all too little for our selues :
for surely we haue heard the Frenchmen report, and I know it
by the Indians, that a very little contenteth them : for the
Indians with the head of maiz rosted, will trauell a whole day,
and when they are at the Spanyards finding, they giue them
nothing but sodden herbs and maiz : and in this order I saw
threescore of them feed, who were laden with wares, and
came fifty leagues off. The Floridians when the trauell,
Tobacco and haue a kinde of herbe dried, who with a cane and an
its virtue earthen cup in the end, with fire, and the dried
thereof. herbs put together, doe sucke thorow the cane the
smoke thereof, which smoke satisfieth their hunger, and there-

with they liue foure or fiue dayes without meat or drinke, and this all the Frenchmen vsed for this purpose : yet do they holde opinion withall, that it causeth water and fleame to void from their stomacks. The commodities of this land are more then are yet knowen to any man : for besides the land it selfe, whereof there is more then any Christian king is able **The variety** to inhabit, it flourisheth with medow, pasture ground, **of commo-** with woods of Cedar and Cypres, and other sorts, as **dities in** better can not be in the world. They haue for **Florida.** apothecary herbs, trees, roots and gummes great store, as Storax liquida, Turpintine, Gumme, Myrrhe, and Frankinsence, with many others, whereof I know not the names. Colours both red, blacke, yellow, and russet, very perfect, wherewith they so paint their bodies, and Deere skinnes which they weare about them, that with water it neither fadeth away, nor altereth colour. Golde and siluer they want not : for at the Frenchmens first comming thither they had the same offered them for little or nothing, for they receiued for a hatchet two pound weight of golde, because they knew not the estimation thereof : but the souldiers being greedy of the same, did take it from them, giuing them nothing for it : the which they perceiuing, that both the Frenchmen did greatly esteeme it, and also did rigourously deale with them, by taking the same away from them, at last would not be knowen they had any more, neither durst they weare the same for feare of being taken away : so that sauing at their first comming, they could get none of them : and how they came by this golde and siluer the French men know not as yet, but by gesse, who hauing trauelled to the Southwest of the cape, hauing found the same dangerous, by means of sundry banks, as we also haue found the same : and there finding masts which were wracks of Spaniards comming from Mexico, iudged that they had gotten treasure by them. For it is most true that diuers wracks haue bene made of Spaniards, hauing much treasure : for the Frenchmen hauing trauelled to the capeward an **Two Span-** hundred and fiftie miles, did finde two Spanyards **yards liued** with the Floridians, which they brought afterward to **long among** their fort, whereof one was in a carauel comming from **ye Floridians.** the Indies, which was cast away foureteene yeeres ago, and the other twelue yeeres ; of whose fellowes some escaped, othersome were slain by the inhabitants. It seemeth they had estimation of their golde and siluer, for it is wrought flat

Pieces of   and grauen, which they weare about their neckes;
Gold grauen othersome made round like a pancake, with a hole in
among yᵉ   the midst, to boulster vp their breasts withall, because
Floridans.   they thinke it a deformity to haue great breasts.   As
for mines either of gold or siluer, the Frenchmen can heare of
Florida   none they haue vpon the Island, but of copper,
esteemed an whereof as yet also they haue not made the proofe,
Island.   because they were but few men : but it is not vnlike,
but that in the maine where are high hilles, may be golde and
This copper siluer as well as in Mexico, because it is all one
was fonnd   maine.   The Frenchmen obteined pearles of them of
perfect golde, great bignesse, but they were blacke, by meanes of
called by the
Sauages,   rosting of them, for they do not fish for them as the
Syeroa   Spanyards doe, but for their meat : for the Spanyards
phyra.   vse to keepe dayly afishing some two or three
hundred Indians, some of them that be of choise a thousand :
and their order is to go in canoas, or rather great pinnesses, with
thirty men in a piece, whereof the one halfe, or most part be
diuers, the rest doe open the same for the pearles : for it is not
suffered that they should vse dragging, for that would bring
them out of estimation, and marre the beds of them.   The oisters
which haue the smallest sort of pearles are found in seuen or
eight fadome water, but the greatest in eleuen or twelue
fadome.

The Floridians haue pieces of vnicornes hornes which they
             weare about their necks, whereof the Frenchmen
Vnicornes
hornes, which obteined many pieces.   Of those vnicornes they
yᵉ inhabitants haue many : for that they doe affirme it to be a
call Soun-   beast with one horne, which comming to the riuer to
namma.
             drinke, putteth the same into the water before he
drinketh.   Of this vnicornes horne there are of our company,
that hauing gotten the same of the Frenchmen brought home
thereof to shew.   It is therefore to be presupposed that there
are more commodities as well as that, which for want of time,
and people sufficient to inhabit the same, can not yet come to
light : but I trust God will reueale the same before it be long, to
the great profit of them that shal take it in hand.   Of beasts
in this countrey besides deere, foxes, hares, polcats, conies,
ownces, and leopards, I am not able certeinly to say : but it is
thought that there are lions and tygres as well as vnicornes ; lions
especially ; if it be true that is sayd, of the enmity betweene

them and the vnicornes;* for there is no beast but hath his
enemy, as the cony the polcat, a sheepe the woolfe, the elephant
the rinoceros; and so of other beasts the like: insomuch, that
whereas the one is, the other can not be missing. And
seeing I haue made mention of the beasts of this countrey,
it shall not be from my purpose to speake also of the venimous
beasts, as crocodiles, whereof there is great abundance, adders of
great bignesse, whereof our men killed some of a yard
and halfe long. Also I heard a miracle of one of
these adders, vpon the which a faulcon seizing, the   Faulcons in
sayd adder did claspe her tail about her; which the   Florida.
French captaine seeing, came to the rescue of the falcon, and tooke
her slaying the adder; and this faulcon being wilde, he did reclaim
her, and kept her for the space of two moneths, at which time
for very want of meat he was faine to cast her off. On these
adders the Frenchmen did feed, to no little admiration of vs, and
affirmed the same to be a delicate meat. And the captaine of the
Frenchmen saw also a serpent with three heads and foure feet, of
the bignesse of a great spaniell, which for want of a harquebuz
he durst not attempt to slay. Of fish also they haue in the riuer,
pike, roch, salmon, trout, and diuers other small fishes,
and of great fish, some of the length of a man and longer,
being of bignesse accordingly, hauing a snout much like a
sword of a yard long. There be also of sea fishes,
which we saw coming along the coast flying, which   Flying
are of the bignesse of a smelt, the biggest sort   fishes.
whereof haue foure wings, but the other haue but two: of these
wee sawe comming out of Guinea a hundred in a company, which
being chased by the gilt heads, otherwise called the bonitos, do
to auoid them the better, take their flight out of the water, but
yet are they not able to fly farre, because of the drying of their
wings, which serue them not to flie but when they are moist, and
therefore when they can flie no further, they fall into
the water, and hauing wet their wings, take a new flight againe.
These bonitos be of bignesse like a carpe, and in colour like
a makerell, but it is the swiftest fish in swimming that is, and
followeth her prey very fiercely, not only in the water, but also
out of the water: for as the flying fish taketh her flight, so doeth
this bonito leape after them, and taketh them sometimes aboue

---

* This legend accounts for the supporters in our National Arms.

the water.   There were some of those bonitos, which being
galled by a fishgig, did follow our shippe comming out of Guinea
500 leagues.   There is a sea-fowle also that chaseth this flying
fish as well as the bonito : for as the flying fish taketh her flight,
so doth this fowle pursue to take her, which to beholde is a
greater pleasure then hawking, for both the flights are as
pleasant, and also more often then an hundred times : for
the fowle can flie no way, but one or other lighteth in her pawes,
the number of them are so abundant.   There is an innumerable
yoong frie of these flying fishes, which commonly keepe about the
ship, and are not so big as butter-flies, and yet by flying do auoid
the vnsatiablenesse of the bonito.   Of the bigger sort of these
fishes wee tooke many, which both night and day flew into the
sailes of our ship, and there was not one of them which was not
woorth a bonito : for being put vpon a hooke drabling in the
water, the bonito would leape thereat, and so was taken. · Also,
we tooke many with a white cloth made fast to a hooke, which
being tied so short in the water, that it might leape out and in,
the greedie bonito thinking it to be a flying fish leapeth thereat,
and so is deceiued.   We tooke also dolphins which are of very
goodly colour and proportion to behold, and no less delicate in
taste.   Fowles also there be many, both vpon land and vpon sea:
but concerning them on the land I am not able to name them,
because my abode was there so short.   But for the fowle of the
fresh riuers, these two I noted to be the chiefe, whereof the
Flemengo is one, hauing all red feathers, and long red legs like a
herne, a necke according to the bill, red, whereof the vpper neb
hangeth an inch ouer the nether ; and an egript, which is all white
as the swanne, with legs like to an hearn-shaw, and of bignesse
accordingly, but it hath in her taile feathers of so fine a plume,
that it passeth the estridge his feather.   Of the sea-fowle aboue
all other not common in England, I noted the pellican, which is
fained to be the louingst bird that is ; which rather then her
yong should want, wil spare her heart bloud out of her belly : but
for all this louingnesse she is very deformed to beholde ; for she
is of colour russet : notwithstanding in Guinea I haue seene of
them as white as a swan, hauing legs like the same, and a body
like a hearne, with a long necke, and a thick long beak, from the
nether iaw whereof downe to the breast passeth a skinne of such
a bignesse, as is able to receiue a fish as big as ones thigh, and
this her big throat and long bill doeth make her seem so ougly.

Here I haue declared the estate of Florida, and the commodities therein to this day knowen, which although it may seeme vnto some, by the meanes that the plenty of golde and siluer, is not so abundant as in other places, that the coast bestowed vpon the same will not be able to quit the charges : yet am I of the opinion, that by that which I haue seene in other Islands of the Indians, where such increase of cattell hath bene, that of twelue head of beasts in fiue and twenty yeeres, did in the hides of them raise a thousand pound profit yerely, that the increase of cattel only would raise profit sufficient for the same : for wee may consider, if so small a portion did raise so much gaines in such short time, what would a greater do in many yeres ? and surely I may this affirme, that the ground of the Indians for the breed of cattell, is not in any point to be compared to this of Florida, which all the yeere long is so greene, as any time in the Summer with vs : which surely is not to be maruelled at, seeing the countrey standeth in so watery a climate : for once a day without faile they haue a shower of raine ; which by meanes of the countrey it selfe, which is drie, and more feruent hot then ours, doeth make all things to flourish therein. And because there is not the thing we all seeke for, being rather desirous of present gaines, I doe therefore affirme the attempt thereof to be more requisit for a prince, who is of power able to go thorow with the same, rather then for any subiect.

Meanes to reape a sufficient profit in Florida and Virginia.

From thence wee departed the 28 of Iuly, vpon our voyage homewards, hauing there all things as might be most conuenient for our purpose : and tooke leaue of the Frenchmen that there still remained, who with diligence determined to make as great speede after,* as they could. Thus by meanes of contrary windes oftentimes, wee prolonged our voyage in such manner that victuals scanted with vs, so that we were diuers times (or rather the most part) in despaire of euer comming home, had not God in his goodnesse better prouided for vs, then our deseruing. In which state of great miserie, wee were prouoked to call vpon him by feruent prayer, which mooued him to heare vs, so that we had a prosperous winde, which did set vs so farre shot, as to be vpon the banke of Newfound land, on Saint Bartholomews eue, and we sounded thereupon, finding ground at an hundred and thirty

* For Laudonnière's own account of Florida, see Vol. II., p. 402.

K 2

fadoms, being that day somewhat becalmed, and tooke a great
number of fresh codde-fish, which greatly relieued vs : and being
very glad thereof, the next day we departed, and had lingring
little gales for the space of foure or fiue dayes, at the ende of
which we sawe a couple of French shippes, and had of them so
much fish as would serue vs plentifully for all the rest of the way,
the Captaine paying for the same both golde and siluer, to the
iust value thereof, vnto the chiefe owners of the saide shippes,
but they not looking for any thing at all, were glad in themselues
to meete with such good intertainement at sea, as they had at
our handes.   After which departure from them, with
Their arriual a good large winde, the twentieth of September we
in Padstow
in the   came to Padstow in Cornewall, God be thanked, in
moneth of safetie, with the losse of twentie persons in all the
September,
1565.   voyage, and with great profit to the venturers of the
said voyage, as also to the whole realme, in bringing
home both golde, siluer, pearles and other iewels great store.
His name therefore be praised for euermore.   Amen.

The names of certaine Gentlemen that were in this voyage.

M. Iohn Hawkins.
M. Iohn Chester, sir William Chesters sonne.
M. Anthony Parkhurst.
M. Fitzwilliam.
M. Thomas Woorley.
M. Edward Lacie, with diuers others.

The Register and true accounts of all herein expressed hath beene approoued by me Iohn Sparke
the younger, who went vpon the same voyage, and
wrote the same.

The third troublesome voyage made with the Iesus of Lubec, the
Minion, and foure other ships, to the parts of Guinea, and
the West Indies, in the yeeres 1567 and 1568 by M. Iohn
Hawkins.

THe ships departed from Plimmouth, the second day of
October, Anno 1567 and had reasonable weather vntill the
seuenth day, at which time fortie leagues North from Cape

Finister, there arose an extreme storme, which continued foure dayes, in such sort, that the fleete was dispersed, and all our great boats lost, and the Iesus our chiefe shippe, in such case, as not thought able to serue the voyage : whereupon in the same storme we set our course homeward, determining to giue ouer the voyage : but the eleuenth day of the same moneth, the winde changed with faire weather, whereby we were animated to followe our enterprise, and so did, directing our course with .the Islands of the Canaries, where according to on order before prescribed, all our shippes before dispersed, met at one of those Ilands, called Gomera, where we tooke water, and departed from thence the fourth day of Nouember, towards the coast of Guinea, and arriued at Cape Verde, the eighteenth of Nouember : where we landed 150 men, hoping to obtain some Negros, where we got but fewe, and those with great hurt and damage to our men, which chiefly proceeded of their enuenomed arrowes : and although in the beginning they seemed to be but small hurts, yet there hardly escaped any that had blood drawen of them, but died in strange sort, with their mouthes shut some tenne dayes before they died, and after their wounds were whole; where I my selfe had one of the greatest woundes, yet thanks be to God, escaped. From thence we passed the time vpon the coast of Guinea, searching with all diligence the riuers from Rio grande, vnto Sierra Leona, till the twelfth of Ianuarie, in which time we had not gotten together a hundreth and fiftie Negros : yet nothwithstanding the sicknesse of our men, and the late time of the yeere commanded vs away : and thus hauing nothing wherewith to seeke the coast of the West Indias, I was with the rest of our company in consultation to goe to the coast of the Mine, hoping there to haue obtained some golde for our wares, and thereby to haue defraied our charge. But euen in that pre-sent instant, there came to vs a Negro, sent from a king oppressed by other Kings his neighbours, desiring our aide, with promise that as many Negros as by these warres might be obtained, as well of his part as of ours, should be at our pleasure : whereupon we concluded to giue aide, and sent 120 of our men, which the 15 of Ianuarie, assaulted a towne of the Negros of our Allies aduersaries, which had in it 8000 Inhabitants, being very strongly impaled and fenced after their manner, but it was so well defended that our men preuailed not, but lost sixe

A towne of 8000 negros taken.

men and fortie hurt : so that our men sent forthwith to me for
more helpe : whereupon considering that the good successe of
this enterprise might highly further the commoditie of our voyage,
I went my selfe, and with the helpe of the king of our side,
assaulted the towne, both by land and sea, and very hardly with
fire (their houses being couered with dry Palme· leaues) obtained
the towne, and put the inhabitants to flight, where we tooke 250
persons, men, women, and children, and by our friend the king
of our side, there were taken 600 prisoners, whereof we hoped
to haue had our choise : but the Negro (in which
No trueth in nation is seldome or neuer found truth) meant nothing
Negros. lesse : for that night he remooued his campe and
prisoners, so that we were faine to content vs with those fewe
which we had gotten ourselues.

Now had we obtained between foure and fiue hundred Negros,
wherewith we thought it somewhat reasonable to seeke the coast
of the West Indies, and there, for our Negros, and other our
merchandize, we hoped to obtaine, whereof to counteruaile our
charges with some gaines, whereunto we proceeded with all diligence, furnished our watering, tooke fuell, and departed the coast
of Guinea the third of Februarie, continuing at the sea with a
passage more hard, then before had bene accustomed till the 27
Dominica. day of March, which day we had sight of an Iland,
called Dominica, vpon the coast of the West Indies,
in fourteene degrees : from thence we coasted from place to
place, making our traffike with the Spaniards as we might, somewhat hardly, because the king had straightly commanded all his
Gouernours in those parts, by no meanes to suffer any trade to
be made with vs : notwithstanding we had reasonable trade, and
courteous entertainement, from the Ile of Margarita vnto Cartagena, without any thing greatly worth the noting, sauing at Capo
de la Vela, in a towne called Rio de la Hacha (from whence
come all the pearles) the treasurer who had the charge there,
would by no meanes agree to any trade, or suffer vs to take
water, he had fortified his towne with diuers bulwarkes in all
places where it might be entered, and furnished himselfe with an
hundred Hargabuziers, so that he thought by famine to haue
inforced vs to haue put a land our Negros : of which purpose he
had not greatly failed, vnlesse we had by force entred the towne :
which (after we could by no meanes obtaine his fauour) we
were inforced to doe, and so with two hundred men brake

in vpon their. bulwarkes, and entred the towne with Rio de la Hacha taken.
the losse onely of two men of our partes, and no
hurt done to the Spaniards because after their volley of shot discharged, they all fled.

Thus hauing the town with some circumstance, as partly by
the Spaniards desire of Negros, and partly by friendship of the
Treasurer, we obtained a secret trade : whereupon the Spaniards
resorted to vs by night, and bought of vs to the number of 200
Negros : in all other places where we traded the Spaniards
inhabitants were glad of vs, and traded willingly.

At Cartagena the last towne we thought to haue Cartagena.
seene on the coast, we could by no meanes obtaine
to deale with any Spaniard, the gouernor was so straight, and
because our trade was so neere finished we thought not good
either to aduenture any landing, or to detract further time, but
in peace departed from thence the 24 of Iuly, hoping to haue
escaped the time of their stormes which then soone after began
to reigne, the which they called Furicanos, but Furicanos.
passing by the West end of Cuba, towards the coast
of Florida, there happened to vs the 12 day of August an extreme
storme which continued by the space of foure dayes, which so
beat the Iesus, that we cut downe all her higher buildings, her
rudder also was sore shaken, and withall was in so extreme a
leake, that we were rather vpon the point to leaue her then to
keepe her any longer, yet hoping to bring all to good passe, we
sought the coast of Florida, where we found no place nor Hauen
for our ships, because of the shalownesse of the coast : thus
being in greater despaire, and taken with a newe Storme.
storme which continued other 3 dayes, we were
inforced to take for our succour the Port which serueth the citie
of Mexico called Saint Iohn de Vllua, which standeth in 19
degrees : in seeking of which Port we tooke in our way 3 ships
which carried passengers to the number of an hundred, which
passengers we hoped should be a meane to vs the better to
obtaine victuals for our money, and a quiet place for the
repairing of our fleete. Shortly after this the 16 of September
we entered the Port of Saint Iohn de Vllua and in The Spaniards deceiued.
our entrie the Spaniardes thinking vs to be the fleete
of Spaine, the chiefe officers of the Countrey came
aboord vs, which being deceiued of their expectation were greatly
dismayed : but immediatly when they sawe our demand was

nothing but victuals, were recomforted. I found also in the same Port twelue ships which had in them by the report two hundred thousand pound in gold and siluer, all which (being in my possession, with the kings Iland as also the passengers before in my way thitherward stayed) I set at libertie, without the taking from them the waight of a groat : onely because I would not be delayed of my dispatch, I stayed two men of estimation and sent post immediatly to Mexico, which was two hundred miles from vs, to the Presidentes and Councell there, shewing them of our arriuall there by the force of weather, and the necessitie of the repaire of our shippes and victuals, which wantes we *Our requests.* required as friends to king Philip to be furnished of for our money : and that the Presidents and ·Councel there should with all conuenient spede take order, that at the arriuall of the Spanish fleete, which was dayly looked for, there might no cause of quarrell rise betweene vs and them, but for the better maintenance of amitie, their commandement might be had in that behalfe. This message being sent away the sixteenth day of September at night, being the very day of our arriuall, in the next morning which was the seuenteenth day of *The fleete of Spaine.* the same moneth, we sawe open of the Hauen thirteene great shippes, and vnderstanding them to bee the fleete of Spaine, I sent immediately to aduertise the Generall of the fleete of my being there, doing him to vnderstand, that before I would suffer them to enter the Port, there should some order of conditions passe betweene vs for our safe being *The maner of the port S. Iohn de Vllua.* there, and maintenance of peace. Now it is to·be vnderstood that this Port is made by a little Iland of stones not three foote aboue the water in the highest place, and but a bow-shoot of length any way, this Iland standeth from the maine land two bow shootes or more, also it is to be vnderstood that there is not in all this coast any other place for shippes to arriue in safety, because the North winde hath there such violence, that vnlesse the shippes be very safely *North windes perilous.* mored with their ankers fastened vpon this Iland, there is no remedie for these North windes but death : also the place of the Hauen was so little, that of neccessitie the shippes must ride one aboord the ‚other, so that we could not giue place to them, nor they to vs : and here I beganne to bewaile that which after followed, for now, said I, I am in two dangers, and forced to receiue the one of them. That

was, either I must haue kept out the fleete from entering the
Port, the which with Gods helpe I was very well able to doe, or
else suffer them to enter in with their accustomed treason, which
they neuer faile to execute, where they may haue opportunitie,
to compasse it by any meanes : if I had kept them out, then had
there bene present shipwracke of all the fleete which
amounted in value to sixe Millions, which was in <sup>1800 thousand
pond.</sup>
value of our money 1800000. li. which I considered I
was not able to answere, fearing the Queenes Maiesties indignation
in so waightie a matter.   Thus with my selfe reuoluing the
doubts, I thought rather better to abide the Iutt of the vncertainty,
then the certaintie.   The vncertaine doubt I account was their
treason which by good policie I hoped might be preuented, and
therefore as chusing the least mischiefe I proceeded to conditions.
Now was our first messenger come and returned from the fleete
with report of the arriuall of a Viceroy, so that hee had authoritie,
both in all this Prouince of Mexico (otherwise called Nueua
Espanna) and in the sea, who sent vs word that we should send
our conditions, which of his part should (for the better maintenance of amitie betweene the Princes) be both
fauourably granted, and faithfully performed with <sup>Faire wordes
beguiled.</sup>
many faire wordes how passing the coast of the Indies
he had vnderstood of our honest behauiour towardes the
inhabitants where we had to doe, aswell elsewhere as in the same
Port, the which I let passe : thus following our demand, we
required victuals for our money, and licence to sell ^{Our requests.}
as much ware as might furnish our wants, and that
there might be of either part twelue gentlemen as hostages for
the maintenance of peace : and that the Iland for our better safetie
might be in our owne possession, during our abode
there, and such ordinance as was planted in the same <sup>The peace
concluded.</sup>
Iland which were eleuen peeces of brasse : and that
no Spaniard might land in the Iland with any kind of weapon : these
conditions at the first he somewhat misliked, chiefly the guard of the
Iland to be in our owne keeping, which if they had had, we had
soone knowen our fare : for with the first North winde they
had cut our cables and our ships had gone ashore : but in the
ende he concluded to our request, bringing the twelue hostages
to ten, which with all speede of either part were receiued, with a
writing from the Viceroy signed with his hande and sealed with
his seale of all the conditions concluded, and forthwith a trumpet

blowen with commandement that none of either part should be
meane to violate the peace vpon paine of death : and further it
was concluded that the two Generals of the fleetes should meete,
and giue faith ech to other for the performance of the premisses
which was so done. Thus at the end of 3 dayes all was concluded and the fleete entered the port, saluting one another as
the maner of the sea doth require. Thus as I said before,
Thursday we entred the port, Friday we saw the fleete, and on
Munday at night they entered the Port : then we laboured 2.
daies placing the English ships by themselues, and the Spanish
ships by themselues, the captaines of ech part and inferiour men
of their parts promising great amity of al sides : which euen as
with all fidelitie it was ment on our part, so the Spaniards ment
nothing lesse on their parts, but from the maine land had furnished themselues with a supply of men to the number of 1000,
and ment the next Thursday being the 23 of September at
dinner time, to set vpon vs on all sides. The same Thursday in
the morning the treason being at hand, some appearance shewed,
as shifting of weapon from ship to ship, planting and bending of
ordinance from the ships to the Iland where our men warded,
passing too and fro of companies of men more then required for
their necessary busines, and many other ill likelihoods, which
A Viceroy caused vs to haue a vehement suspition, and there-
false of his withall sent to the Viceroy to enquire what was ment
faith. by it, which sent immediatly straight commandement
to vnplant all things suspicious, and also sent word that he in
the faith of a Viceroy would be our defence from all villanies.
Yet we being not satisfied with this answere, because we suspected a great number of men to be hid in a great ship of 900
tunnes, which was mored next vnto the Minion, sent againe to
the Viceroy the master of the Iesus which had the Spanish
tongue, and required to be satisfied if any such thing were or
The treason not. The Viceroy now seeing that the treason must
brake foorth. be discouered, foorthwith stayed our master, blew the
Trumpet, and of all sides set vpon vs : our men which
warded a shore being stricken with sudden feare, gaue place,
fled, and sought to recouer succour of the ships ; the Spaniardes
being before prouided for the purpose landed in all places in
multitudes from their ships which they might easily doe without
boates, and slewe all our men ashore without mercie, a fewe of
them escaped aboord the Iesus. The great ship which had by

the estimation three hundred men placed in her secretly, immediatly fell aboord the Minion, but by Gods appoint- The Minion
ment, in the time of the suspicion we had, which was   escaped
onely one halfe houre, the Minion was made readie   hardly.
to auoide, and so leesing her hedfasts, and hayling away by the
sternefastes she was gotten out: thus with Gods helpe she
defended the violence of the first brunt of these three hundred
men. The Minion being past out, they came aboord the Iesus,
which also with very much a doe and the losse of manie of our
men were defended and kept out. Then there were   The Iesus
also two other ships that assaulted the Iesus at the   escaped
same instant, so that she had hard getting loose, but   hardly.
yet with some time we had cut our head-fastes, and gotten out
by the stern-fastes. Nowe when the Iesus and the Minion were
gotten about two shippes length from the Spanish Sharpe wars.
fleete, the fight beganne so hotte on all sides that
within one houre the Admirall of the Spaniards was
supposed to be sunke, their Viceadmirall burned, and   3. ships of
one other of their principall ships supposed to be sunke,   the
so that the shippes were little able to annoy vs.   Spaniards
                                                    consumed.
Then it is to be vnderstood, that all the Ordinance vpon the
Ilande was in the Spaniardes handes, which did vs so great
annoyance, that it cut all the mastes and yardes of the Iesus in
such sort that there was no hope to carrie her away: A hard case.
also it sunke our small shippes, whereupon we determined to place the Iesus on that side of the Minion, that she
might abide all the batterie from the land, and so be a defence
for the Minion till night, and then to take such reliefe of victuall
and other necessaries from the Iesus, as the time would suffer
vs, and to leaue her. As we were thus determining, and had
placed the Minion from the shot of the land, suddenly the
Spaniards had fired two great shippes which were comming
directly with vs, and hauing no meanes to auoide the fire, it
bredde among our men a maruellous feare, so that some sayd,
let vs depart with the Minion, other said, let vs see whether the
winde will carrie the fire from vs. But to be short, the Minions
men which had alwayes their sayles in a readinesse, thought to
make sure worke, and so without either consent of the Captaine
or Master cut their saile, so that very hardly I was receiued into
the Minion. /
The most part of the men that were left aliue in the Iesus,

made shift and followed the Minion in a small boat, the rest
Small hope to be had of tyrants. which the little boate was not able to receiue, were
inforced to abide the mercie of the Spaniards (which
I doubt was very little) so with the Minion only and
the Iudith (a small barke of 50 tunne) we escaped, which barke
the same night forsooke vs in our great miserie : we were now
remooued with the Minion from the Spanish ships two bow-
shootes, and there rode all that night : the next morning we
recouered an Iland a mile from the Spaniardes, where there
A storme. tooke vs a North winde, and being left onely with two
ankers and two cables (for in this conflict we lost
three cables and two ankers) we thought alwayes vpon death
which euer was present, but God preserued vs to a longer time.

The weather waxed reasonable, and the Saturday we set saile,
Small hopes of life. and hauing a great number of men and little victuals
our hope of life waxed lesse and lesse : some desired
to yeeld to the Spaniards, some rather desired to
obtaine a place where they might giue themselues to the Infidels,
Hard choice. and some had rather abide with a little pittance the
mercie of God at Sea : so thus with many sorowful
hearts we wandred in an vnknowen Sea by the space of 14 dayes,
Miseries. till hunger inforced vs to seek the land, for hides were
thought very good meat, rats, cats, mice and dogs,
none escaped that might be gotten, parrats and monkeyes that
were had in great price, were thought there very profitable if they
serued the turne one dinner : thus in the end the 8 day of
October we came to the land in the botome of the same bay of
Mexico in 23 degrees and a halfe, where we hoped to haue found
inhabitants of the Spaniards, reliefe of victuals, and place for the
repaire of our ship, which was so sore beaten with shot from our
enemies and brused with shooting off our owne ordinance, that
our wearie and weake armes were scarce able to defende and
keepe out water. But all things happened to the contrary, for
we found neither people, victuall, nor hauen of reliefe, but a
place where hauing faire weather with some perill we might land
a boat : our people being forced with hunger desired to be set
on land, whereunto I consented.

And such as were willing to land I put them apart, and such
as were desirous to goe homewardes, I put apart, so that they
were indifferently parted a hundred of one side and a hundred of
the other side : these hundred men we set a land with all dili-

gence in this little place beforesaid, which being landed, we determined there to take in fresh water, and so with our little remaine of victuals to take the sea.*

The next day hauing a land with me fiftie of our hundreth men that remained for the speedier preparing of our water aboord, there arose an extreame storme, so that in three dayes we could by no meanes repaire aboord our ship : the ship also was in such perill that euery houre we looked for shipwracke.

The greatest miserie of all.

But yet God againe had mercie on vs, and sent faire weather, we had aboord our water, and departed the sixteenth day of October, after which day we had faire and prosperous weather till the sixteenth day of Nouember, which day God be praysed we were cleere from the coast of the Indies, and out of the chanell and gulfe of Bahama, which is betweene the Cape of Florida, and the Ilandes of Lucayo. After this growing neere to the colde countrey, our men being oppressed with famine, died continually, and they that were left, grew into such weakenesse that we were scantly able to manage our shippe, and the winde being always ill for vs to recouer England, we determined to goe with Galicia in Spaine, with intent there to relieue our companie and other extreame wantes. And being arriued the last day of December in a place neere vnto Vigo called Ponte Vedra, our men with excesse of fresh meate grew into miserable diseases, and died a great part of them. This matter was borne out as long as it might be, but in the end although there were none of our men suffered to goe a land, yet by accesse of the Spaniards, our feeblenesse was knowen to them. Whereupon they ceased not to seeke by all meanes to betray vs, but with all speede possible we departed to Vigo, where we had some helpe of certaine English ships and twelue fresh men, wherewith we repaired our wants as we might, and departing the 20 day of Ianuary 1568 arriued in Mounts bay in Cornewall the 25 of the same moneth, praised be God therefore.

If all the miseries and troublesome affaires of this sorowfull voyage should be perfectly and throughly written, there should

---

* Two accounts, the one by Miles Philips, the other by Job Hortop, two of the men set ashore by John Hawkins, will be found in Vol. III., pages 187 and 226. This narrative, with those of Philips and Hortop, has been extensively used by Charles Kingsley throughout his " Westward Ho !"

neede a painefull man with his pen, and as great a time as he had
that wrote the liues and deathes of the Martyrs.

IOHN HAWKINS.

THE END.

ImTheStory.com

Lightning Source UK Ltd.
Milton Keynes UK
UKOW06f2224290315

248738UK00004B/43/P

9 781314 564006